The Usborne
Complete Jane Austen

ALL THE NOVELS RETOLD

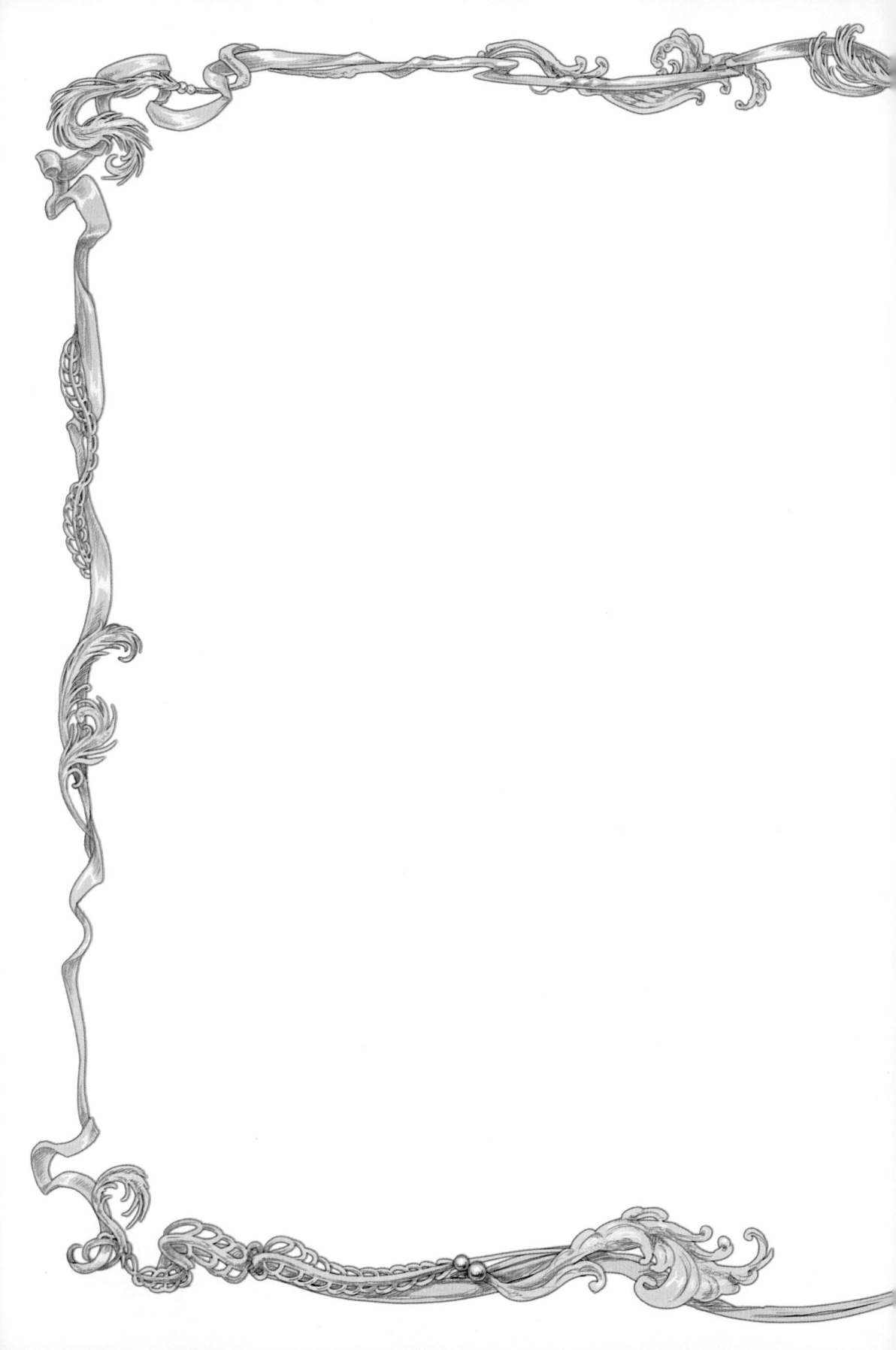

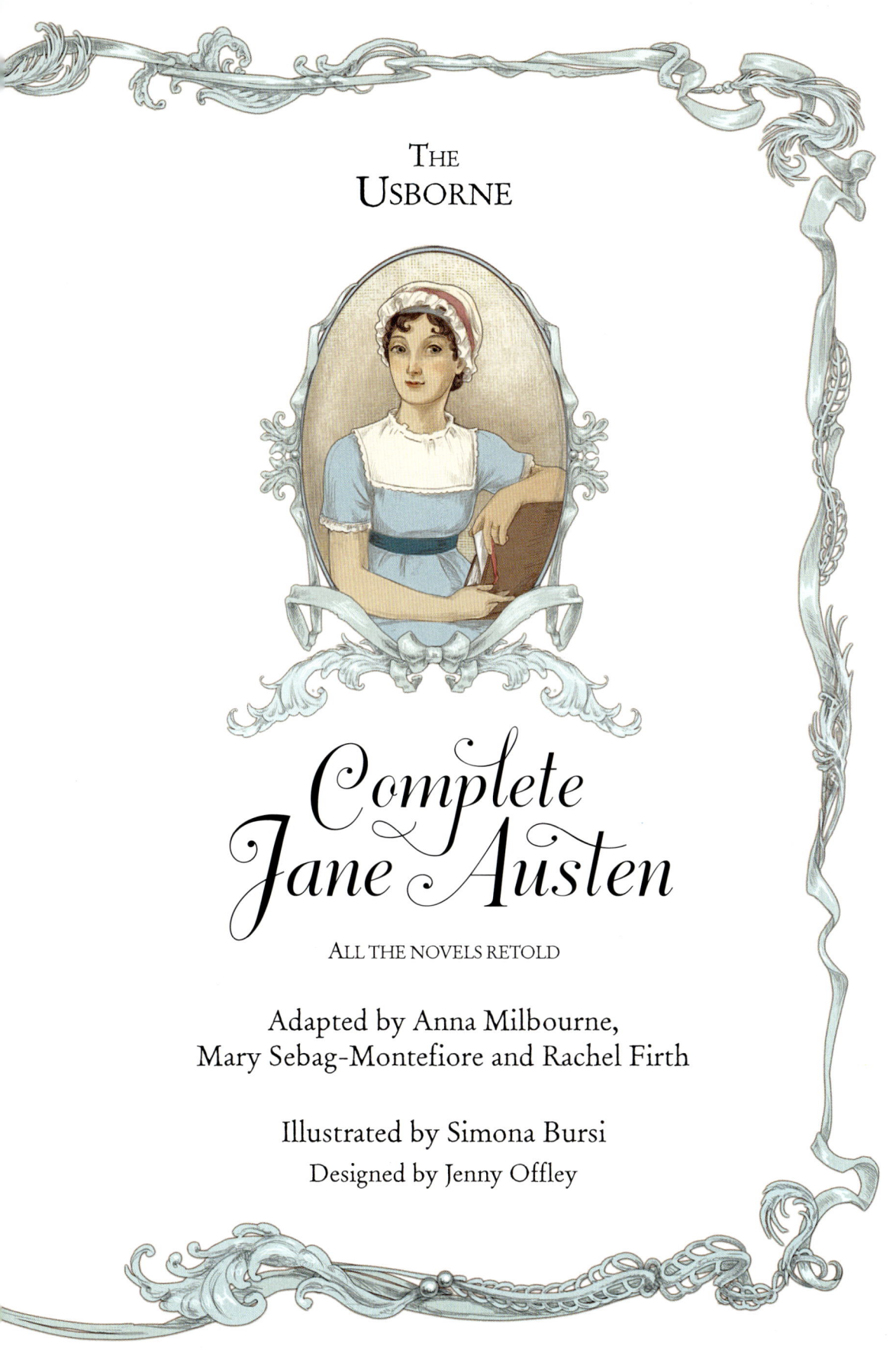

THE USBORNE

Complete Jane Austen

ALL THE NOVELS RETOLD

Adapted by Anna Milbourne,
Mary Sebag-Montefiore and Rachel Firth

Illustrated by Simona Bursi
Designed by Jenny Offley

Mr. Darcy and Elizabeth
PRIDE AND PREJUDICE

Contents

Pride and Prejudice 8

Northanger Abbey 66

Emma 128

Sense and Sensibility 184

Mansfield Park 244

Persuasion 306

Lady Susan 368

Jane Austen: Life and Times 393

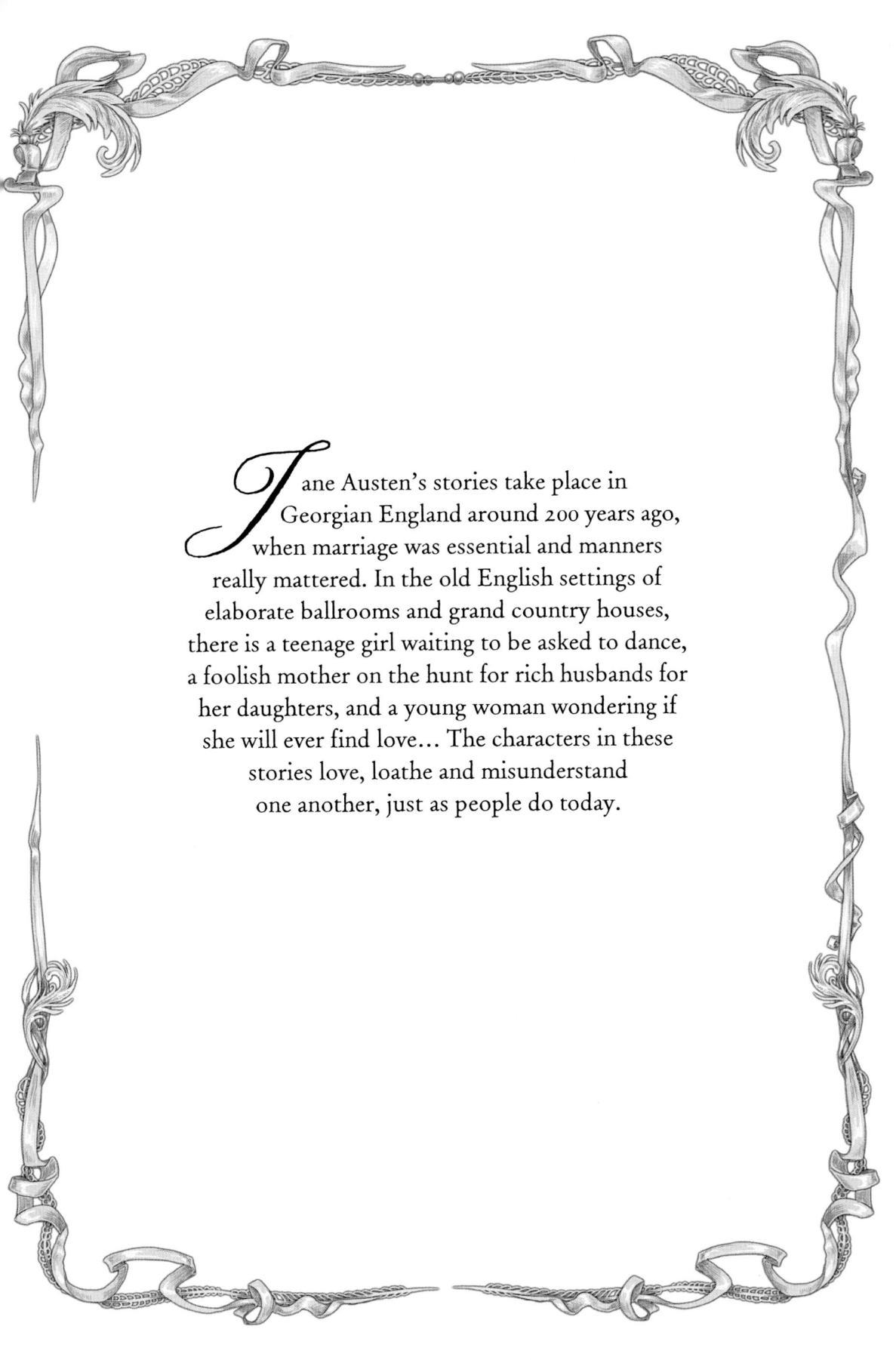

Jane Austen's stories take place in Georgian England around 200 years ago, when marriage was essential and manners really mattered. In the old English settings of elaborate ballrooms and grand country houses, there is a teenage girl waiting to be asked to dance, a foolish mother on the hunt for rich husbands for her daughters, and a young woman wondering if she will ever find love… The characters in these stories love, loathe and misunderstand one another, just as people do today.

Pride and Prejudice

Mrs. Bennet is looking for husbands for her five daughters. When Mr. Bingley, a rich bachelor, moves into the area, all eyes are on him. He and Jane Bennet seem to be falling for one another. Jane's clever sister Elizabeth thinks his friend Mr. Darcy horribly proud, but somehow sparks fly between them. Is Darcy everything he appears?

Mr. Bennet
Affectionate but sarcastic father.

Mrs. Bennet
Foolish mother whose aim in life is to get her daughters married.

Jane Bennet
Eldest, prettiest and most kind-hearted Bennet daughter.

Mary Bennet
The bookish daughter.

Elizabeth Bennet
Sharpest of the Bennet daughters. Particularly beloved of her father. Also known as 'Lizzy'.

Mr. & Mrs. Gardiner
The Bennet girls' uncle and aunt.

Kitty Bennet
The silly, youngest daughter.

Lydia Bennet
The flirtatious daughter.

Charlotte Lucas
Lizzy's sensible best friend.

*I*T IS A TRUTH UNIVERSALLY ACKNOWLEDGED, THAT A SINGLE man in possession of a good fortune, must be in want of a wife. Whatever the feelings of the man in question as he moves into a new area, the families around agree on it so well, that he is immediately considered to be the property of one of their daughters.

"My dear Mr. Bennet," said Mrs. Bennet one day, "have you heard? Netherfield Park has been let out at last!"

Mr. Bennet made no answer.

"Do you not want to know who has taken it?" cried his wife impatiently.

"You want to tell me, and I have no objection to hearing it."

This was invitation enough.

"A single man with a large fortune. His name is Bingley. What a fine thing for our girls!"

"Why?"

"How can you be so tiresome!" scolded Mrs. Bennet. "You must know that I am thinking of his marrying one of them. You must visit him as soon as he comes."

"I shall do no such thing."

"But Sir William and Lady Lucas are going for their daughters, and they never visit newcomers. You must go, for we cannot visit him if you do not."

"I shall send Mr. Bingley a letter to say he can marry whichever of the girls he chooses, though I must throw in a good word for my little Lizzy."

"You will do no such thing. Lizzy is no better than the others, not half so beautiful as Jane nor so good-tempered as Lydia."

"They are all silly, ignorant girls, but Lizzy is somewhat cleverer than her sisters."

"How can you insult your own children in such a way? You have no compassion for my poor nerves."

"On the contrary, your nerves are my oldest friends. I have heard you talk about them for the last twenty years."

"Ah, you do not know what I suffer."

"But I hope you will get over it, and live to see many rich young single men come to the neighbourhood."

"But if twenty should come, it would still be no use, since you will not visit them."

Mr. Bennet smiled. "I promise, my dear, when there are twenty, I will visit them all."

Mr. Bennet was such a strange mixture of humour, sarcasm, detachedness and contrariness that after twenty-three years of marriage his wife still did not understand him. Her mind was less difficult. She was a woman of small brain and uncertain temper. The business of her life was to get her daughters married; its comfort was visiting and gossip.

Mr. Bennet was one of the first to call on Mr. Bingley. He had always intended to, despite telling his wife that he would not. Till the evening after the visit, she did not know of it. He revealed it as he watched his second daughter trimming a hat. "I hope Mr. Bingley will like it, Lizzy," he said suddenly.

"We will never know what Mr. Bingley likes, since you will not visit," said Mrs. Bennet resentfully. "Do not keep coughing so, Kitty, for heaven's sake. Have a little compassion for my nerves. You are tearing them to pieces."

Pride and Prejudice

"Kitty times her coughs very badly," said her father.

"I am not coughing for my own amusement," replied Kitty fretfully. "When is the Assembly Rooms Ball, Lizzy? At least we shall see Mr. Bingley there."

"A fortnight tomorrow."

"But we cannot speak to him. No one will have introduced us," snapped Mrs. Bennet.

"I shall introduce you," said Mr. Bennet.

The girls stared at their father, and Mrs. Bennet said, "Nonsense!"

"Are all forms of introduction nonsense?" he asked. "What do you say, Mary? You are a young lady of deep reflection."

Mary wanted to say something clever but did not know how.

"While Mary is thinking," her father continued, "let us return to Mr. Bingley."

"I am sick of Mr. Bingley," cried his wife.

"I am sorry to hear that. If I had known, I certainly would not have called upon him. It is very unlucky, for we cannot escape the friendship now."

The astonishment of his family was just what he wished.

When the first burst of joy was over, Mrs. Bennet declared that she had always expected it. "I knew it! What a good joke! Girls, what a good father you have got! Lydia, my love, though you are the youngest, I dare say Mr. Bingley will dance with you."

"Oh," said Lydia. "I am not afraid, for though I am the youngest, I am the tallest."

"Now, Kitty, you may cough as much as you choose," said Mr. Bennet as he left the room, exhausted by his wife's delight.

Mr. Bingley attended the ball at the Assembly Rooms with a small party consisting of his two sisters, the husband of the elder sister, and another young man. Mr. Bingley was good-looking, with pleasant, easy manners. His sisters were women of high fashion. His brother-in-law, Mr. Hurst, looked like a gentleman, but his friend, Mr. Darcy, drew the attention of the entire room by his height, handsome features, and the rumour of his having ten thousand pounds a year.

He was admired for about half the evening until he was discovered to be proud, haughty and conceited, and not even his enormous estate in Derbyshire could save him from being thought disagreeable and unworthy of his friend.

Mr. Bingley danced every dance and talked of giving a ball himself at Netherfield. Mr. Darcy danced only once with Mrs. Hurst and once with Miss Bingley, refused to be introduced to any other lady, and spent the rest of the evening walking about the room speaking to no one except his own party.

Among the most violently against him was Mrs. Bennet, who particularly resented his having slighted one of her daughters.

Owing to the scarcity of gentlemen, Elizabeth had to sit down for two dances, and overheard Mr. Darcy and Mr. Bingley talking.

"Come, Darcy. I hate to see you stand about in this stupid manner. You ought to dance."

"I certainly shall not. You know how I detest it, unless I know my partner. Your sisters are already dancing, and it would be a punishment to stand up with any of the other women here."

"I have never met so many charming girls in my life as I have this evening!" cried Bingley.

"You are dancing with the only pretty one in the room," said Mr. Darcy, looking at the eldest Miss Bennet.

"Oh, she is the most beautiful creature I ever saw! But her sister is sitting just behind you, who is very pretty and I dare say pleasant. Do let me ask my partner to introduce you."

Darcy turned round, looked at Elizabeth, till, catching her eye, he withdrew his own and said coldly, "She is tolerable, but not handsome enough to tempt *me*. I am in no mood to pay attention to young ladies who have been ignored by other men. You had better return to your partner, for you are wasting your time with me."

Mr. Darcy walked off, leaving Elizabeth torn between anger and laughter. She told the story with great spirit to her friends, however, for she delighted in anything ridiculous.

The evening passed pleasantly for the rest of the family. Mrs. Bennet was thrilled that Mr. Bingley danced with Jane twice. Jane was as pleased as her mother, but more quietly. Elizabeth felt Jane's pleasure. Mary heard herself described to Miss Bingley as the most accomplished girl in the neighbourhood, and Kitty and Lydia were never without partners.

When Jane and Elizabeth were alone that evening, after their sisters were in bed, Jane confided how very much she admired Mr. Bingley. "He is exactly what a young man ought to be: good-humoured, lively and kind."

"Handsome too – as a young man ought to be, if he can possibly help it!" Elizabeth said playfully.

"I was flattered he asked me to dance a second time," Jane said. "I did not expect such a compliment."

"No? I did for you. But that is the great difference between us. Compliments always take you by surprise, and me never. I give you permission to like him. You have liked many a stupider person."

"Oh Lizzy!"

"You never see a fault in anybody. All the world is good in your eyes. I have never heard you speak badly of anyone in my life."

"I never want to be quick to judge," Jane protested mildly.

"I know," said Lizzy. "You are unique. To take the good of everybody's character and make it still better, and say nothing of the bad, that is a quality which belongs to you alone."

"His sisters seemed charming too."

Lizzy, who was both more observant and quicker to judge than her sister, was not so sure.

Within walking distance of Longbourn lived a family who were friends of the Bennets. Sir William Lucas had been given a knighthood for addressing the king when he was mayor and now he occupied himself in being friendly to everyone. Lady Lucas was not too clever to be a good companion to Mrs. Bennet. Their daughter, Charlotte Lucas, was Elizabeth's particular friend.

That the Lucases and the Bennets should meet to talk over the events of a ball was absolutely necessary. So the morning after, they gathered at Longbourn to do just that.

"You began the evening well, Charlotte," said Mrs. Bennet. "You were Mr. Bingley's first choice."

"Yes, but he seemed to like his second better."

"Oh, you mean Jane, I suppose. I heard that he thought her the prettiest woman in the room… but it may all come to nothing."

"To overhear that comment was nicer than what you overheard, Lizzy," said Charlotte. "Poor Lizzy! To be only just *tolerable*."

"Mr. Darcy is a very disagreeable man," said Mrs. Bennet. "If he ever asks you to dance, Lizzy, you should refuse him."

"Mama, I can safely promise *never* to dance with him."

"Perhaps he has a right to be proud," said Charlotte, "being a handsome man from a high family, with all that wealth."

"I could easily forgive *his* pride if he had not mortified *mine*," said Elizabeth.

"Pride and vanity," announced Mary, finding words of wisdom at last, "are very different. Pride relates to our opinion of ourselves; vanity to how we wish others to see us."

Lydia yawned, "Oh, be quiet, Mary." A quarrel ensued, which ended only with the visit.

Pride and Prejudice

The Longbourn ladies and the Netherfield ladies soon began to pay one another visits. Jane Bennet's manners pleased Mrs. Hurst and Miss Bingley, though they found her mother impossible and her younger sisters not worth speaking to. Nevertheless, they expressed a wish to get to know the two eldest Bennet sisters.

Jane was delighted, but Elizabeth did not like them, feeling they were snobbish and sneering. Their approval of Jane, she thought, arose only from their brother's admiration.

His high regard for Jane was obvious. And to Elizabeth it was equally clear that Jane was falling in love with him. No one else was likely to discover this, however, since Jane had an air of general cheerfulness and calm which kept her true feelings from showing.

Elizabeth mentioned this to Charlotte Lucas.

"It is a disadvantage to be so very guarded," said Charlotte. "Mr. Bingley undoubtedly likes Jane, but he may never do more than that without some encouragement from her."

"She does as much as she can. If I can see what she feels, he must be a fool not to know it too," Elizabeth said.

"But he does not know Jane as you do," Charlotte replied. "Though they meet fairly often, it is never for long, and always in large parties. Jane should make the most of every half hour. When she is certain of him, there will be time enough to fall in love."

"That is all very well if you are only trying to get a husband, but Jane is not plotting that. She can only feel what she feels, and hardly knows him yet – she has not seen him enough to understand his character."

"Happiness in marriage is entirely a matter of chance," said Charlotte. "Understanding your spouse before the wedding does not make any difference to your happiness in the marriage."

"You make me laugh, Charlotte, but you know that makes no sense. You would never act that way yourself."

Pride and Prejudice

Elizabeth was so busy observing Mr. Bingley's attentions to Jane, that she was unaware of being observed herself by his friend. Darcy had at first scarcely thought her pretty. When they next met, he looked at her only to criticize. But no sooner had he told himself and his friends that her face had no good features, than he began to find it was made unusually intelligent by the beautiful expression of her dark eyes. Though he had criticized her figure, he was forced to acknowledge that it was light and graceful, and in spite of claiming that her manners were not those of the fashionable world, he was caught by their playfulness.

Elizabeth knew none of this. To her, he was only the man who had not thought her pretty enough to dance with.

He began to wish to know more of her. It was at a party given by Sir William Lucas that she noticed his attention.

"What does he mean by listening in on my conversations?" she asked Charlotte.

As she spoke, Sir William called out to her, "My dear Miss Eliza, why are you not dancing? Mr. Darcy, let me present this young lady to you as a very desirable partner." And taking her hand, he gave it to Mr. Darcy, who put out his own to receive it, but she instantly drew back.

"I do not wish to dance, sir."

"You dance so well, Miss Elizabeth, that this gentleman could not object to giving us all the pleasure of seeing you."

"Mr. Darcy is all politeness," Elizabeth said with a smile. And she would not be persuaded.

Her resistance intrigued Mr. Darcy, and he was lost in thought about the matter when Miss Bingley accosted him. "I can guess what you are thinking of."

"I imagine not."

"You are thinking this is an intolerable way to spend an evening. I agree. The nothingness, and yet the self-importance of these people! And the noise! Am I not right?"

"You are wrong," replied Mr. Darcy. "My thoughts were happier. I have been thinking about the very great pleasure which a fine pair of eyes in a pretty face can give."

Miss Bingley immediately fixed her eyes on his face and demanded: "Whose eyes?"

"Miss Elizabeth Bennet's," replied Mr. Darcy.

"I am astonished!" cried Miss Bingley. "When do I congratulate you on your engagement? You will have a charming mother-in-law, and of course, she will always be at Pemberley with you."

He listened with indifference but, as his silence convinced her that her wit had struck home, she did not stop for the rest of the evening.

Mr. Bennet's property, Longbourn, gave him an income of two thousand pounds a year. Unfortunately for his daughters, it would be inherited on his death by a distant male relative. Their mother's inheritance from her father was not enough to make up the shortfall. Her father had been a lawyer in Meryton, the nearest town to Longbourn. She had a sister living there, who had married a lawyer in their father's firm, and another brother in London.

The Bennet sisters often went to Meryton, for shopping, and to see their aunt. Kitty and Lydia went the most frequently, following the enticing news from their aunt that army officers had settled in Meryton for the winter.

Every day added to their knowledge. They learned the officers' names, and made their acquaintance. Mr. Bingley's large fortune could not compare, in their eyes, to the glittering braid on an officer's coat. They talked of nothing but officers.

After listening to them one morning, Mr. Bennet coolly observed, "You must be two of the silliest girls in the country."

"How can you think your own children silly?" demanded

Pride and Prejudice

Mrs. Bennet. "They are all very clever. I remember, when I was a girl, I liked a red coat myself, and if a smart young colonel with five or six thousand pounds a year came along for one of my girls, I should not say no to him."

Mr. Bennet was saved from having to reply by the arrival of a note from Netherfield for Jane.

"Well, Jane? What does it say? Make haste, my love, and tell us!" said her mother.

"It is from Miss Bingley," said Jane, and read aloud:

My dear Friend,

If you do not come to dinner today with Louisa and me, we shall die of boredom. My brother and the gentlemen are dining out with the officers. Come as soon as you can.

Yours as ever,

Caroline Bingley

"With the officers!" cried Lydia. "Lucky them!"

"Dining out," said Mrs. Bennet. "How unlucky for you, Jane."

"Can I have the carriage?" Jane asked.

"No, you must go on horseback, because it looks like rain, and if it rains you will have to stay the night," said her mother, taking her to the door with cheerful hopes of bad weather.

Jane had not been long gone before it began to rain hard. The rain continued the whole evening. She would certainly not be able to come back.

"Such a lucky idea of mine," said Mrs. Bennet several times, as if the weather were all her own making.

But the next day brought a note for Elizabeth from Netherfield.

Pride and Prejudice

My dearest Lizzy,

I am very unwell this morning, which I suppose is the result of getting wet through yesterday. My kind friends will not hear of my returning home till I am better.

With love,

Jane

"Well, my dear," said Mr. Bennet to his wife, "if Jane should die, it will be a comfort to know that it was all under your orders, in pursuit of Mr. Bingley."

"Oh, people do not die of little colds. As long as she stays there, it could not be better."

But Elizabeth was anxious, and determined to go to see Jane. As the carriage was not to be had, and she was no horsewoman, she declared that she would walk to Netherfield.

"How can you be so silly to think of such a thing in all this dirt?" cried her mother. "You will not be fit to be seen."

"I shall be fit to see Jane, which is all I want," Elizabeth replied.

She walked at a quick pace through field after field, jumping over stiles, springing over puddles, and found herself at last at Netherfield. She was shown into the breakfast room with dirty stockings and a face glowing with exercise.

Her appearance created great surprise. That she should have walked three miles, unaccompanied, and in such weather, was incredible to Miss Bingley and Mrs. Hurst. Mr. Darcy was silent, divided between thinking about the brilliance of her complexion and the boldness of her coming alone. Mr. Hurst was also silent, but he was thinking about his breakfast.

Elizabeth found Jane very ill. She stayed with her till the clock

Elizabeth was shown into the breakfast room with dirty stockings and a face glowing with exercise.

struck three, when Jane, feverish, with an aching head, was too upset to part with her. The ladies changed their offer of a carriage to take Elizabeth home into an invitation to stay. A servant was sent to Longbourn to tell the family and bring her clothes.

Elizabeth joined the Netherfield party for dinner. The sisters said several times how shocking it was to have a bad cold, and how they disliked being ill themselves, and then thought no more of it. Their indifference towards Jane, when she was not right in front of them, restored Elizabeth to the complete enjoyment of her original dislike.

Only Mr. Bingley showed real concern for Jane, and his careful attention to Elizabeth stopped her from feeling so much like the outsider she felt the others considered her.

As soon as dinner was over, she returned to Jane. Miss Bingley and her sister began insulting her the minute she was out of the room. They decided her manners were bad, a mixture of pride and cheek, she had no style, no conversation, no taste, no beauty…

"She has nothing to recommend her but being an excellent walker," sneered Mrs. Hurst. "Her appearance this morning! She really looked wild."

"Very nonsensical to come at all," Miss Bingley agreed. "Why should she be scampering about the countryside because her sister has a cold? She looked so untidy."

"Did you see her dress, six inches deep in mud, and shoes and stockings too?"

"What you say may be true," said Mr. Bingley, "but I thought she looked remarkably well. I never noticed her muddy dress."

"You saw it, Mr. Darcy," said Miss Bingley. "You would not like your sister to make such an exhibition."

"Certainly not."

"I am afraid that this adventure has rather affected your opinion of her fine eyes."

"Not at all," he replied. "They were brightened by the exercise."

A short pause followed and then Mrs. Hurst began again. "Jane Bennet is a very sweet girl, but with such a father and mother, and such common relations, she has no hope of marrying well."

"One of their uncles is only a lawyer in Meryton," Miss Bingley sneered.

"And they have another who lives in *Cheap*side!" added Mrs. Hurst, and they both laughed.

"If they had uncles enough to fill *all* of Cheapside, it would not make them any less agreeable!" cried Mr. Bingley.

"But it must seriously affect their chances of marrying men of any consequence," said Darcy.

To this, Bingley made no answer, but his sisters heartily agreed.

Elizabeth sat with Jane till she fell asleep and then thought it was right, rather than pleasant, to go downstairs. The others were playing cards. She was asked to join them, but the stakes appeared high, and she said she would rather sit with a book.

"Miss Eliza Bennet," said Miss Bingley, "despises cards. She is a great reader and has no pleasure in anything else."

"I deserve neither such praise nor such censure," said Elizabeth. "I am *not* a great reader, and I have pleasure in many things."

"You have a delightful library at Pemberley, Mr. Darcy," said Miss Bingley. "Tell me, how is your sister, dear Georgiana? Her manners, her performance on the piano – oh! she is exquisite!"

"All young ladies are accomplished these days," said Mr. Bingley. "They all play an instrument and paint."

"I only know around half a dozen who are really accomplished," said Darcy.

"Then you must think being accomplished includes a lot more

than that," Elizabeth said.

"Oh, yes, to be truly accomplished," cried Miss Bingley, "a woman must have a thorough knowledge of music, singing, drawing, dancing and the modern languages, and besides all this, she must possess a certain something in her air and manner of walking and speaking, and her expressions."

"And she must add something more," said Darcy, "in improving her mind by constant reading."

"Now I am surprised that you know any accomplished women at all!" Elizabeth remarked. "I have never met such a woman!"

"Eliza Bennet," said Miss Bingley, when Elizabeth had left the room, "is one of those young ladies who tries to attract the other sex by undervaluing their own. It is a mean, underhand art."

"There is a meanness in all the arts which ladies use to capture men," said Darcy, to whom this remark was addressed. "All cunning is despicable."

Miss Bingley was not happy enough with this reply to continue talking on the subject.

Mrs. Bennet, Kitty and Lydia called at Netherfield the following day. Seeing that Jane was not alarmingly ill, Mrs. Bennet had no desire for her to get better immediately. "She is much too ill to be moved," she declared when she came downstairs. "We must trespass a little longer on your kindness."

"She must not think of going till she is well," cried Bingley.

"She shall have every possible attention while she stays with us," said Miss Bingley with cold politeness.

The two younger girls had been whispering throughout the visit, and Lydia now asked Mr. Bingley if he would give a ball at Netherfield.

Lydia was a well-grown girl of fifteen, and was her mother's most beloved daughter. She had high spirits and a natural self-confidence which the attentions of the officers had increased. "It would be shameful not to keep your word," said Lydia. "I shall tell Colonel Forster he must give one too."

Bingley's answer delighted her mother: "As soon as your sister is better, you shall name the day of the ball."

Elizabeth asked after Charlotte.

"She was with us yesterday," Mrs. Bennet said. "She is so very plain. Not like Jane. Do you not think, Mr. Bingley? Mrs. Lucas often envies us Jane's beauty. Jane was nearly snapped up by an officer when she was only fifteen. He wrote verses about her too."

"And so ended his love," Elizabeth said, blushing for her mother, while Caroline Bingley directed her eye to Mr. Darcy with a very expressive smile.

"I thought poetry was the food of love," Mr. Darcy said.

"Of stout, hearty love, maybe. But if the love is only slight, a good poem could starve it completely to death!" Elizabeth replied.

Mr. Darcy smiled, and the ensuing silence made Elizabeth tremble in case her mother said anything else… But Mrs. Bennet, Lydia and Kitty soon left, and Elizabeth returned to Jane.

The rest of the day passed much like the day before. When Elizabeth joined the others downstairs in the evening, she could not help noticing that Mr. Darcy's eyes were fixed on her. She did not think it possible that he could admire her, but to look at her because he disliked her was still more strange. She concluded he must be finding something wrong with her, but she did not care.

Miss Bingley played a Scottish tune on the piano, and Mr. Darcy asked Elizabeth if she would like to dance a reel. She did not answer, and so he asked again.

"I was trying to work out what to reply," Elizabeth said. "You can only have asked me so that I would say yes, and you could despise my taste. Since I delight in overthrowing such plans, I shall answer no, I do not. So now despise me if you dare."

"Indeed, I do not dare."

Elizabeth, having expected to annoy him, was amazed at his gallant reply. There was a mixture of sweetness and playfulness in her manner, and Darcy found he had never been so bewitched by a woman as he was by her. He really believed that were it not for the inferiority of her family, he would be in danger of falling in love.

Miss Bingley suspected enough to be jealous, and her anxiety for Jane's recovery was founded on her desire to get rid of Elizabeth. "I hope you will give your future mother-in-law a few hints on holding her tongue," she whispered to Darcy, "and stop the younger girls running after officers. You must hang a picture of the Cheapside uncle in the portrait gallery at Pemberley."

"Have you any other ideas for my domestic happiness?" asked Darcy, picking up a book.

Miss Bingley was desperate. She wanted him to look at her. Turning to Elizabeth, she said, "Will you walk around the room with me? It is refreshing after sitting still."

Elizabeth was surprised, but she agreed. Mr. Darcy put down his book. Triumphantly, Miss Bingley asked him to join them.

He declined. "I can imagine only two motives for your exercise. Either you have secrets to discuss, which means I should leave you alone, or you wish to be admired, which I can do better from here."

"Shocking!" cried Miss Bingley. "How shall we punish him for such a speech?"

"Tease him – laugh at him," replied Elizabeth.

"I never tease Mr. Darcy."

"Mr. Darcy is not to be laughed at!" cried Elizabeth. "That is an uncommon advantage. I hope it remains uncommon among the people I know, however, for I dearly love a laugh."

"It is easy enough to make anything – even wisdom – seem ridiculous by a joke," said Darcy.

"I hope I never ridicule what is wise and good," said Elizabeth.

"Foolishness amuses me, but I suppose you are free of that."

"I have tried," said Darcy solemnly, "all my life to avoid those weaknesses which lend themselves to ridicule."

"Such as vanity and pride?"

"Vanity certainly. But pride – where the mind is truly superior, pride is acceptable, within reason."

Elizabeth turned away to hide her smile.

"Is your examination of Mr. Darcy over?" asked Miss Bingley. "What have you learned from it?"

"That he has no defects. He admits it himself," said Elizabeth.

"I make no such claim," said Darcy. "I have a temper. It yields too little. I cannot easily forget the wrongdoings of others. My good opinion, once lost, is lost for ever."

"You have chosen well. I cannot laugh at your defect, Mr. Darcy," said Elizabeth. "You are safe from me."

"Everyone has some fault in their character," he said.

"Yours is a propensity to hate everybody?"

"And yours," he replied with a smile, "is to deliberately misunderstand them."

"Do let us have a little music," cried Miss Bingley, tired of a conversation in which she had no share. She opened the lid of the piano, and Darcy was not sorry. He began to feel he was paying Elizabeth too much attention.

The next day, Jane was so much better that Elizabeth asked to borrow Mr. Bingley's carriage to take them home. Mr. Bingley agreed, with genuine sorrow that they were leaving. To Mr. Darcy, however, it was welcome news. Elizabeth attracted him more than he liked to admit to himself. He wisely resolved not to show her any admiration from then on, and hid his nose in his book until she had left.

Jane and Elizabeth were not welcomed home enthusiastically by their mother. Mrs. Bennet had wanted them to stay longer, but Mr. Bennet, though he did not say so, had missed them very much.

"I hope, my dear," said Mr. Bennet to his wife at breakfast the next morning, "you have ordered a good dinner today, as there will be one extra with us. A gentleman— "

"Mr. Bingley!" cried Mrs. Bennet. "Why Jane – you sly thing! You never dropped a word."

"It is *not* Mr. Bingley," her husband said. "It is someone I have never seen before in my life: my cousin, Mr. Collins, who, when I am dead, may turn you all out of this house as soon as he pleases."

"Oh, him! I cannot bear to have that odious man mentioned. It is the hardest thing in the world that your estate should be entailed away from your own children, and if I had been you, I should have tried to do something about it."

Jane and Elizabeth had often tried to explain to her the legal complexities of an entail – that an estate thus burdened must be inherited by the nearest male heir, but it was a subject on which Mrs. Bennet was beyond the reach of reason.

"Nothing can clear Mr. Collins from the guilt of inheriting Longbourn, my dear," said Mr. Bennet, "but if you listen to his letter, you may be a little softened."

"I am sure I shall not be. It was very wrong of him to write at all. Why could he not keep on quarrelling with you, as his father did before him?" Mrs. Bennet sniffed.

"Listen," said Mr. Bennet, and he read aloud:

Dear Sir,

The disagreement between yourself and my late father has always made me uneasy, and since his death, I have wanted to heal the breach between us. Having been ordained at Easter,

Pride and Prejudice

I have been fortunate to have been given the attentions of the Right Honourable Lady Catherine de Bourgh, and now I gratefully live in the vicarage of her parish, where I will for ever show respect to Her Ladyship and be ready to perform the rites and duties of the Church.

As a clergyman, I feel it my duty to promote the blessing of family peace, and, if you can kindly overlook my being next in the entail of Longbourn, and not reject the offered olive branch, I beg to propose myself for Monday, November 18th at four o'clock, and shall probably stay a fortnight. I apologise for being the means of depriving your daughters, and assure you of my readiness to make amends, but more on this hereafter.

I remain your well-wisher and friend,

William Collins

"Today, then, we may expect this polite, peacemaking young gentleman," said Mr. Bennet as he folded up the letter.

"How can he make amends?" Jane wondered.

Elizabeth was chiefly struck by his attitude to Lady Catherine, and his kind intention of christening, marrying and burying his parishioners when required. "He must be an oddity," she said. "He writes very pompously. Can he be a sensible man?"

"I think not. There is a mixture of toadying and self-importance in the letter which promises well. I am impatient to see him," said Mr. Bennet wryly.

"It is not badly constructed," said Mary, "though the olive branch idea is not original."

To Kitty and Lydia, the letter and its writer were of no interest. He would not be wearing a scarlet coat, and so held no attraction for them.

Mr. Collins turned out to be a heavy-looking young man with very formal manners. He admired everything at Longbourn – the hall, the dining room and the furniture – which would have touched Mrs. Bennet's heart but for the mortifying thought that it would all one day be his. At dinner, Mr. Bennet led him on to talk of Lady Catherine, hoping to be entertained. He could not have chosen better. Mr. Collins was eloquent in her praise.

"She is all condescension. She has actually asked me to dine at Rosings – twice! There is nothing she is not interested in. She has advised me to get a wife, and she has called on my humble abode, and instructed me to build shelves in the cupboards!"

"Shelves, eh? She must indeed be a great lady," said Mr. Bennet. "I think you said she is a widow. Does she have children?"

"She has a charming daughter, unfortunately sickly, which prevents her from an active life. I told Lady Catherine that the British Court has thus been deprived of one of its brightest stars. I also said her daughter seemed born to be a duchess. These are the sort of little remarks which please Her Ladyship."

"You have the talent of flattery," said Mr. Bennet. "May I ask if these remarks come from the speed of the moment, or are the result of previous study?"

"I amuse myself with planning elegant little compliments that can be adapted to all occasions. I try to give them as unstudied an air as possible."

Mr. Bennet's expectations were fully answered. His cousin was as absurd as he had hoped and he listened to him with the keenest enjoyment. But when dinner was over, he had had quite enough.

Mr. Collins was not a sensible man, and the deficiency of nature had not been helped much by good education or company. He had come to Longbourn expressly to choose a wife from one

Pride and Prejudice

of Mr. Bennet's daughters, to make amends for inheriting their father's estate. He thought it an excellent plan, full of suitableness and generosity on his part. Jane's lovely face confirmed his views, but a tête-à-tête with Mrs. Bennet the next morning made a small alteration to his plans.

"I must just hint that my eldest daughter is likely to be very soon engaged," Mrs. Bennet told him. "But my younger daughters..." Mr. Collins had only to change from Jane to Elizabeth, and it was done while Mrs. Bennet was stirring the fire.

Mrs. Bennet trusted she would soon have two daughters married, and the man she could not bear to speak to yesterday, today she was prepared to love.

Later that morning, every sister except Mary wanted to walk to Meryton. Mr. Collins was to go too, at the request of Mr. Bennet, who was anxious to get rid of him for a while. Mr. Bennet liked reading in his library, but Mr. Collins kept following him there, talking incessantly.

In Meryton, their attention was caught by a handsome young gentleman, whom they had never seen before, walking with an officer Lydia knew, Captain Denny. Captain Denny introduced him as Mr. Wickham, who had just joined the regiment. As they were all talking, Darcy and Bingley rode down the street. Bingley bowed and said they had been on their way to Longbourn to ask after Jane. Darcy bowed and, determined not to fix his eyes on Elizabeth, caught sight of the stranger. Elizabeth happened to see them as they looked at each other, and was astonished. Both of their faces changed at once – one turned white, one red. What could be the meaning of it? It was impossible not to be curious.

In a minute, Mr. Bingley and Mr. Darcy went on their way.

The Bennet party called on Mrs. Bennet's sister, Mrs. Philips. Mr. Collins, on his return to Longbourn, delighted Mrs. Bennet by his praise of Mrs. Philips, for she had included him in an invitation for the very next evening. He had never met such politeness, he declared, apart from Lady Catherine's.

Elizabeth was delighted to hear that Mrs. Philips had also invited Mr. Wickham. He was the happy man to whom all the women's eyes turned when he entered, and she was the happy woman he sat next to. The agreeable way in which he immediately fell into conversation, though it was only about it being a wet night, made her feel that the commonest, dullest, most threadbare topic might be made interesting by the skill of the speaker.

She held back from asking him about Mr. Darcy, but her curiosity was unexpectedly relieved.

"How long has Mr. Darcy been staying here?" Mr. Wickham asked her.

"About a month," she replied, then, unwilling to let the subject drop, continued, "He has a very large property in Derbyshire, I understand."

"Yes, a noble estate. A clear ten thousand a year. You could not have better information than from myself, for I have known the family from childhood. I was the godson of Mr. Darcy's late father, and my father was the steward of Pemberley. Do you know Mr. Darcy well?"

"As well as I ever wish to," Elizabeth said warmly. "I have spent four days in the same house with him, and think him very disagreeable. Everyone around here thinks him horribly proud."

"His behaviour to me has been scandalous," said Wickham.

Elizabeth listened eagerly as Mr. Wickham continued.

"I did not set out to be a soldier. The Church ought to have been my profession; Mr. Darcy's father, the kindest gentleman, left me a very valuable living when he died, but when a position became available, Mr. Darcy gave it away elsewhere."

"Good heavens!" Elizabeth exclaimed. "How could the will be disregarded? Why did you not take legal action?"

"There was just enough informality in the wording as to give me no hope from the law. No man of honour would have doubted the meaning, but Mr. Darcy chose to. He dislikes me because his father doted on me, rather than him."

"Shocking. People should know about this!" cried Elizabeth.

"I could never make it publicly known. In memory of his kind father, I could never do such a thing."

Elizabeth thought his feelings were noble, and thought him handsomer than ever as he expressed them.

"It is strange that his pride did not make him behave better," she said.

"He has family pride – he is generous to his tenants; and he has brotherly pride. You will find him well spoken of as a careful guardian to his sister, Georgiana."

"What sort of girl is she?"

"I wish I could call her amiable. She is too much like her brother – *very* proud. As a child she was fond of me. She is a pretty girl, about fifteen years old, and lives in London with a guardian."

Mr. Wickham's attention was now caught by hearing Mr. Collins talking to Mrs. Philips about Lady Catherine de Bourgh.

"Did you know," he asked Elizabeth, "that Lady Catherine is Mr. Darcy's aunt?"

"I did not. I had never heard of her till two days ago."

"Her daughter, Miss de Bourgh, will have a very large fortune, and it is believed she and her cousin, Mr. Darcy, will marry and unite their estates."

Elizabeth smiled as she thought of poor Miss Bingley, whose efforts would all be in vain.

The evening ended, and all the way home, she could think of nothing but Mr. Wickham and everything he had told her.

Pride and Prejudice

The next day, as they walked in the garden, Elizabeth told Jane what Mr. Wickham had said about Mr. Darcy. Jane was astonished. It was not in her nature to question the truthfulness of such a pleasant man as Wickham. Nor could she believe that Darcy was as bad as he had been painted, or Bingley would not have him as a friend.

"There must be more to the story on each side. It is difficult indeed," she said. "One does not know what to think."

"One knows exactly what to think," said Elizabeth.

They were summoned indoors by the arrival of Mr. Bingley and his sisters with their invitation for the long-awaited ball at Netherfield, fixed for the following Tuesday. The two ladies were delighted to see Jane, but avoided Mrs. Bennet, did not say much to Elizabeth and said nothing at all to the others. They were soon gone again.

Everyone in the family was pleased about the Netherfield ball. Mrs. Bennet was certain it was a compliment to Jane. Elizabeth thought with pleasure of dancing with Wickham. Her spirits sank when Mr. Collins asked her to keep the first two dances for him. She had hoped Wickham would ask her for those very dances. There was nothing she could do apart from accept with good grace, but Elizabeth began to suspect Mr. Collins's gallantry of hiding a deeper purpose: that she was the selected sister to be the mistress of his vicarage and dine sometimes at Rosings with the great Lady Catherine.

As for Kitty and Lydia, and even Mary, Tuesday could not come too soon.

Elizabeth looked in vain for Wickham at the ball. She wondered if Darcy had prevented his invitation, till Captain Denny told her he had gone to London on business, as, "he wished to avoid a certain gentleman." Now she was angry with Darcy, and she turned away from his polite enquiries with distaste. But she was not made for ill-humour, and her spirits were not depressed for long.

The first two dances, however, were dances of mortification. Mr. Collins was awkward and solemn, always moving wrong, filling her with shame. The moment of release from him was ecstasy.

She danced next with an officer, and heard from him how Mr. Wickham was liked by everyone. Then she went to chat to Charlotte Lucas. Almost immediately, she found Darcy by her side, asking her to dance. It surprised her so much that she accepted.

They were silent for a while, till, deciding it would punish him to make him talk, Elizabeth said something about the dance.

He replied and fell silent again.

After a pause of some minutes, Elizabeth said, "It is your turn to speak now, Mr. Darcy. I said something about the dance and you ought to say something about the number of couples."

"Do you always talk as a rule, when you are dancing?" he asked.

"Sometimes. One must speak a little, you know, to be polite." She glanced at him, and added pointedly, "For the advantage of some, the conversation ought to be arranged so one may say as little as possible."

"Are you consulting your own feelings, or mine?" he asked.

"Both," replied Elizabeth, "for I have seen similarities between us. We are each of us unsocial creatures, unwilling to speak unless we expect to say something that will amaze the whole room."

"That is no portrait of you," he said. "How near it may be to me, I cannot say."

They were silent again till he asked her if she and her sisters often walked to Meryton.

"Fairly often," she said, then, unable to resist the temptation, continued, "when you met us there the other day, we had just been making a new friend."

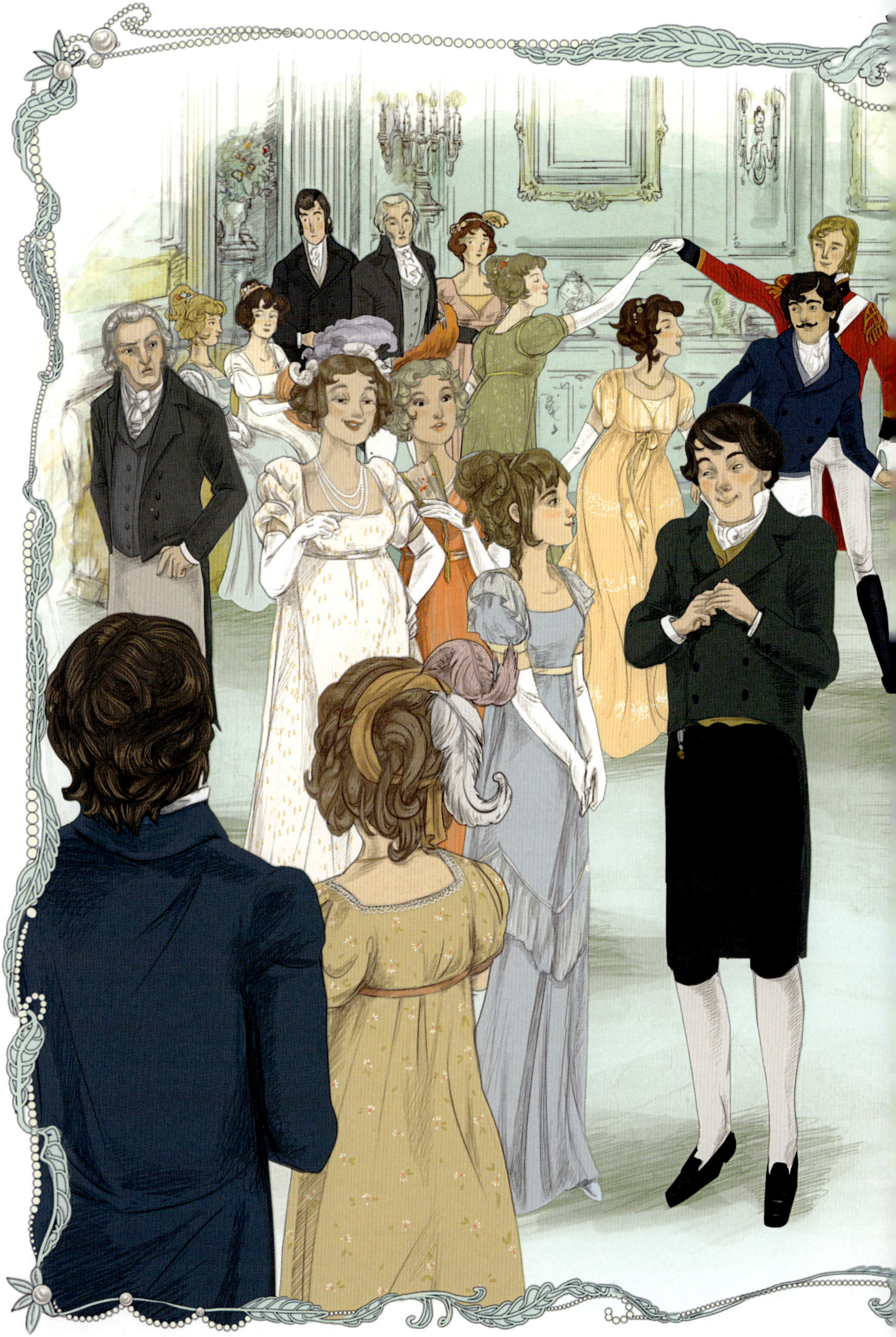

*Elizabeth found Darcy by her side, asking her to dance.
It surprised her so much that she accepted.*

Pride and Prejudice

The effect was immediate. A deeper look of haughtiness spread over his face as he said, "Mr. Wickham has such happy manners that he makes friends easily. Whether he is equally capable of keeping them is less certain."

"He is unlucky to have lost *your* friendship," said Elizabeth, "in a manner he is likely to suffer from all his life."

Darcy did not answer.

"I remember you once said, Mr. Darcy, that you hardly ever forgave – that your resentment, once created, was fixed. You are very careful, I suppose, as to its being created in the first place?"

"I am," he said firmly.

"And you never allow yourself to be blinded by prejudice?"

"I hope not. Why do you ask?"

"I am trying to work out your character, but I cannot. I have such different accounts of you that I am exceedingly puzzled."

"That does not surprise me," Mr. Darcy said, and they finished the dance, each dissatisfied; in Darcy, however, a powerful feeling towards Elizabeth soon made him forgive her and direct his anger against someone else.

Jane was dancing with Bingley, in a glow of delight. Watching her, all Elizabeth's thoughts gave way to the hope that Jane was on the path to happiness.

Mr. Collins interrupted her dreams, saying eagerly, "I have just discovered that Mr. Darcy is Lady Catherine's nephew."

"You are not going to introduce yourself to him?"

"Indeed I am, with apologies for not having done so earlier. I can assure him that she was well a fortnight ago."

Elizabeth begged him not to. He ignored her, and she watched Mr. Darcy regard him with an air of astonishment that increased with Mr. Collins's every grovelling word. At the end of it, Mr. Darcy made a slight bow and moved away.

When they sat down to supper, her attention was caught by

her mother talking to Lady Lucas. "Yes, Jane will soon be married to Mr. Bingley," she was saying. "He is so charming, and so rich, and Jane marrying him will be a good thing for my other girls, throwing them into the path of other rich men."

In vain did Elizabeth beg her to talk more quietly, fearing that Mr. Darcy, sitting opposite them, would hear.

"What do I care if Mr. Darcy hears?" asked Mrs. Bennet loudly.

At last, however, the comforts of cold chicken and ham overpowered her speech, and Elizabeth could breathe again.

Not for long. Mary was asked to play and sing. Such a request pleased her, but her powers were not equal to it. Her voice was weak, and her manner pretentious. Elizabeth was in agonies. She saw Bingley's sisters snigger and she glanced at her father in desperation. He took the hint after Mary's second song. "That will do extremely well, child. You have delighted us long enough."

To Elizabeth it seemed her family had an agreement to make themselves look ridiculous. Bingley did not seem to notice, but his sisters and Darcy had ample opportunity to mock her relations. She could not bear his grave silence or their insolent smiles.

They were the last to depart. Mrs. Bennet arranged for their carriage to arrive a quarter of an hour after everyone else's, which allowed Elizabeth to see how heartily they were wished away. Mrs. Bennet was perfectly satisfied, dreaming of wedding clothes and having a daughter settled at Netherfield. On having another daughter married to Mr. Collins, she dwelt with equal certainty. Elizabeth was her least beloved child, and she thought the man and the match quite good enough for her.

The next day, Mr. Collins proposed. Elizabeth saw it coming and tried to escape him, but at her mother's cry of: "Lizzy, I insist upon your staying and hearing Mr. Collins," she thought it might be wisest to get it over with.

"Your modesty does you credit," said Mr. Collins, as soon as her mother had gone. "Before I run away with my feelings…"

The idea of Mr. Collins running away with his feelings made Elizabeth so close to laughing that she could not prevent him from continuing.

"…I must give you my reasons for marrying. Lady Catherine told me to find a wife. 'Choose a gentlewoman, for my sake,' she said, 'an active, useful sort of person, not brought up too high.' Your wit and liveliness will, I think, be acceptable to her, especially if you restrain yourself by your respect for her rank. Secondly, I wished to choose a wife from among you all, to make amends for my gain when your father dies."

"Stop!" cried Elizabeth. "Accept my thanks; I am aware of the honour, but I must decline your proposal."

"Ladies often refuse two or three times," he replied. "I am not discouraged. I will lead you to the altar before long."

"Your hope is rather extraordinary after what I have said," said Elizabeth. "You could not make me happy, and I am the last woman in the world who would make you so. I am sure Lady Catherine would find me ill-qualified. Can I speak plainer?"

"You are charming," he cried, with awkward gallantry. "And soon you will bow to the wishes of your parents!"

Mr. Collins went to tell Mrs. Bennet, who was shocked at Lizzy's refusal.

"I will bring her to reason," she promised. "She is a very foolish, headstrong girl, but I will make her see sense."

"If she is really headstrong, then perhaps…"

"No, no! Only in matters like this! In every other way she is very good-natured." She gave him no time to reply, but hurried to Mr. Bennet's library, crying: "You must make Lizzy marry Mr. Collins at once! If you do not hurry, he will change his mind and not have her."

"Call her here," said Mr. Bennet.

"Well, child," he said when she appeared, an expression of calm unconcern on his face, "an unhappy prospect lies before you. Your mother will never see you again if you do not marry Mr. Collins, and I will never see you again if you do."

"Oh! Mr. Bennet," cried Mrs. Bennet. She did not give up easily, using coaxing and threats, but Elizabeth stood firm.

Mr. Collins thought far too well of himself to understand why Lizzy could possibly have refused him. His pride was a little hurt, but he suffered in no other way. In fact the hint of Elizabeth's headstrong nature meant he was somewhat relieved.

While the family were in this confusion, Charlotte Lucas called, and with great tact, and to everyone's relief, took Mr. Collins off to spend the day at Lucas Lodge.

The next day brought a letter written on elegant paper for Jane from Netherfield. "It is from Caroline Bingley," she said. Alone with Elizabeth, she read part of it aloud. The whole party were to quit Netherfield, with little chance of returning. "We will all go to London. Mr. Darcy is anxious to see his sister again, as are we all. Dear Georgiana is unequalled for beauty and elegance. My brother admires her greatly, and there is nothing to prevent our happy expectations."

Jane looked at her sister unhappily. "Caroline wants to put me off," she said.

"She sees her brother is in love with you; she whisks him away. We are not rich or grand enough for them," Elizabeth said. "But he does love you, Jane. You will see."

The next day, Charlotte again offered to spend time with Mr. Collins. Elizabeth was grateful to her for keeping him out of the way, but Charlotte's kindness extended further than Elizabeth could have imagined. She was trying to prevent a return of Mr. Collins's advances toward Elizabeth by securing them for herself. The stupidity with which he was blessed prevented his proposal to her, when it came, from being all that charming. But Charlotte overlooked that for the sake of marriage.

Without thinking highly either of men or matrimony, marriage had always been her aim: it was the only honourable way for a well-educated young woman with little money to provide for herself. However uncertain of giving happiness, it was the best way to keep her from living in poverty. At twenty-seven, without ever having been beautiful, she felt lucky to have secured it. The least pleasant part was the view of her dearest friend on the matter.

When Charlotte told her, Elizabeth could not help bursting out, "Engaged to Mr. Collins? Impossible!"

"I am not romantic," replied Charlotte. "I never was. I ask only for a comfortable home, and I am certain my chance of happiness with him is as fair as most people can expect."

Elizabeth was so disappointed with Charlotte that she could hardly bear to speak to her after that. She turned even more to Jane, growing more and more anxious for her happiness, since a week had passed, and nothing had been heard from Mr. Bingley.

Her mother was in a pitiable state. "To think that Charlotte Lucas will be mistress of this house! To think Elizabeth could have married him..." she complained. "And Jane, why does Mr. Bingley *not* come?"

It took all Jane's steady mildness for her to bear these attacks from her mother with anything like her usual calm.

Another letter from Miss Bingley put an end to any doubt. The Bingleys were settled in London for the winter, and Miss Bingley hinted again that her brother was partial to Mr. Darcy's charming, wealthy sister.

Pride and Prejudice

Jane gave up all hope. "He will live in my memory as the most amiable man I ever met," she told an indignant Elizabeth. "A little time... and I shall recover..."

A week later, Mrs. Bennet's brother and his wife, Mr. and Mrs. Gardiner, came to stay for Christmas. Mr. Gardiner was a sensible man, whom the Netherfield ladies would have found difficult to believe could be so well-bred, working in trade and living in Cheapside. Mrs. Gardiner was amiable and intelligent, and her nieces loved her. Seeing Jane's unhappiness, they offered to take her back to London with them for a change of scene. Jane accepted the invitation with pleasure.

After they had left, Charlotte Lucas and Mr. Collins were married. "You must write – and visit!" Charlotte told Elizabeth as she left for her new home in Kent. Elizabeth agreed, wondering if they could ever be truly close friends again.

Indeed, Charlotte's letters, which Elizabeth read eagerly, said nothing of what she thought of Lady Catherine, and spoke cheerfully about the house and neighbourhood. Elizabeth realized she would have to wait until she herself visited, to know the rest.

Jane's letters from London were full of hope of seeing Miss Bingley. She called on her, but Miss Bingley was out. At last came news that Miss Bingley had returned the call. "But, oh my dear sister, how mistaken I was in her. She was very cold and formal, and made no mention of wanting to see me again. She told me he knows I am in town, but will not see me. She also said something about his never returning to Netherfield again."

This letter gave Elizabeth more pain than the other news she had recently received, that Mr. Wickham was engaged to a rich heiress, a Miss King. She had thought him the most agreeable man she had ever met, and yet she found the news not so very painful. Her heart had been only lightly touched, and she flattered herself that she would have been his choice, had their fortunes allowed it. But young gentlemen, even very handsome ones, must have something to live on, after all.

January and February passed with no more diversion than muddy walks to Meryton. Then Elizabeth received an invitation from Charlotte to visit. Absence had increased her desire to see Charlotte, and weakened her disgust for Mr. Collins, so she went.

Mrs. Collins welcomed her friend with pleasure. She showed Elizabeth the vicarage, but within a day, Elizabeth noticed how well Charlotte managed to organize Mr. Collins out of it, encouraging him to garden and sending him on errands. When Mr. Collins could be forgotten, everything seemed very comfortable, and judging by Charlotte's happiness, Elizabeth supposed he must often be forgotten.

Elizabeth felt that everything Mr. Collins said regarding his house was pointed at her, in an attempt to make her realize what she had lost in refusing him. But she felt no repentance, wondering how Charlotte could be so cheerful with such a companion.

They were asked to dinner at Rosings, Lady de Bourgh's house, the following day. "I thought she might ask us to drink tea, but dinner…!" exclaimed Mr. Collins. "Such condescension! Such kindness! We are indeed fortunate. Do not be overpowered, cousin, by the number of servants, or the fine rooms. Do not be uneasy about your clothing. Lady Catherine will prefer you simply dressed. She likes to have the distinctions of rank observed."

Elizabeth found herself perfectly equal to the occasion.

Lady Catherine was a large woman, with a manner that made visitors aware of their inferiority. Whatever she said was spoken in so authoritative a tone as marked her self-importance. Miss de Bourgh was pale and sickly looking, and spoke very little. To

Elizabeth's astonishment, dinner was graced by the presence of two other gentlemen: Lady Catherine's nephews, Colonel Fitzwilliam and Mr. Darcy.

Nothing escaped this great lady's attention. Lady Catherine inquired about Elizabeth's sisters, what sort of carriage her father kept, her mother's maiden name… Elizabeth felt it rude, but answered composedly.

"Do you play and sing, Miss Bennet?" asked Lady Catherine.

"A little."

"You should practise every day or you will not improve. You may practise here in the housekeeper's room; you would be quite out of the way."

Mr. Darcy looked rather ashamed of his aunt.

"Has your governess left you?" she continued.

"We never had one," said Elizabeth.

"Really? Five daughters and no governess? Your education must have been sorely neglected."

"Those of us who wished to learn did so. We were always encouraged to read and had all the necessary books."

"You give your opinions very decidedly."

Colonel Fitzwilliam, unlike his aunt, talked very pleasantly with the well-bred readiness and ease of a gentleman. He sat beside Elizabeth, and they talked so much of books and music that Lady Catherine called out, "What are you saying? Let me hear."

"We are speaking of music, madam."

"There are few people in England who have more enjoyment of music than I. If I had ever learned to play, I should have been an expert. And so would my daughter, if her health had allowed her. You may play to us now, Miss Bennet."

Lady Catherine listened to half a song and turned away, but Darcy moved to the piano and stood beside Elizabeth.

"You mean to frighten me, Mr. Darcy, but I will not be

alarmed," said Elizabeth. "I know I am not accomplished, but my courage always rises when someone intimidates me."

"You could not really believe I want to alarm you," Darcy said. "I know you enjoy announcing opinions you do not really believe."

Elizabeth laughed at this picture of herself, and said to Colonel Fitzwilliam, "Your cousin will not allow you to believe a word I say. But I can retaliate. The first time I met him, he would not dance, even though there were ladies without partners."

"I did not have the pleasure of knowing them," said Darcy.

"True, and no one can ever be introduced in a ballroom."

"Perhaps I should have sought an introduction but I am ill-qualified to recommend myself to strangers."

"Shall we ask him why?" Elizabeth said to Colonel Fitzwilliam.

"I have no talent for easy conversation with people I have never seen before," said Darcy.

"My fingers," said Elizabeth, "do not move over this instrument with ease, but I have always supposed it my fault – because I do not practise enough."

Darcy smiled. "You are perfectly right. You have employed your time better than I. No one listening to you could find anything wanting."

Several times on walks in the countryside around the vicarage, Elizabeth met Darcy. It was very unexpected, and he seemed to think it necessary to walk with her. He never said much, nor did she give herself the trouble of talking, but she did think it odd that his few questions were so unconnected – directed at her love of solitary walks and the happiness of Mr. and Mrs. Collins.

Once on such a walk, she saw that Colonel Fitzwilliam had come to meet her. Their conversation turned to Bingley and his sisters. "Mr. Darcy really does take care of his friend," said Colonel Fitzwilliam. "He told me that he had saved Mr. Bingley from a very bad marriage."

"Did Mr. Darcy say anything more?"

"He said there were some strong objections against the lady."

They talked of other matters till she reached the vicarage. There, she shut herself in her room, too distressed for company. It was Darcy who had ruined Jane's happiness. He – and his pride – were the cause of all she suffered. "Strong objections" no doubt meant an uncle who was a lawyer in Meryton and another in Cheapside. To Jane herself, all loveliness and goodness, there could be no possible objection.

Her anguish brought on a headache. She refused an evening invitation to Rosings, ignoring Mr. Collins's dread of Lady Catherine's displeasure.

It was a relief that her visit to Charlotte would be over the following day. While they were gone, she was startled by the doorbell. Who could be calling so late? To her utter amazement, Mr. Darcy came walking in. In a hurried manner he enquired after her health. She answered him with cold politeness.

He was silent for a few minutes, then came towards her, agitated, and began: "In vain have I struggled. It will not do. My feelings will not be repressed. You must allow me to tell you how ardently I admire and love you."

Elizabeth's astonishment was beyond expression.

He took this as encouragement and went on. He spoke well, but he dwelt with warmth on other feelings beside the heart, such as her inferiority, of its being a degradation to him, and of family obstacles. Her anger mounted, coming to a head when she saw he expected her to accept him.

She flushed and said, "If I could feel gratitude, I would thank you, but I cannot. I have never desired your good opinion, and you have certainly bestowed it most unwillingly."

Pride and Prejudice

Mr. Darcy grew pale. At last, with forced calmness, he said, "Is this all you have to say? With so little attempt at politeness? You give no reason why I am thus rejected."

"I might as well enquire," she replied, "why, with so evident a desire of offending and insulting me, you told me you liked me against your better judgement. Had my own feelings not dissuaded me, do you think I could ever marry the man who ruined the happiness of my sister? I have every reason to think ill of you. How can you defend your treatment of Mr. Wickham? You withheld from him the living which was promised him."

"And this," cried Darcy, "is your opinion of me! I am not ashamed of my feelings for you. They were natural and just. Could you expect me to rejoice in the inferiority of your family connections, so decidedly beneath my own?"

"I might have refused you more kindly had you behaved more like a gentleman. But from the moment I met you, your manners have only shown me your arrogance, your conceit and your selfish disdain for the feelings of others. As I already felt within a month of knowing you, you are the last man in the world whom I could ever be persuaded to marry!"

"You have said enough. I perfectly comprehend your feelings and all that remains is for me to be ashamed of what mine have been. Forgive me for taking your time. I wish you happiness."

With these words he left the room. Elizabeth sat down and cried. That Mr. Darcy should love her! But he had been so cruel to Jane and Mr. Wickham! His behaviour overcame any feeling which his declaration of love might for a moment have aroused.

The next morning, Elizabeth went for a walk. She was striding along, when who should she see coming towards her but Mr. Darcy! He held out a letter which she instinctively took. He said, "Will you do me the honour of reading this?" Then, with a slight

Pride and Prejudice

bow, he turned and walked away.

Elizabeth opened the letter with curiosity, finding two pages of closely written lines. It was as follows:

Be not alarmed of a renewal of my words which were so disgusting to you yesterday, but my character requires this letter to be written and read. I appeal to your sense of justice.

You accused me of two offences: that I detached Mr. Bingley from your sister and that I blasted Mr. Wickham's prospects. After watching my friend with your sister, I realized that his feelings were deeper than any he had felt before. However, your sister's calm behaviour towards him convinced me that she did not feel deeply for him in return. I may have been mistaken in this. Apart from your sister and yourself, I disapproved of your family's status, not merely your mother's family, but the lack of propriety displayed by her and your younger sisters, and even - pardon me, it pains me to offend you - by your father. I persuaded Mr. Bingley that your sister did not love him. If I wounded your sister's feelings, it was unknowingly done.

As for Mr. Wickham, he was the son of my father's steward. My father paid for his schooling, and before he died, asked me to give him a valuable living in the Church, as well as £1,000. Wickham told me he had no interest in the Church, and asked me for money instead. I gave him £3,000. After this, he led a life of idleness and extravagance. I ask for your secrecy in what follows. About a year ago, my sister, Georgiana, then only fifteen years old, confessed to me that she was about to elope with Mr. Wickham. He had been visiting her in London and had

Pride and Prejudice

gained her innocent heart. His aim, of course, was not love, but her fortune of thirty thousand pounds. You can imagine how I felt and acted. I do not know what falsehoods he has told you. If you doubt my account of him, Colonel Fitzwilliam will vouch for the truth of what I say.

I will only add, God bless you,

Fitzwilliam Darcy

At first Elizabeth was struck by the letter's pride and haughty style. When she reached the part about Wickham, she felt astonishment and horror. But she had no doubt that it was true. She remembered how Wickham had avoided Darcy at the Netherfield ball – not the other way around. His pursuit of Miss King was entirely mercenary. And then she thought of Jane. She remembered Charlotte's opinion that Jane was too reserved in expressing her affection. She could not deny that his description of Jane was fair. His description of her family filled her with shame. She remembered her humiliation at the Netherfield ball when his impression of her family evidently equalled her own. When she thought that Jane's disappointment had been the work of her nearest relations, depression overwhelmed her.

How different everything seemed now. She grew ashamed of herself, and could not think of Wickham or Darcy without feeling that she had been prejudiced and blind. "How badly I have acted!" she thought. "I – who prided myself on my clear judgement. Till this moment, I never knew myself."

She wandered in the country lanes for hours. When she returned, she learned that Mr. Darcy and Colonel Fitzwilliam had called to bid her goodbye. She was glad to have missed them; she could think only of the letter.

Her feelings varied every minute. She was still angry at the haughty style of his address, but when she remembered how unjustly she had condemned him when he had proposed, her anger turned against herself. She felt more compassionate towards him, although she had no wish ever to see him again. She saw no remedy for the unhappy defects of her family. And her father, content with laughing at his younger daughters, would never constrain their giddiness. While there were officers in Meryton, Kitty and Lydia would follow them for ever.

Elizabeth and Jane arrived home at the same time. Mrs. Bennet rejoiced to see Jane's beauty undiminished, and several times Mr. Bennet said, "I am glad you are back, Lizzy."

Elizabeth had the time now to observe Jane's manner. She came to the conclusion that Jane was not happy – she still cherished feelings for Mr. Bingley. Elizabeth could not bring herself to tell Jane what Darcy's letter had contained about her, but she did confide in her the business about Wickham.

Jane, with all her goodness, could scarcely believe that such wickedness could exist in the world. "And poor Mr. Darcy, having to bear your ill opinion with all he felt!" she exclaimed.

"Have you heard, Lizzy?" asked Lydia soon after. "The officers are going to Brighton, and I am going too as Mrs. Forster's guest!"

"She should have asked me as well," lamented Kitty.

"And," Lydia continued, "Mr. Wickham is safe! He has broken his engagement to Miss King."

"So Miss King is safe," thought Elizabeth.

Later, when she was alone with her father, she spoke to him. "Is it wise to let Lydia go to Brighton?"

"Lydia will not be content till she has disgraced herself, and much better that she should do so away from her family."

Pride and Prejudice

"If you knew the disadvantages to her family she had already caused, you would judge differently," said Elizabeth.

"Has she frightened away your lovers? Never mind. Such squeamish men who cannot manage a little absurdity are not worth any regrets," her father said wryly.

"I have no injuries to resent," Elizabeth told him. "But if you do not rein in her wildness – she is, at sixteen, the most determined little flirt – then she will be despised wherever she goes, and her sisters will be involved in her disgrace."

"We shall have no peace unless she goes to Brighton, and she is too lacking in wealth for anyone to prey upon her."

With this answer Elizabeth was forced to be content.

Lydia went off to Brighton, and Mr. and Mrs. Gardiner came to Longbourn and took Elizabeth with them on a tour of Derbyshire. That county held a particular attraction for Mrs. Gardiner, for she had spent her childhood there.

Elizabeth could not see the word Derbyshire without thinking of Mr. Darcy. "But surely," she thought, "I may enter his county without his knowledge."

They stayed in a comfortable inn at Lambton. Within five miles of Lambton, Elizabeth learned from her aunt, was Darcy's grand house and estate, Pemberley.

"My love, would you not like to see a place of which you have heard so much?" asked Mrs. Gardiner.

"Thank you, but I am tired of great houses," Elizabeth told her, "and fine carpets and satin curtains. We have seen so many."

"But it is not only a fine house. The grounds are delightful. They have the finest woods in the country."

The possibility of meeting Mr. Darcy while viewing his house was dreadful.

"I hear the family is away," her aunt insisted. She was clearly longing to see it. Elizabeth finally agreed, with a pretence of indifference. To Pemberley, therefore, they were to go.

As they drove there, Elizabeth's spirits were in a high flutter. The house rose into view, a large, beautiful building, with a wood behind, and a river in front. Elizabeth was delighted. Never had she seen such a perfect setting. At that moment she felt that to be mistress of Pemberley might have been something.

The housekeeper showed them over the house, reassuring Elizabeth that Mr. Darcy was indeed away. He was expected the following day, with a party of friends. Elizabeth rejoiced that their own journey had not been delayed by a day.

The rooms were superb, but not uselessly lavish. They had less splendour and more real elegance than Lady Catherine's house. "To think all this might have been mine," thought Elizabeth. "But my uncle and aunt would have been lost to me. I would never have been allowed to invite them here." This was a lucky recollection – it saved her from something uncomfortably like regret.

Her aunt now called her to look at a picture: a miniature of Wickham. "He was the son of my late master's steward," said the housekeeper. "But I am afraid he has turned out very wild. He left a lot of debt in his wake, which my master has paid off. And that is a picture of my master."

"Well, Lizzy," said her aunt. "Is it like him? Is he as handsome?"

"Does the lady know Mr. Darcy?" asked the housekeeper.

"A little," Elizabeth replied.

"A better gentleman never lived," said the housekeeper. "I have known him since he was four years old, and there is no sweeter-tempered, more generous man. He is the best landlord and the best master one could hope for. All his tenants and servants would say the same."

This praise was the opposite of all Elizabeth's ideas. His ill-temper had been her firmest opinion. As she gazed at the portrait, its expression seemed to soften with the housekeeper's praise. And she remembered his proposal to her with more warmth, and gratitude. This smile was like the one he had often had when he looked at her.

When they had finished seeing the house, they were handed over to a gardener who showed them the enormous grounds. But as they crossed the lawn to the river, and Elizabeth turned back to look at the house… its owner suddenly came forward.

So abrupt was Mr. Darcy's appearance that it was impossible to avoid him. Their eyes instantly met and the cheeks of each were overspread with the deepest blush. Darcy recovered himself and spoke to Elizabeth, if not with perfect composure, with perfect politeness, asking after her family with a gentle warmth.

The next few minutes were the most uncomfortable of her life. Oh, why had she come? It must seem as if she had purposely thrown herself in his way. If they had been ten minutes sooner, they would not have seen him.

She was amazed, with every word he spoke, at the alteration in his manner from their last encounter. He asked if she would do him the honour of introducing her friends.

Elizabeth smiled, thinking how fast he would decamp from her disgraceful relations, and introduced them as her uncle and aunt. To her astonishment, he was politeness itself.

Hearing Mr. Gardiner was a keen fisherman, Darcy immediately invited him to fish in his lakes and rivers.

It was consoling to know she had some relations for whom there was no need to blush. But still Elizabeth could not think what had made him so different. "It cannot be for me. It cannot be for my sake that he has changed his manners," she thought. "It is impossible that he could still love me…"

"My sister particularly wants to meet you, Miss Bennet," he was saying now. "Will you do us the honour of dining with us

*Elizabeth was amazed at the alteration
in his manner from their last encounter.*

tomorrow? Mr. Bingley and his sisters will also be there."

Elizabeth was surprised. She agreed, relieved; perhaps he did not really think so badly of her after all. He pressed her to go to the house for some refreshment, and when she declined, helped her into her carriage with the utmost politeness.

The very next day, Darcy, Miss Darcy and Bingley came to call on them at the inn in Lambton. Miss Darcy, described as so proud, turned out to be only exceedingly shy. She was sixteen, unassuming and gentle.

In seeing Mr. Bingley, Elizabeth's thoughts naturally flew to her sister. She could detect no hint that Miss Darcy, whom his sisters had set up as a rival to Jane, was the object of his affection.

"It is a long time since we met," he said. "I have not seen you since the 26th of November, when we all danced at Netherfield."

Elizabeth was pleased to find his memory so exact.

Over the next few days, they met frequently at Pemberley, at Mr. Darcy's invitation. To Mr. and Mrs. Gardiner, it was obvious that Mr. Darcy was very much in love.

Elizabeth's feelings were confused. She did not hate him. No; hatred had vanished long ago. She felt gratitude, not merely for his having once loved her, but for loving her still well enough to forgive the manner of her rejection.

She saw she was closely watched by Miss Bingley. After her departure the first evening, Miss Bingley cried, "How coarse and brown Eliza Bennet has grown! I remember when we first knew her, how amazed we were to find her a reputed beauty, and I particularly recollect you, Mr. Darcy, saying, 'She, a beauty! I should as soon call her mother a wit!'"

"Yes," said Darcy, who could contain himself no longer. "But that was when I first knew her. For many months I have thought her one of the most beautiful women I know."

Pride and Prejudice

Miss Bingley was left to all the satisfaction of having forced him to say what gave no one any pain but herself.

Back at the inn Elizabeth received a letter, written in haste:

Dearest Lizzy,

Lydia has run away with Wickham. We do not know where they are. Our poor mother is ill, and our father is powerless. There is no indication that he will marry her. Our sister is ruined. I long for your return.

Jane

As she read it, her head swimming with distress, Darcy knocked at her door. "What is the matter?" he cried, seeing her pale face. "You look ill!"

Wordlessly she showed him Jane's letter. "When I think that I might have prevented it!" cried Elizabeth. "I knew what he was, but I said nothing. Oh, it is horrible! She has nothing – no money, no connections – to tempt him to marry her."

"I am grieved – shocked…" he began, after reading it. Then he fell silent, and began walking to and fro, deep in thought.

Elizabeth understood. His opinion of her was sinking because of her family's disgrace. This thought made her understand her own wishes as never before. Now, when it was all in vain, she finally realized that she could have loved him.

"I am afraid you would rather I went," said Darcy. "There is nothing I can say to comfort you. I expect you will not want to dine at Pemberley this evening." Mr. Darcy left, looking grave.

It was all over, she thought with regret. She was desperate to be at home.

Pride and Prejudice

On the journey back to Longbourn, her uncle said, "I think they may be in London, where it is easiest to hide. Do you think he will marry her?"

"I do not," said Elizabeth. "He has neither integrity nor honour."

At home, they found Mrs. Bennet wailing, "I know Mr. Bennet will fight Mr. Wickham when he sees him, and then he will be killed, and what is to become of us all? Mr. Collins will turn us out!"

They all exclaimed against such dreadful ideas, while Mr. Bennet said as little as possible, remarking only to Elizabeth: "If I had only listened to you, Lizzy. I blame myself."

The Gardiners returned to London, and within a few weeks Mr. Bennet received a letter from Mr. Gardiner. "All is well," he announced. "They have been found. All I have to do is give Lydia now her share of the five thousand pounds she will inherit after my death, and Wickham will marry her. Wickham is taking her for very little. Your uncle must have given at least ten thousand more. Oh, that good, generous man. How can I possibly repay him?"

Only Mrs. Bennet was delighted. "My dear, dear Lydia!" she crowed. "She will be married at sixteen! How merry we will be when we meet!"

Lydia and Wickham came back to Longbourn, with Lydia in the highest spirits. "I take your place now, Jane," she cried as she went first through the door, "for I am a married woman!"

"I must tell you about my wedding," she said later, alone with her sisters. "Uncle Gardiner was to give me away, and I was upset because he was late, but it would not have mattered – Mr. Darcy would have done instead—"

"Mr. Darcy!" said Elizabeth, astonished.

"Gracious me! I forgot! That was a secret!"

"Then I will not ask," said Elizabeth, burning with curiosity.

She could not work out the meaning of it. She wrote to her aunt. Back came the reply:

Pride and Prejudice

Dearest Lizzy,

On the very day we returned from Longbourn, Mr. Darcy called. He told us he had come to London to find Mr. Wickham and Lydia – and that he had succeeded. Mr. Wickham had no intention of marrying her, hoping to make a richer catch elsewhere, but Mr. Darcy has paid all his debts, purchased his commission in the army, and induced him to marriage by the gift of a large sum. Your uncle and I believe Mr. Darcy's real motive is not unknown to you, dear niece. His behaviour to us has been as pleasing as when we were in Derbyshire.

Your loving aunt

Very soon, Wickham and Lydia left for the north, where Wickham's regiment had been sent. The absence of her most beloved Lydia made Mrs. Bennet very dreary for several days, but her mood was relieved by the sudden and surprising news that Mr. Bingley was returning to Netherfield.

Jane turned white at the news. Later, she said to Elizabeth, "I dread other people's remarks about it, that is all. I no longer have feelings for him. I have nothing to resent him for."

After seeing him in Derbyshire, Elizabeth was sure Bingley still had feelings for Jane, but said nothing for fear of distressing her.

Mrs. Bennet told her husband to call on Mr. Bingley.

"I will not," he replied. "I did what you wanted when he first came here, but it ended in nothing. He knows where we live, if he wants to see us. I will not spend my hours running round after neighbours every time they go away and come back again."

But on the third morning after his arrival, Kitty saw two gentlemen riding towards the house.

"One is Mr. Bingley," she announced, "and the other is that tall, proud man…"

"Mr. Darcy!" exclaimed Mrs. Bennet. "I hate the sight of him!"

Both Jane and Elizabeth felt awkward when the gentlemen came in. Elizabeth was astonished that Darcy had come. It made her wonder whether it meant that his affection was unshaken. The thought brought a flush to her cheeks, but she could not be sure. "Let me see how he behaves," she thought, and she bent over her embroidery, giving it more attention than she ever had before.

Jane was pale but calm; she was as warm and mild as ever, if a little more subdued.

Their mother welcomed Mr. Bingley with effusive warmth, and Mr. Darcy with a noticeable chill. Darcy was quiet, and Elizabeth, mortified, hardly had courage to speak.

"What a delight it is, to have one daughter well married," Mrs. Bennet said. "Lydia and Mr. Wickham have gone north, with his new regiment. Thank goodness he has *some* friends, though not as many as he deserves."

Elizabeth knew this to be directed against Darcy, and was in a misery of shame, knowing all Darcy had done for Wickham. But Mrs. Bennet had not finished talking.

"No doubt you will be going out shooting, while you are in the country? Well, when you have killed all your own birds, Mr. Bingley, I hope you will come here and shoot as many as you please. Mr. Bennet will keep the best for you."

Such fawning attention was unbearable.

But Elizabeth's mind was eased as she watched Jane and Bingley who, after the first few uneasy minutes, were talking quietly in a corner, looking as though they had never parted.

When the visitors left, Mrs. Bennet was in great spirits, for she had seen enough of Bingley's behaviour to Jane to be certain that Jane would get him at last. And she was right.

Pride and Prejudice

Later, Jane told Elizabeth, "He loves me. But he never realized that I loved him. That is really why he went away. I am so happy."

So was her mother. "Ten thousand pounds a year," she clucked. "I always knew her beauty would do the trick."

A few days later, a smart carriage drawn by four horses clattered to the door. Out stepped Lady Catherine de Bourgh.

She marched through the house with an ungracious air, nodding her head at Mrs. Bennet. "This must be a very inconvenient sitting room in the summer," she announced. "The windows face west."

Elizabeth wondered why she had come, half expecting a message, perhaps, from Charlotte.

Mrs. Bennet begged Lady Catherine to take some refreshment, but she refused. Then Lady Catherine said, "Miss Elizabeth Bennet, there seems to be a prettyish kind of little wilderness on one side of your lawn. I should like to walk there with you."

"Go, my dear," cried Mrs. Bennet, and Elizabeth led her noble guest outside. As soon as they were alone, Lady Catherine began.

"You know why I am here?"

"Indeed, I have no idea," replied Elizabeth.

"I have heard worrying rumours of your intended marriage to my nephew. Such a thing is impossible," Lady Catherine said coldly. "Has he asked you to marry him?"

"Your Ladyship has declared it impossible."

"It ought to be. But your machinations may have drawn him in. Who are you? A young woman without a good family, connections or fortune. Your marriage would be a disgrace."

"Mr. Darcy is a gentleman. I am a gentleman's daughter. Thus far, we are equals," said Elizabeth.

"But who is your mother? Your uncles and aunts? And your sister's marriage I know was a botched, patched-up affair. Is such a girl to be my nephew's sister-in-law? And Wickham, the son of his father's steward, to be his brother-in-law? It cannot be. Let me tell you, Darcy is engaged to my daughter! His mother and I planned the marriage years ago. What have you to say?"

"Only this: if he is, then you have no reason to suppose he will marry me."

"Insolent, wicked girl! Is Pemberley to be polluted by a girl like you? If you marry him, your name will never be mentioned by any of us. You will be despised by everyone connected to him. Tell me once and for all, are you engaged to him?"

"I am not."

Lady Catherine seemed pleased. "And you promise never to marry him?"

"I will make no such promise."

"I am shocked," said Lady Catherine. "I am not used to being spoken to in such a way. Is this your gratitude for my kind attention to you at Rosings? I shall not go away until you have given me your promise."

"I shall never give it. I will not be intimidated. You have insulted me in every possible way, Lady Catherine. I am going to return to the house."

Elizabeth turned and walked away. Lady Catherine shook her fist, shouting after her: "I am most seriously displeased!" But she could do nothing else but get into her carriage and drive away.

Mrs. Bennet asked why Lady Catherine had not come in. "I suppose she was on her way somewhere, and kindly wanted to see you. She had nothing particular to say, did she?"

Elizabeth was forced into telling a small lie, for telling the truth was impossible.

Soon after Lady Catherine's visit, Bingley and Darcy called at Longbourn. Bingley proposed that they all go for a walk, for he wanted to be alone with Jane. And it worked out as he wished.

Pride and Prejudice

Mrs. Bennet never walked; Mary was too busy. Jane and Bingley were soon far ahead of Kitty, Elizabeth and Darcy. When they got near the Lucases' house, Kitty decided she wanted to call on them, which left Elizabeth and Darcy alone together.

Elizabeth had been secretly resolving to speak to him. Now she felt the time had come, and she must make herself brave enough. "Mr. Darcy, I am so grateful for your kindness to my sister," she said. "Ever since I knew what you did, I have wanted to thank you again and again, on behalf of all my family."

"Your family owes me nothing. Much as I respect them, I never thought of your family. I thought only of *you*."

Elizabeth was too embarrassed to speak.

After a short pause, he added, "You are too honest not to tell me the truth. If your feelings for me are still what they were, tell me so at once. *My* affections and wishes are unchanged, but one word from you will silence me on this subject forever."

Elizabeth, feeling so full of emotion, began to speak. Although not very fluently, she managed to make him understand that her feelings since his first proposal had completely changed.

Her answer gave Darcy more happiness than he had ever felt before, and he spoke as warmly as a man violently in love will do. She saw how important she was to him, and every moment his affection seemed to her more precious.

They walked on without knowing in what direction. There was too much to be thought and said for any other consideration. Elizabeth learned that they were indebted for their understanding to none other than Lady Catherine.

"She came to see me. She told me of your conversation, and that made me hope, as I had scarcely ever allowed myself to hope before," said Darcy. "I knew that if you had decided against me, you would have told her so frankly."

Elizabeth reddened and laughed. "Yes, you know enough of

my nature to believe me capable of that. After abusing you so abominably to your face, I would not hold back in abusing you to your relations. I blush to think of what I said to you that day."

"What did you say that I did not thoroughly deserve?" Darcy cried. "I cannot think of my behaviour now without shame. And my letter – did it – did it make you think any better of me?"

She explained its effect on her. How it had gradually removed all of her prejudices.

"I hope you burned that letter," Darcy said. "I thought I wrote it calmly, but I realize I did not. Some of it was dreadfully bitter."

"It is all forgotten now," Elizabeth assured him. "You must learn some of my philosophy. Only remember the pieces of the past that give you pleasure."

"Dearest, loveliest Elizabeth. I owe you everything. You taught me a lesson; you humbled me. I came at first without a doubt that you would accept me. You showed me how much better I had to be, in order to please a woman so worth pleasing."

After Darcy had asked Mr. Bennet's permission to marry his daughter, Mr. Bennet called Elizabeth into his library.

"Are you out of your mind?" he asked. "You have always hated the man. We all know him to be proud and disagreeable. You will be very rich, but is that enough to make you happy? My child, I know that you will only be happy if you marry someone your equal. I beg you, do not tie yourself into an unequal marriage of minds."

"But I do, truly, love him," Elizabeth said. "You do not know what he really is." When she told her father what Darcy had done for Lydia, he was astonished.

"So it was Mr. Darcy? Well! This will save me a world of trouble. Had it been your uncle's doing, I would have had to repay him, but if I offer to repay Darcy, he will storm about his love for

Pride and Prejudice

you, and there will be an end of it."

Mrs. Bennet was delighted to hear Elizabeth's news. "Oh my dearest, sweetest Lizzy, how rich you will be! Oh my! Three daughters married!"

Lady Catherine, of course, was not at all pleased. But after the wedding, she did bring herself to visit Pemberley, out of curiosity, to see how Elizabeth was doing there.

Bingley and Jane stayed at Netherfield for a year, and then moved to Derbyshire too. Mr. Bennet missed Elizabeth exceedingly, and often went to stay, as did Kitty, who was much improved by the company of her two elder sisters.

Mr. and Mrs. Gardiner were always welcome guests at Pemberley. Darcy, as well as Elizabeth, really loved them, and never ceased to be grateful to them for bringing Elizabeth to Derbyshire, the visit that had led to their marriage and happiness.

Northanger Abbey

Catherine is delighted with her first experience of going to balls in fashionable Bath, but the rules of polite society prove tricky. When she is invited to stay at her dream house, Northanger Abbey, her love of Gothic horror novels clouds her judgement. Is her imagination running away with her?

Catherine Morland

An impressionable teenager, and keen reader of Gothic horror novels. Eldest of nine children, she is eager to go to her first ball. But can she see what is going on around her?

Mr. Allen

A kindly, sensible, rich friend of Catherine's family. His poor health leads him to Bath.

Mrs. Allen

Passionate about fashion, she is a rather dubious chaperone for Catherine.

Henry Tilney
A handsome, funny young man who likes to tease people. Takes a liking to Catherine in Bath, but will they be able to keep touch?

Eleanor Tilney
Henry's quiet, pretty and modest sister who becomes Catherine's friend.

General Tilney
Henry and Eleanor's domineering father. Owner of the impressive, Gothic Northanger Abbey.

Captain Tilney
Henry and Eleanor's dashing elder brother. Charming and dangerous, he sweeps into Bath and ruins everything.

Isabella Thorpe
Catherine's lively new friend in Bath. Charming and chatty, and rather a flirt. Is she as true a friend as she claims to be?

John Thorpe
James Morland's friend from Oxford. A brusque, boastful young man who takes a liking to Catherine.

James Morland
Catherine's affectionate elder brother. Studying at Oxford with John Thorpe, and rather smitten with John's sister, Isabella.

No one who met Catherine Morland as a child would ever have supposed she was born to be the heroine of a story. She had kind, sensible parents, who seemed very unlikely ever to leave her an orphan. And she had nine brothers and sisters, all as plain and ordinary as herself.

At ten, Catherine was skinny and pale, with dark hair, and loved nothing in the world more than rolling down the grassy slope at the back of her house. By fifteen, her face had grown soft and rosy. She began to curl her hair and long to go to balls. She finally got around to reading books, and developed a taste for horrifying, romantic, spine-chilling novels. By seventeen, she was warm and cheerful, not vain or pretentious in any way, and very, very naive.

So far she fell miserably short of any heroic height, not least because she had never yet fallen in love. That was strange indeed. But the truth of it was, there was not a single worthy hero in the whole neighbourhood. But when a young lady is destined to be a heroine, her surroundings cannot stop her. Something must and will happen to throw a hero in her path.

A family friend named Mr. Allen, who owned a lot of property around Fullerton, the village in Wiltshire where Catherine lived, had been advised to visit the spa town of Bath for the benefit of his health. His wife was fond of Catherine, and invited her to go with them. Catherine's parents were happy to agree, and Catherine herself was delighted.

As the hour of Catherine's departure drew near, one might

suppose her mother to be anxious about evils she could encounter, such as dastardly noblemen stealing her away in the dead of night; but Mrs. Morland knew little of dastardly noblemen, and merely warned Catherine to wrap up warmly and to be careful how much she spent. In fact, there was no drama at all. The Morlands said goodbye calmly and sensibly – as was their way.

The journey to Bath was uneventful. They encountered no robbers or tempests. In fact, nothing more alarming happened than Mrs. Allen worrying that she had left her clogs behind at an inn, and finding that, in fact, she had not. They arrived in Bath, and were soon settled in comfortable lodgings in Pulteney Street.

Mrs. Allen was neither beautiful nor intelligent, but she was good-tempered. In one way, she was well qualified to introduce a young lady into polite society, for she was just as fond of going to balls as any young lady, and she was passionate about fashion.

On the evening of Catherine's very first ball, her hair was cut and styled, she dressed with care, and Mrs. Allen declared she looked just right. Mrs. Allen took so long getting dressed herself that it was late when they entered the ballroom. Bath was teeming with visitors and so the room was horribly crowded.

The two ladies squeezed in as best they could, while Mr. Allen went off to the card room. Paying rather more attention to the safety of her new dress than her protégée, Mrs. Allen battled through the throngs. Catherine held her arm and stuck with her.

There she was at her first ball. She could see nothing of the dancing at all but the feathers on top of some ladies' heads. Catherine longed to dance, but they did not know anyone who could ask her. Mrs. Allen did all she could, which was to murmur feebly, "I wish someone would ask you to dance."

Before long, everybody began to surge out of the room for tea, and they had to squeeze out with them. Catherine began to feel a little disappointed. No one spoke to them all evening until, when it was all over, Mr. Allen joined them. "Have you had a pleasant first ball?" he asked.

"Very," Catherine replied, smothering a yawn.

As the crowds thinned, our heroine had more chance of being noticed. There were no gasps at her beauty, but Catherine did overhear a gentleman say she was pretty. She felt more grateful for this humble praise than a heroine would for twenty pages of poetry, and went home perfectly happy with her first ball.

There was something different to do every day in Bath – shops to visit, sights to see, and the Pump Room to attend, where visitors went to drink Bath's healing mineral waters. They walked up and down there, looking at everybody and speaking to no one.

In the evening, there was another ball, where our heroine's fortune changed for the better. The master of ceremonies introduced her to a dancing partner named Mr. Tilney. He was about twenty-five, tall and pleasant-looking with an intelligent twinkle in his eye.

They scarcely had a moment to talk while they were dancing, but when they sat down for tea, his conversation was lively and intriguingly teasing. After chatting a while, he suddenly said, "Oh, I have forgotten to ask you the usual questions one is supposed to ask: how long you have been in Bath, and so on. I shall begin now."

"You need not worry," Catherine said.

"It is no trouble," he said. Putting on a fixed smile, and a false, simpering voice, he asked, "Have you been in Bath long, madam?"

"About a week, sir," replied Catherine, trying not to giggle.

"Indeed!" he simpered on. "And are you pleased with Bath?"

"I like it very much," Catherine said, with genuine enthusiasm.

"And so I can smirk one more time, and we can go back to being normal," Mr. Tilney joked.

Northanger Abbey

Catherine turned away to hide her mirth, unsure whether it was proper to burst out laughing.

"Oh dear," said Mr. Tilney. "I know what you will write in your journal about me: 'Friday. Was harassed by odd, half-witted man who made me dance with him and talked utter nonsense.'"

"I shall write no such thing," Catherine protested.

"I will tell you what I would like you to write," Mr. Tilney continued. "'I danced with a pleasant young man and had a delightful conversation with him. He seems to be some kind of genius, and I hope to get to know him better.'"

Catherine smiled.

Mrs. Allen bustled up to them. "Catherine, please take this pin out of my sleeve," she said. "It has torn a hole. And this dress is my favourite, even though the muslin was only nine shillings a yard."

"That is exactly what I would have guessed it cost," Mr. Tilney said solemnly, looking at the cloth of Mrs. Allen's sleeve.

"You know about muslin?" Mrs. Allen said, very impressed.

"Indeed," replied Mr. Tilney airily. "The other day I bought some for my sister, a fabulous bargain at only five shillings a yard."

Mrs. Allen clearly thought him some kind of genius. "What do you think of the muslin on Miss Morland's dress?" she asked.

He pretended to study it gravely. "Very pretty," he pronounced, "but I do not think it will wash well."

Catherine laughed. "How can you be so…?" she began, but trailed off, as she did not dare to say "strange".

They danced some more, and when they parted at the end of the evening, Catherine very much wanted to see him again.

Mr. Allen, without any idea of them falling in love, found out that the gentleman was a suitable companion for his charge, being a vicar from a respectable family in Gloucestershire.

Catherine hurried to the Pump Room eagerly the following

day, ready to meet Mr. Tilney with a smile. But he did not appear. Everyone else in Bath was there, it seemed, but him. After wandering up and down for an hour, she and Mrs. Allen sat down near the great clock. "I wish we knew someone," said Mrs. Allen. Just then, a lady sitting nearby looked up and said, "Excuse me, is your name Allen?"

It turned out that the lady was Mrs. Thorpe, a school friend whom Mrs. Allen had not seen for years. They both proceeded to give news of their families, each more keen to give than receive information, hearing little of what the other said. Mrs. Thorpe had an advantage, as she had children to boast about. Mrs. Allen, while pretending to listen, took comfort in noticing that the lace on Mrs. Thorpe's jacket was nowhere near as pretty as her own.

Presently, three smart young ladies came along. "Here come my girls," cried Mrs. Thorpe. "This is Isabella, my eldest. Is she not beautiful?" Mrs. Allen introduced Catherine.

"How very like her brother Miss Morland is!" Isabella declared.

Catherine remembered that James, her eldest brother, had recently made friends with a young man named Thorpe from his college at Oxford, and had spent the last week of the Christmas vacation staying at his family home near London.

Isabella invited her to link arms and walk around the room. Catherine was so delighted, she almost forgot all about Mr. Tilney. Friendship is certainly the finest balm for the pangs of disappointed love.

The two walked around chatting about everything from dresses to balls. They got along so well that they were relieved to find they would see one another at the theatre that very night. Catherine said goodbye, feeling grateful to have found such a friend.

At the theatre that evening, Catherine was not so busy smiling at her new friend as to forget to look for Mr. Tilney. But she looked in vain. She hoped to have more luck the following day.

Northanger Abbey

However, despite a pleasant walk in the Crescent with the Thorpe family and, it seemed, the rest of Bath, Catherine was still disappointed in her hope of seeing Mr. Tilney. He must have left Bath. He became a well-discussed subject with Isabella.

Mrs. Allen was quite satisfied with Bath now. She was happy to have met an old friend, and even happier that this friend was not as expensively dressed as herself. So the Allens and their charge spent a lot of time with the Thorpes. Catherine and Isabella quickly became close friends, walking arm in arm everywhere. And, when the weather was too bad to go out, they even sat and read sensational, gory, spine-chilling novels together.

The following conversation will give you an idea of how close Catherine and Isabella were after only eight or nine days.

They had arranged to meet at the Pump Rooms and Isabella had arrived a few minutes before Catherine. Her first words were, "Where were you? I have been waiting for ages! I saw the prettiest hat in a shop window just now, like yours only with a red ribbon instead of green. I longed to buy it. So what have you been doing all morning? Did you carry on reading that novel, *Udolpho*?"

"Yes, since I woke up. I am up to the part with the black veil…"

"Oh, that part! Are you dying to know what is under the veil?"

"I think it is a skeleton! But do not tell me! I am so enjoying it. If I were not meeting you, I would have kept on reading all day."

"When you have finished *Udolpho*, we can read more. I have made a list of more hair-raising stories… Oh! When you left yesterday, I saw a man looking at you – I think he was in love!"

Catherine blushed.

"I see," said Isabella knowingly. "You do not care to be admired by anyone other than a certain gentleman…"

"I might never see him again," Catherine said.

"You would be utterly miserable!" exclaimed Isabella.

"No, actually, I would not," Catherine replied thoughtfully. "I did like him, but while I have a good novel to read, I do not think anyone could make me truly miserable."

"Oh, I meant to ask – do you prefer dark or fair men?"

"I have never really thought about it. Maybe something between the two?" Catherine replied.

"Like Mr. Tilney – you said he had brown hair and dark eyes. I prefer light eyes and a pale complexion." Isabella's eyes narrowed. "You will not betray me if you meet anyone of that description?"

"Betray you? What do you mean?" Catherine asked innocently.

"Never mind. Let us drop the subject."

Catherine could not think of anything else to say. But Isabella said, "Let us move. Those two young men are staring at us."

They went to the other end of the room. "They are not coming this way, are they?" Isabella hissed.

"No need to worry; they have left," Catherine reassured her.

"Oh no, which way did they go?" said Isabella disappointedly. "One of them was very good looking!"

"Towards the churchyard," Catherine replied in surprise.

"Let us go and look at that new hat," Isabella suggested.

Catherine agreed. "But shall we wait a few moments so we do not catch up with those men?" she asked.

"Oh we will not wait on their account!" Isabella exclaimed. "You cannot treat men with respect. It spoils them."

With nothing to say against such an argument, Catherine followed her friend out of the door. And so, to prove Isabella's independence, and to humble the opposite sex, they set off as fast as they could in hot pursuit of the two young men.

They had reached the main road, but were stopped by traffic. Carriage after carriage passed, making it impossible for anyone to cross, no matter how important their business was, whether in quest of pastries, hats or even, as in this case, young men.

"I detest these horrid carriages," Isabella declared. But almost immediately contradicted herself with, "How delightful! Your brother with my brother John!"

"James!" cried Catherine at the same moment.

A carriage stopped by them and two gentlemen leaped out.

Catherine and her brother greeted one another fondly, and Miss Thorpe fluttered her bright eyes at James. He showed a mixture of joy and embarrassment, which might have told Catherine, had she been better at detecting other people's feelings, that her brother found Isabella every bit as pretty as she did herself.

John Thorpe handed the reins to a servant, then joined them. He greeted Isabella carelessly, but bowed to Catherine. He was a stout young man, a little scruffy and rather rude. "Miss Morland, look at my horse. Did you ever see another animal so made for speed? And guess how much the carriage cost?"

"I have no idea," Catherine replied.

"Fifty guineas!"

"I know little of such things," Catherine admitted, "so I do not know if that is cheap or dear."

The gentlemen decided to come with the ladies to visit Mrs. Thorpe. James and Isabella led the way, and Isabella was so happy that when they passed the two young men from the Pump Rooms she only looked back at them three times.

John Thorpe walked with Catherine. "Are you fond of riding in an open carriage such as mine?" he asked.

"Yes!" Catherine said. "I have scarcely ever had the chance."

"Then I will drive you out in mine every day!" said Mr. Thorpe.

"Thank you," said Catherine worriedly, wondering whether it was proper to accept such an offer from someone she barely knew.

"I will drive you to Lansdown Hill tomorrow," he said.

Isabella turned around, "Oh, will there be room for me too?"

"No! Besides, I did not come to Bath to drive my sisters about," Thorpe said. "Morland will have to take care of you."

This comment led to a discussion between Isabella and James, which Catherine could not hear, as John Thorpe had taken to condemning the looks of every woman who passed. Catherine did not trust herself to offer an opinion. Finally she ventured, "Have you read *Udolpho*, Mr. Thorpe?"

"Heavens, no. I have better things to do than read novels."

Catherine felt ashamed of having asked.

They had reached the door of the house where Mrs. Thorpe was staying, and Mr. Thorpe demonstrated what a caring son he was. "Good day, Mother," he said. "Where did you get that hat? It makes you look like an old witch!"

His mother seemed happy enough to see him nonetheless.

These manners did not please Catherine, but what was she to think? He was James's friend and Isabella's brother, after all. In any case her judgement was thrown when John asked her to dance with him that evening, and Isabella told her that he thought her the most charming girl in the world. It was difficult, young as she was, to resist such flattery. Consequently, as she and her brother set off for Mrs. Allen's, and James asked how she liked his friend, instead of replying, "Not at all," she said, "Very much."

"He is a chatterbox but so good-natured. And do you like the rest of the family?" James asked.

"Very much. Isabella particularly."

"I am so glad. She is just the right kind of friend for you."

They chatted on until they reached Pulteney Street, where James dropped her off. Catherine was left to sink back into her thrilling book, barely stopping for a moment to consider the happy fact that she had been asked to dance that very evening.

At that evening's ball, when the dancing began, James and

Northanger Abbey

Isabella were ready, but John had gone off to talk to a friend. "I would not dance without you for the world!" Isabella declared. But a minute later, she said, "I must dance. John will be back soon."

Catherine could not help but be a little annoyed at John Thorpe. After ten minutes, however, a sight raised her spirits. It was Mr. Tilney, walking right past where they sat. He had a young, fashionable woman on his arm. Catherine took her to be his sister.

They paused, held up by the crowd, and Catherine caught Mr. Tilney's eye. He smiled and came over. "How lovely to see you again," said Mrs. Allen. "I was afraid you had left Bath."

Mr. Tilney said he had been away for a week. After chatting a little more, Mrs. Thorpe went to sit down. Mr. Tilney and Catherine were left together, and that was the moment Mr. Tilney asked Catherine to dance.

Catherine was delighted and mortified all at once. She had promised the first two dances to Mr. Thorpe. She said how sorry she was, and she looked it. Mr. Thorpe, who joined them half a minute later, might have been sorry himself to see it. He did not seem at all sorry for having kept her waiting, however. Nor did the details he told her about the dogs and horses of his friend in the card room cheer her up. She found herself glancing mournfully toward Mr. Tilney. Having somebody to dance with at a ball did not, she realized, necessarily make one happier after all.

She was roused from her thoughts by Mr. Tilney's sister coming to dance beside her. Miss Tilney seemed very pleasant. She was pretty and elegant, without Isabella's pretentiousness, and she did not express dramatic opinions about every little thing. Her manners were perfect, and she seemed perfectly capable of being young and pretty at a ball without having to attract the attention of every man around her. Catherine talked to her eagerly whenever she could find anything worth saying.

Northanger Abbey

After barely two dances, Catherine found her arm seized by Isabella, who exclaimed, "Why did you dance so far away?"

Catherine pointed out Miss Tilney, who was now a little way across the room. "She is beautiful!" Isabella exclaimed. "Where is her brother? I am dying to see him."

But she chattered on, seeming to forget all about it instantly, which made Catherine wonder whether she could really have been dying to see Mr. Tilney after all.

As the promised dances had been danced with Mr. Thorpe, Catherine hurried back to the rest of their group, hoping to find Mr. Tilney still with them. Sadly he was not. She saw him leading someone else off to dance, and was very disappointed.

John Thorpe bowled up to her, "I suppose you and I had better get up and do another jig then?" he said.

"Thank you, but I am tired now," Catherine said politely.

"Then let us walk around and laugh at people," John offered, "such as my sisters and their dance partners."

But Catherine excused herself again, and he walked off without her. The rest of the evening was very dull. Mr. Tilney was with other people. Miss Tilney sat nowhere near her, and Isabella was so busy chatting to James, she had no time for Catherine whatsoever.

When Catherine left the ballroom that night she was fed up with everyone. But after a good meal and nine hours deep sleep, she emerged in good spirits, with fresh hopes and plans.

Firstly, she wished to get to know Miss Tilney better. That afternoon, she would find her in the Pump Rooms and do just that. In the meantime, she settled down to read her novel all morning.

At about half past twelve, there was a loud knock at the door. Two carriages were outside, and John Thorpe came running up the stairs calling, "Come on Miss Morland, we are in a hurry to go!"

Northanger Abbey

"What do you mean?" Catherine asked.

"Have you forgotten? We agreed to drive to Claverton Down!"

"Oh," Catherine said. "I was not expecting you." But she did not feel there could be anything wrong with going for a drive, especially as Isabella and James were going too. Getting to know Miss Tilney could wait for another day.

After asking Mrs. Allen if she could go, Catherine ran to get ready. Within moments, she was climbing into Mr. Thorpe's open carriage. "Do not be frightened if my horse dances about as we set off," said Thorpe. "He will soon settle."

It had not occurred to Catherine to be frightened until this point, but it was too late to go back now, so she sat down. Thorpe climbed in too and they were off. The horse started very quietly. When Catherine said so, Thorpe assured her it was down to the way he held the reins. Why then, Catherine wondered, had he needed to alarm her in the first place?

After a short silence, Thorpe said abruptly, "That Mr. Allen. He is very rich, is he not? Does he not have any children?"

"No, he has no children," Catherine replied.

"Is he your godfather?"

"No," Catherine said. "He is very kind to me though."

Thorpe asked what she thought of his carriage, but then talked so effusively of it himself, that it was impossible for her to add a thing. Before long, he had established that his carriage was the best in the country and he was the best driver.

"Your brother's carriage is so rickety!" Thorpe cried. "I would not ride in it even if you gave me fifty thousand pounds!"

"Good heavens," said Catherine, frightened. "Then we should turn back. We need to tell my brother that it is unsafe!"

"Oh it is not in the least bit unsafe. I would drive it to York and back again for a mere five pounds!" Thorpe declared.

Catherine listened in astonishment, uncertain how to

understand two such different descriptions of the same thing. Her family were matter-of-fact people who did not exaggerate or contradict themselves. She was perplexed. But, she reasoned, he would not be likely to leave his own sister and friend in real danger, when he could easily avoid it, so he must think them safe after all.

Mr. Thorpe, in the meantime, continued to talk entirely about himself – how perfect his aim was, how well he rode over rough ground when all around him riders were breaking their necks…

Catherine was not used to judging people for herself, but nonetheless a doubt was creeping into her mind, while he listed his endless accomplishments, as to whether John Thorpe was altogether that likeable. By the time they returned to Pulteney Street, she was extremely weary of his company.

After the others had left, Mrs. Allen told her that she had been to see Mrs. Thorpe. "We met Mr. and Miss Tilney. And I spoke to a Mrs. Hughes, who told me about them," she said. "Apparently they are a very good family, and very rich."

"Are Mr. and Mrs. Tilney in Bath?" Catherine asked.

"I think she said Mrs. Tilney had died," Mrs. Allen replied. "But she said Mr. Tilney, your dancing partner, is a fine young man, and likely to do very well for himself."

It was unfortunate to have missed seeing the Tilneys. In this light, Catherine thought the drive and Mr. Thorpe seemed even more unpleasant than she had thought before.

The Allens, Thorpes and Morlands all met that evening at the theatre. As Isabella sat down beside Catherine, she began chatting. "Now I have you to myself, I shall not talk to anyone else all evening. Your hairstyle is heavenly – all the men will be in love with you. My brother already is. Is Mr. Tilney here?"

"I cannot see him anywhere," Catherine replied.

Northanger Abbey

"I am growing rather tired of Bath. James and I were talking about how we prefer the countryside. We share so many opinions it is ridiculous!" Isabella declared. "If you had heard, you might have said we were born for each other, and made me blush."

"It would never have entered my head," Catherine protested.

Isabella smiled disbelievingly, and spent the rest of the evening talking to James.

The following morning, Catherine finally managed to chat to Miss Tilney in the Pump Room. "Your brother dances so well," Catherine enthused innocently.

Eleanor Tilney smiled. "Henry? Yes I suppose he does."

"He must have been surprised when I said I could not dance the other evening, but I had promised Mr. Thorpe the first two dances... Do you think the lady he danced with was very pretty?"

"Not so very," Eleanor said kindly.

"Will I see you – and your brother – tomorrow at the ball?"

"Yes, I think we will be there," Eleanor said.

"I am so glad!" Catherine beamed.

They parted, with Eleanor Tilney having some knowledge of Catherine's feelings towards her brother, yet with Catherine having no knowledge whatsoever of having revealed them.

Catherine entered the ballroom on Thursday evening with very different feelings to those of the Monday before. Then she had revelled in the prospect of dancing with Mr. Thorpe; now she was anxious to avoid him, in case he asked her to dance.

As the Thorpes joined them, her agony increased: she hid from John Thorpe as much as possible. The first dance was over, and the second began and still she saw no sign of the Tilneys. Isabella whispered, "I am going to dance with your brother again."

Catherine did not answer. The others walked away. John

Thorpe was close, and she gave herself up for lost. She kept her gaze firmly fixed on her fan, so as not to catch his eye, and was busy berating herself for even supposing it possible to find the Tilneys in time, when someone asked her to dance.

She looked up to find Mr. Tilney standing there.

You might easily imagine her sparkling eyes and fluttering heart, as she eagerly accepted and went with him onto the dance floor. It was the greatest happiness Catherine could imagine.

They had scarcely taken their place, however, when John Thorpe came up behind Catherine and said, "What is all this? I thought you and I were going to dance together!"

"That surprises me, as you did not ask me," Catherine replied.

"That is a good one! I only came here for the sake of dancing with you. Who is this fellow?"

Catherine told him, and he said, "I do not know him. But tell him if he wants a horse, I have a friend selling one. Forty guineas…"

Thankfully, he was borne away into the crowd by a passing tide of young ladies.

"It was rude of that gentleman to talk to you when you were about to dance with me," Mr. Tilney said. "Agreeing to dance with someone is like marriage – there should be only one partner!"

"Oh it is hardly the same!" Catherine protested. "Mr. Thorpe is a friend of my brother, so I had to answer him. But you do not need to worry – I do not know anyone else here."

"Is that the only thing stopping you?" Mr. Tilney asked.

"No. I do not *want* to talk to anybody else!" Catherine added.

Mr. Tilney smiled. "Ah, that makes me feel more secure… So, have you grown tired of Bath yet?"

"No, I like it even more! There is so much to do. The fact that James, my brother, has come is delightful, and we have friends here. Oh, who could ever be tired of Bath?"

"Not those who bring such fresh, honest feelings to it,"

*Catherine looked up to find
Mr. Tilney standing there.*

Northanger Abbey

Mr. Tilney said approvingly.

The dancing began. As they reached the end of one line, Catherine noticed an older gentleman staring at her. She blushed and turned her face away. As Mr. Tilney came closer in the dance, he said, "That gentleman is my father, General Tilney."

"Oh!" replied Catherine, relieved.

Before the evening was over, something else arose which made her happy. She chatted to Miss Tilney, who told her of various country walks around Bath, and suggested she and her brother could take Catherine on one. "I would like that more than anything in the world! Could we go tomorrow?" Catherine gasped.

They arranged to call for her at twelve o'clock in Pulteney Street. "Do not forget," were her parting words to her new friend, and her spirits danced all the way home.

The next morning, the weather was dull, but Catherine felt optimistic. Cloudy mornings almost always improved. At eleven o'clock, however, the rain began. It increased steadily. "Perhaps it will stop soon," Catherine said to herself hopefully.

At half past twelve, when Catherine had finally given up hope, the sky began to clear. The clouds parted and the sun broke through. It looked as if it would be a sunny afternoon. Catherine was at the window when she saw two carriages approaching.

"It is Isabella, my brother and Mr. Thorpe!" she cried. "They probably expect me to go with them, but I shall not go this time."

Moments later, John Thorpe hurried inside crying, "Put on your hat! We are going to Bristol!"

"I cannot go. I am waiting for some friends," Catherine said.

Mr. Thorpe laughed at this as no reason at all. "We shall be visiting Blaize Castle too," he added.

Catherine loved the sound of a castle, and this made her pause. "Is that a real, old castle, like in a book?" she asked.

"Yes, the finest place to visit in England!" Mr. Thorpe declared.

"Oh, then I should have really liked to come," Catherine said wistfully, "but I have a prior engagement. Mr. and Miss Tilney are coming to take me for a walk. We were meant to go at twelve…"

"Tilney? The fellow you danced with? I saw him just now with a lady in a carriage. They were driving out of town."

"That is odd," said Catherine. "Perhaps they thought it was too muddy for a walk."

"Of course they did. It is ankle deep everywhere!"

Isabella had come in now too, and said, "You must come, Catherine. There is no reason not to now."

And so it was agreed, and they set off, with Catherine's feelings very mixed. She was sad to miss her walk with the Tilneys, unsettled that they had driven off without a word to her, and rather looking forward to seeing the castle. It would be like the one in her novel, *Udolpho*, and as such would be a great consolation.

But as they drove through Bath, Thorpe said, "Who is that looking at you?"

On the pavement, arm in arm with her brother, was Miss Tilney. "Stop!" cried Catherine to Mr. Thorpe. "Stop the carriage. It is Miss Tilney. How could you have told me they were gone? I need to speak to her right away. Stop!"

But Mr. Thorpe did not stop. He urged his horse into a faster trot, and the carriage drove right past the Tilneys and around the corner. Still Catherine begged Mr. Thorpe to stop, but he just laughed and drove on. "How could you deceive me like that?" Catherine said heatedly. "They will think me very rude. I will not enjoy this outing now one little bit!"

Mr. Thorpe protested that he had seen a man driving out of town who had looked like Mr. Tilney, and the subject was closed. They drove on for a long way, with Mr. Thorpe chatting away,

*"Stop!" cried Catherine to Mr. Thorpe...
But Mr. Thorpe did not stop.*

until a call from James in the carriage behind stopped them. "We had better turn around," he told Thorpe. "We have gone less than halfway. It is too far to go today."

"It is all the same to me," said Thorpe angrily. He turned his horse and they began to head back to Bath. "It is your brother's fault. He is a fool not to buy his own carriage and a better horse!"

"He does not have that kind of money!" Catherine retorted.

"Well, whose fault is that? What a miserly family – rolling in it and unwilling to buy things…" Thorpe ranted. But Catherine was not really listening. Now she was disappointed she had missed the castle too, and hardly spoke a word all the way back.

As she entered the house, the servant told her that a lady and gentleman had called for her twenty minutes after she had left. That evening, Catherine went to bed very unhappy indeed.

The next morning, Catherine asked Mrs. Allen, "May I call on Miss Tilney? I cannot rest until I have explained everything to her."

"By all means, dear," Mrs. Allen replied.

Catherine set off shortly afterwards. Having found out where the Tilneys were staying from the Pump Rooms, she hurried there with a beating heart. She knocked, and asked to see Miss Tilney. The servant went upstairs and returned to say she was not at home. Catherine blushed. She felt sure Miss Tilney *was* there, but had not wanted to let her in! And, it seemed, she was right. Glancing back from the end of the street, she saw Miss Tilney herself coming out of the front door with her father! Catherine was mortified.

She was so miserable, she almost refused to go to the theatre that night. But it was a play she very much wanted to see. And so she went, and found herself quite enjoying it. But the appearance of Mr. Tilney and his father halfway through, in a box opposite, brought her worries rushing back.

Northanger Abbey

She watched Henry Tilney without being able to catch his eye. At length he looked at her, and bowed – but oh, what a bow; no smile accompanied it. His eyes immediately returned to the stage, and Catherine was miserable for the rest of the play.

The play ended, the curtain fell, and in a few minutes Henry appeared by them, greeting them all calmly. Catherine answered him in a manner far from calm. "Oh, Mr. Tilney! I have been desperate to apologize. You must have thought me so rude, but it was not my fault. They told me you had gone out in a carriage! I begged Mr. Thorpe to stop but he would not," she continued. "I would a thousand times rather have been with you."

Who in the world could have resisted such a declaration? Evidently not Henry Tilney. The warmth returned to his smile, and he said that his sister was by no means angry either.

"Do not say that," Catherine cried. "I know she was. She would not see me when I called, but I saw her leave only moments later."

"Yes, Eleanor told me. Our father was just going out with her when you called, and ordered her to say she had already gone, so he would not have to wait. She has been wanting to apologize."

Catherine felt greatly relieved.

Before long, they were back on as good terms as ever, and they rearranged their walk for two days' time. By the time he left, Catherine was the happiest creature in the world.

While they had been talking, Catherine had noticed John Thorpe talking to General Tilney. They seemed to be talking about *her*. What could they be saying?

"What do you think the General and I were talking of?" Mr. Thorpe said slyly as they were leaving the theatre. "You! The General thinks you are the finest girl in Bath! And what do you think I said?" Thorpe continued in a low voice. "'Well done, General,' I said, 'I agree completely.'"

Catherine was much less pleased with his approval than with

Northanger Abbey

General Tilney's, and was relieved when she was called away by Mr. Allen.

The highs and lows of almost a whole week have been described; only the pangs of Sunday now remain.

In a walk in the Crescent, the Thorpes and James revived their plan to drive out into the countryside. They had agreed to set off early the following morning. When they told Catherine, however, she told them she could not go, as she had arranged her walk with the Tilneys for then.

The Thorpes cried that she must. "Tell them that you have remembered a prior engagement," Isabella insisted.

"No, I will not. That is not true," Catherine replied firmly.

Isabella pleaded, flattered and, in the end, scolded, accusing Catherine of paying the Tilneys more attention than she paid her. Catherine thought this unkind and, for the first time, thought Isabella rather selfish. But she said nothing.

"If you go on Tuesday, instead, I can come," Catherine offered.

"No!" came Isabella's immediate reply. "John said he had something to do in town on Tuesday."

"Sorry, I cannot offer more than that," Catherine said sadly.

The walk continued, rather awkwardly, with Isabella and Catherine arm in arm although their hearts were at war.

"I think," muttered Isabella, "that you simply do not care."

Catherine withdrew her arm from her friend's, very upset. A long few minutes passed, until they were rejoined by John Thorpe, who had gone off somewhere, and now said, "I have settled it. I have told Miss Tilney that you are coming with us, and she agreed you can go on Tuesday with her instead."

"Lovely!" cried Isabella.

"No!" Catherine cried heatedly. "I will not submit to this! I will run after Miss Tilney and put it right."

But Isabella held her arm, and Thorpe her other, so she could not go, and even James was against her.

"If I had wanted to put off my walk with Miss Tilney I could have told her myself," Catherine argued. "Mr. Thorpe had no business to tell her any such thing! It was very rude. Let me go."

She broke away from them and hurried off. She caught up with the Tilneys just as they had gone inside their lodgings. The servant was still standing at the open door, and Catherine hurried past. She opened a door, and found herself in the drawing room with General Tilney and his son and daughter. "It was all a mistake," she burst out breathlessly, "I never agreed to go with them!"

It did not take long to set everything straight. Miss Tilney was happy to go back to their original plan. Once it was settled, Miss Tilney introduced Catherine to her father. General Tilney was so polite to her, Catherine thought John Thorpe must have told him something positive, and her feelings towards him softened a little.

As Catherine was leaving, the General came with her to the door, and said she must come to dinner with them soon. He bowed very gallantly as they said goodbye.

Catherine walked happily back to Pulteney Street. Only when she reached home did her anxiety about her friends' ruined plan return. To ease her mind, and to gain an objective view, she explained everything to Mr. Allen. "I had made an arrangement, so it would not have been right for me to break it off, would it?"

"Certainly not," he replied. "And in any case, I am not sure it is proper for young women to drive about in open carriages with gentlemen they barely know."

"Oh dear," said Catherine, "I wish you had told me before. I would never have gone in the first place if I had known!"

"No harm done," Mr. Allen assured her. "I would just advise you not to go again."

Northanger Abbey

The next morning was fair, and the Tilneys called for Catherine as arranged. Despite fears that it would never happen, our heroine was finally able to go out with the hero himself.

As they walked along, Catherine said, "This reminds me of the country in the novel I am reading, *The Mysteries of Udolpho*... But I suppose you have not read it? You probably do not read novels..."

"Whoever cannot enjoy a good novel must be unbearably stupid! I have read it, and enjoyed it so much I could not put it down," Henry declared. "I finished it in two days flat, my hair standing on end the whole time."

"I am glad to hear you liked it," Catherine said happily. "Now I will never be ashamed of liking *Udolpho* or novels like that myself. Do you not think *Udolpho* is the nicest book in the world?"

"The *nicest*? I am never sure what 'nice' is supposed to mean," Henry Tilney remarked wryly. "This is a *nice* day, and you two are *nice* young ladies. Originally 'nice' meant neat, or precise, but now it is used for anything, and means altogether less."

"Do not mind him," Eleanor said. "He is treating you exactly as he does me. He is forever finding fault with some inaccurate use of language..." She smiled. "Come, Miss Morland, let us leave him to contemplate our faults while we praise *Udolpho* in any way we like. Are you fond of that kind of book?"

"Oh yes!" Catherine told her. "I read poetry and plays too, but I am not interested in solemn history. Are you?"

"Yes, I am fond of history," Miss Tilney replied.

"You are? Then I shall not pity its writers any longer," Catherine declared. "I used to think they went to all that trouble of filling all those huge volumes only to torture children."

Henry laughed. "The great historians might be offended by the assumption that they had no better aim than torturing children!"

"If you were used to watching little children struggle to learn to read with my poor mother, you might think that 'torture' and 'learning' were interchangeable words too!" Catherine insisted.

"Very probably," Henry Tilney allowed. "Although historians are not to answer for the torture of learning to read. Besides, you must admit that it is worth being tortured for a few years to be able to read novels like *Udolpho*!"

Catherine agreed heartily, and the subject was closed.

Next, the Tilneys started talking about drawing. This was another subject Catherine knew little of. Eventually, she confessed her lack of knowledge, and Henry Tilney gave her an enthusiastic lecture, using the landscape around them. She soon began to see the beauty in everything he admired, which pleased them both.

As they reached the top of Beechen Cliff, the subject dwindled, and Catherine's thoughts returned to novels. "I have heard something really shocking is coming from London," she said.

Miss Tilney had no idea what she was talking about. Aghast, she said, "Good heavens! Where did you hear such a thing?"

"A friend of mine said it is more hair-raising than anything yet, with murder and everything!" Catherine said.

"Surely the government will put a stop to it!" said Eleanor.

Henry Tilney grinned. His sister may not have realized what Catherine was talking about, but he had. "Oh, it is the kind of murder the government are not the least bit interested in," he said.

Both women looked baffled, and he burst out laughing. "Shall I let you work it out for yourselves, or help a little? Miss Morland has been talking of a fictional murder, Eleanor – of a new book about to be published. Miss Morland, my sister was imagining London streets flowing with blood. Please forgive her stupidity. Her assumption *was* rational, after all, given the way you introduced the subject! Ah, dear me, and some say that women lack the intelligence of men. How could they!"

Eleanor looked scoldingly at him. "Now you have made us understand one another, you must make Miss Morland understand you. She is not used to you and does not know that, in fact, you believe women to be just as intelligent as men."

"I do, oh I do," Mr. Tilney said laughing helplessly. "Women have so much intelligence, they usually only bother using half!"

"Ignore him! We will not get anything sensible out of him now," Eleanor said to Catherine. "But I assure you, if he appears to say unkind things about women it is not his real opinion."

But Catherine needed no convincing of the correctness of Henry Tilney's opinions. She admired him so much, she believed him to be right about – well – just about everything.

The rest of the walk was delightful. As they parted at the Allens', the Tilneys invited Catherine to dine with them the day after next. Catherine could have burst with happiness.

Early the next day, Catherine received a note from Isabella, urging her to come quickly. The moment she entered the Thorpes' lodgings, Isabella burst out. "I am so excited. No doubt you have guessed my news? Your brother is so charming!"

Catherine had not guessed, but began to get an inkling of what the news could be. "Are you in love with James?" she asked.

But that, as she soon found out, was only half the story. The other half was that James had confessed yesterday that he loved her too, and that they were engaged to be married.

Catherine was delighted, and hugged Isabella with tears of joy. "You will be dearer to me than my real sisters!" Isabella declared.

As happy as Catherine was, this declaration surpassed any she could offer. But Isabella did not notice. "The first moment I saw your brother," she continued blithely, "my heart was his. I had my yellow dress on and my hair up, and when John introduced me, I thought I had never seen anyone so handsome. I nearly gave myself away – but I knew my secret would be safe with you."

"It could not have been safer!" thought Catherine, who had not suspected a thing.

Isabella told her that James was about to set off for home, to ask for his parents' consent and to see what their situation would be, in other words, how much money his father would grant him to live on with his new wife. This was a source of great worry for Isabella, who said, "They might want a richer wife for their son…"

"I do not think it will matter to them," Catherine assured her.

"Well, if I were a millionairess and he were poverty-stricken, he would still be my only choice," Isabella declared.

The next day, Catherine waited with Isabella for a letter from James with their father's answer. When at last it came, Isabella glowed with happiness as she read: "My parents consent, and will do everything in their power to ensure our happiness."

The details of exactly what the Morlands would do to ensure their happiness remained to be told, but Isabella's imagination took flight, certain that they would be very comfortably off. She imagined herself admired by everyone in a new carriage, leaving a grand house, with a brilliant ring on her finger…

John Thorpe, who had waited for the letter before setting off for London himself, now came to take his leave of Catherine. "Miss Morland, I have come to say goodbye."

"Have a good journey," Catherine replied, but he did not seem to hear her. He went and stood by the window, humming and fidgeting in the most peculiar manner.

"Will you not be late?" Catherine asked.

After a silence, John suddenly burst out, "Jolly good idea, this marrying business, do you not think?"

"I think it is a good idea," Catherine agreed.

"Oh, I am glad. Do you know the song, 'Going to one wedding brings on another'? You are coming to Bella's wedding, I hope."

Northanger Abbey

"Yes, of course."

"Then you know," John gave a foolish laugh, "we might try the truth of the old song…"

"Might we?" said Catherine, completely missing his meaning. "I do not know. I never sing. Well, I hope you have a good journey. I am invited for dinner with Miss Tilney today, so I must go."

"Who knows when we will see each other again?" John said. "Actually, I will be back in a fortnight but it will seem long to me."

He appeared to be waiting for an answer, so Catherine said, "Well, could you not just come back sooner?"

"That is so kind. I do not know anybody like you," John said.

"There are lots of people like me," said Catherine. "Goodbye!"

"But may I visit Fullerton, when you return home?"

"Yes, I am sure my mother and father would like to see you."

"But *you* would not be sorry to see me?"

"Oh, I would not be *sorry* to see anybody," Catherine said.

"My opinion exactly. You and I think alike about most things!" John said eagerly.

"I am not sure *what* I think about most things," Catherine said.

"See? Even on that point, we agree. I am not sure either. All I know is I want a roof over my head, and a nice girl. Her fortune is not important as I have an income myself."

"There we agree," Catherine said. "As long as there is enough to live on – it makes no difference whose side it comes from. I hate the idea of marrying for a fortune. To marry for money I think is the wickedest thing of all. Anyway, goodbye."

And off Catherine went, leaving John Thorpe with the happy certainty that he had told her how he felt, and she felt the same. Catherine, however, was none the wiser.

Catherine was a little disappointed by her dinner with the Tilneys. Although they were polite, their father overwhelmingly so,

Northanger Abbey

Eleanor and Henry said very little. It was almost a relief to get away. It puzzled her. Could it be the presence of the General that had made the difference?

When she told Isabella, her friend exclaimed: "How rude!"

"No, it was not as bad as all that…"

"Do not defend them! I cannot bear inconsistency. He does not deserve you, Catherine!" Isabella said. "How different he is to your brother – and to mine. John has a very constant heart, you know…"

But Catherine's mind was elsewhere. "General Tilney was so polite. He seemed anxious to make me happy," she mused.

"Well, John says he is a gentleman, and John always—"

"I will just see how they are this evening in the ballroom," Catherine said, almost to herself.

"Oh dear, do I have to go too?" said Isabella. "I expect I should. Even with my heart forty miles away. But do not ask me to dance – that is out of the question. I expect I will be plagued with offers…" She sounded enthusiastic, and Catherine's mild, "You do not have to go if you do not want to," went almost unheard.

The Tilneys' behaviour to Catherine that evening was back to its usual warmth. Eleanor spent a lot of time with her, and Henry asked her to dance.

During her visit they had told her that their brother, Captain Tilney, was coming to Bath, and so when a handsome young man turned up, Catherine knew who he must be. He could be considered handsomer still than his brother, she pondered, but his face was not as attractive, nor were his manners. He refused to dance, and laughed at Henry for suggesting it.

She, however, was her usual happy self, being with Henry Tilney, listening with sparkling eyes to his every word and, in finding him irresistible, becoming so herself.

At the end of the first dance, Captain Tilney pulled Henry

away to talk to him. When they returned, Henry asked Catherine whether she thought Isabella would dance with his brother. "No. She has decided not to dance this evening," Catherine replied. When Henry told Captain Tilney, he turned and walked away.

"He does not like dancing, so he will not be upset, will he?" Catherine asked Henry. "He was probably just asking to be kind."

"Your belief in my brother's good intent reveals little more than your own good nature," Henry said.

Catherine blushed, unsure how to take this, and almost confused the steps of the dance in thinking about it. She looked up to find Captain Tilney and Isabella dancing right next to her. She stared in astonishment at Isabella, who shrugged and smiled.

"I cannot think how that happened. Isabella was so determined not to dance!" Catherine said to Henry Tilney.

"Has Isabella never changed her mind before?" he replied.

"But – and – but your brother must have asked her anyway, despite what I said!" Catherine said.

"That does not surprise me in the least. But only you can know your friend's firm mind," he chuckled.

"You are laughing, but Isabella is normally very firm-minded."

After the dance, Isabella told Catherine, "I would have given the world to just sit and not dance."

"Then why did you not?" Catherine asked, bewildered.

"He would not take no for an answer," Isabella smirked. "He would not dance with anyone in the room apart from *me*."

"He is very handsome," Catherine said.

"Is he? I suppose so," said Isabella.

By the time Catherine and Isabella next met, James Morland had sent another letter, with details of his father's intentions. He was to give James an income of four hundred pounds a year, which was no small amount considering the nine other children, and

Northanger Abbey

James would inherit property in the future too. James wrote that they would only have to wait two years before they could afford to get married. He said he would gladly wait for her.

Catherine congratulated her warmly, but Isabella's face was grave. "Nobody could think more highly of Mr. Morland than I do," she said, "but everyone has their failings, and everyone has a right to do what they like with their own money…"

Catherine was hurt by the insinuation. "I am sure my father has promised as much as he can afford," she said.

Isabella changed tack. "Oh, it is not really the money that bothers me," she said hurriedly, "but the long wait. Two years!"

Catherine tried her best to believe that the only thing disappointing Isabella was the wait. When James returned, Isabella received him cheerfully, and so Catherine put aside her unease.

The Allens were now in the sixth week of their stay at Bath. To Catherine's relief, they decided to stay on for two more weeks. But when she visited Miss Tilney, she was upset to learn that her father had decided they would leave in a week.

"But I wondered, perhaps…" Miss Tilney began shyly.

Just at that moment, her father came in. "Eleanor, have you asked your friend yet?" he said. But then, without waiting, he went on himself, "Would you like to come and stay at our home in Gloucestershire when we leave Bath? Eleanor would love your company. Northanger Abbey is quiet, but not disagreeable."

Catherine's head was awhirl. Northanger Abbey! She accepted eagerly, provided her parents were in agreement. "I will write home today. I am sure they will not object…"

With Henry in her heart, and Northanger Abbey on her lips, Catherine ran home to write the letter.

The Allens and her parents, relying on the Allens' judgement, gave their permission, and Catherine felt like the luckiest creature

Northanger Abbey

in the world. Everything seemed to be cooperating for her benefit: the Allens bringing her to Bath, gaining Isabella as a sister-in-law, and her friendship with the Tilneys. And now, she was to spend weeks under the same roof as Henry Tilney – under the roof of a real abbey, no less! Its long, damp, dark passages and ruined chapel were to be within daily reach, and she could not subdue the vague hope of some awful memorial to some ill-fated nun or other...

With a mind so full of happiness, two or three days flew by. One morning, Catherine was at the Pump Rooms, when she realized she had not seen Isabella for days. Luckily, her friend arrived that very moment and, saying she wanted a private chat, led Catherine to a bench between the two doors, from which there was a view of everyone entering the Pump Rooms.

Noticing Isabella's eyes scanning everyone who came in, Catherine said, "James will be here soon, Isabella."

Isabella said, "Pah! I am not looking for him. We are not glued together... So, I heard you are going to Northanger Abbey?"

"Yes – but who were you looking for?" Catherine asked.

"Nobody," Isabella insisted, her eyes still darting to the door.

"Oh... Did you have something to tell me?" Catherine asked.

"Oh yes!" Isabella said. "I had quite forgotten. I had a letter from my brother, John. You can guess what it said, of course?"

"No," Catherine replied, bemused.

"My sweet thing, do not pretend. You must know. He is head over heels in love with you!" Isabella told her.

Catherine gasped. "With *me*?"

"Modesty is one thing, but this is just fishing for compliments," Isabella snapped. "He says before he left Bath he told you and you encouraged him. It is silly to pretend you do not know."

Catherine protested that she had no idea he felt that way. "I – I am not sure what to say – but can you set him straight for me? I mean your brother no offence, but if I were to value one man over another, he would not be the one."

Isabella was silent.

"Do not be angry," Catherine pleaded. "We can still be sisters!"

Isabella blushed. "There is more than one way we can be sisters," she said obscurely. "Oh dear, so you refuse poor John?"

"I cannot return his affection, and never meant to encourage it," Catherine said.

"Then we will never mention it again…"

"So you do not blame me?" Catherine asked anxiously. "You understand that I never meant to deceive him?"

"I do not blame you," Isabella said. "But as for your intention – how do I know? A little flirtation is nothing. It happens now and then. One often gives more encouragement than one wishes to stand by. Feelings can change…"

"But that is not what happened. My feelings to your brother have always been the same," Catherine insisted.

"My dearest Catherine," Isabella continued, hardly seeming to be speaking to Catherine, "I would not want you to hurry into an engagement that you might regret. You should not stay engaged to someone's brother for their sake. Even your friend's. Captain Tilney says people can be wrong about their affections… Ah, here he comes. Do not worry, I am sure he will not see us."

Through the doors came Captain Tilney, and he could not have missed Isabella if he had tried, she was gazing so intensely at him. He sat down on the seat Isabella had patted beside her, and murmured to her, "How I wish we were alone…" He gazed at Isabella intently. "My eyes torment me."

"Do they? I am sorry," Isabella turned away with a coy smile. "I hope your eyes are not tormented now."

"Never more so. I can still see the edge of a blooming cheek…"

Catherine, hearing all of this, surged with indignation on her brother's behalf. She was surprised Isabella could bear it. Standing up, she said, "Let us go and join Mrs. Allen."

But Isabella refused. When Catherine went home with Mrs. Allen a little later, Isabella was still sitting with Captain Tilney.

Catherine's mind churned. It was plain to her that Captain Tilney was falling in love with Isabella, and that Isabella was encouraging him without knowing. She could *not* know, as she loved James… did she not? Catherine wished Isabella had not looked so very glad to see Captain Tilney.

A few days passed, and to Catherine's dismay she found Isabella a changed creature. She paid Captain Tilney as much attention as she ever gave James. She saw her brother grow solemn and uneasy, and could not bear his suffering. Captain Tilney could not be aware of Isabella's engagement, considering the way he was behaving. And, when she learned that he planned to stay in Bath after his family had left, she decided to talk to Henry about it. She asked him to tell his brother of Isabella's engagement.

To her surprise, he replied, "I have told him already."

"Then why is he going to stay in Bath?" Catherine asked. "He will only be miserable. Why do you not persuade him to leave?"

"Sorry, but I cannot. He knows full well what he is doing."

"He does not know full well what he is doing. He does not know the pain he is causing my brother," Catherine said, upset.

"Is it my brother's attention to Miss Thorpe, or Miss Thorpe's reaction that is causing you pain?" Henry asked gently.

Catherine thought about it, and blushed for Isabella. "Isabella is wrong. But I cannot believe she means to torment my brother. She said she has been in love with him since they first met."

"She is in love with James yet flirts with Frederick?"

"No! A woman in love with a man cannot flirt with another!" Catherine exclaimed. She thought for a moment, and added slowly,

Northanger Abbey

"You do not believe Isabella is in love with my brother after all?"

"I could not possibly say," said Henry.

"Can your father not stop your brother?" said Catherine.

"Is Miss Thorpe's heart only true to your brother if nobody else wants it?" Henry asked. "Do they need to live in isolation? If they truly love each other, this cannot come between them."

Thinking Henry Tilney must know best, Catherine decided not to worry about it anymore. She spent her last evening in Bath with the Thorpes. Catherine and Isabella said goodbye with embraces, tears and fervent promises to write to one another.

The next morning, Catherine was almost bursting with excitement as Mr. Allen walked her to the Tilneys' lodgings, where she was to have breakfast before the journey. Her friends welcomed her kindly, but the General somehow made it impossible to relax: he worried about breakfast; scolded Captain Tilney for coming to breakfast late; and was cross that they were late setting off.

But when at last they did set off, Catherine was in a luxurious carriage just with Eleanor, and began to enjoy herself. She felt very special, travelling in such style towards a real abbey!

After a break in the journey while the horses were rested and fed, the General suggested that she take his place in Henry's open carriage. "It is a fine day, and you will see more of the countryside."

Catherine blushed, thinking of Mr. Allen's disapproval of open carriages, but her respect for General Tilney convinced her that it must not be improper in this case. In a few minutes' time, she found herself sitting beside Henry, and was the happiest girl alive.

Henry Tilney drove quietly and well, without boasting, unlike the only other gentleman she had ridden with so far. And he looked so smart and important in his hat and overcoat. To be driven along by him, as to dance with him, was the best thing in the world. In addition to this, he even *thanked* her for agreeing to come. He said

Northanger Abbey

his sister was often lonely when their father was away.

"How can that be? Are you not with her?" Catherine asked.

"Northanger is only half my home," Henry answered. "I have my own house in Woodston, about twenty miles away."

"You must be so sorry to leave Northanger Abbey!" Catherine exclaimed. "Such a fine old place as those I have read about."

"Ah yes," said Henry, glancing at her with a smile, "have you solid enough nerves for that kind of place?"

"I think so," Catherine replied earnestly. "Besides, the building has not been deserted for years and years as in the books…"

"No. We shall not have to explore a dark building, lit only by the embers of a dying fire…" Henry's eyes glinted with mischief as he added, "But you do realize that when a young lady visits this kind of place, she is always put in a room far from the family? Dorothy the housekeeper leads her along many gloomy passages to a room that has not been used since some relative died in it years ago… Can your nerves take it?"

Catherine laughed nervously. "I am sure that will not happen."

"And when you examine your room, what will you find? Perhaps a chest that will not open. Dorothy tells you the building is haunted, and that no one will hear you if you call, then leaves you… her footsteps fading into silence."

"How frightful – that is just like in a book!" Catherine cried, trembling with excitement. "What then?"

"You fall into an uneasy sleep but awake to a terrible storm. As the wind howls around the building, you notice that the tapestry on the wall is moving. You investigate, with your flickering lamp, and discover a secret passageway…"

Catherine shivered in delight, "I would be too terrified to go in!"

"In a secret room you find, perhaps, a dagger with blood on it. Your lamp is nearly out, so you return to your room. You discover an ebony and gold cabinet you had not noticed before. You open

Northanger Abbey

it, and search every drawer but discover nothing. Then your hand touches a secret spring, and a compartment opens. You see a roll of paper! Trembling, you open it, and read, 'Whosoever reads these, the memoirs of poor, wretched Matilda…' then suddenly your lamp goes out, plunging you into pitch darkness!"

Catherine squealed in delight and terror, and begged him to continue, but Henry Tilney was too consumed with laughter to go on. Catherine, rather ashamed of her eagerness, calmed down and assured him that she was not really afraid that anything like that would happen to her at the Abbey.

As they drew near the end of the journey, she imagined coming upon its huge stone walls with gleaming Gothic windows reflecting the setting sun. But she found herself passing through the gates without having seen so much as an antique chimney.

She did not have time to think about it, however, as a sudden scud of rain in her face made her more worried about her new straw bonnet. And then she was under the Abbey walls, springing down from the carriage, and entering the drawing room, where Eleanor and the General were waiting to welcome her.

Looking around, she could scarcely believe she was in a real abbey. The room was furnished with elegant, modern furniture. The fireplace, instead of being a Gothic one, was plain marble, with pretty English china on it. The windows, although they had pointed Gothic arches, were so bright and clear. To someone who had hoped for gloom and cobwebs, it was all very distressing!

The General followed her gaze around the room, and said he hoped it was comfortable enough for her. Then, taking out his watch, he suddenly exclaimed that it was already twenty to five, and Eleanor hurried Catherine away to dress for dinner.

She was led up a broad, shining oak staircase to a long, wide gallery with doors along one side and windows along the other that

Northanger Abbey

looked outside into a quadrangle. Catherine scarcely had time to look before being left in her room to get ready.

The room was entirely unlike Henry's alarming description. It had neither tapestries nor velvet; the walls were papered and the floor was carpeted. The windows were bright, the furniture comfortable, and it was altogether rather cheerful. Feeling relieved, she started to get ready for dinner. She was just throwing off her cloak, when her eye fell on a large chest, pushed back into an alcove on one side of the fireplace.

"How strange," she thought. "I wonder what can be inside it? Why is it pushed back like that?" She decided to examine it right away, by daylight, so there was no fear of her candle going out.

With trembling hands, she began to pull the lid open. It was stiff and heavy. Just as it began to rise… there was a sudden knocking at the door. She jumped and the lid crashed shut. Miss Tilney's maid came in to ask if she could be of any help. Catherine declined and the maid left, but, reminded that she should be getting ready, Catherine continued to do so.

Eyeing the unexplored chest, she changed her dress hurriedly, then darted across the room and threw back the lid. What should be revealed to her waiting, astonished eyes but… a small, white cotton bedcover, folded neatly in the bottom of the trunk.

She was gazing at it in surprise, when Miss Tilney came in to see whether she was ready. Catherine blushed, ashamed of being caught investigating the chest with such absurd expectations. She closed the lid hastily and turned away.

"Strange old thing, is it not?" Miss Tilney said. "I thought it might be useful, but it is so awkward to open… at least it is out of the way in that corner."

Catherine, busy blushing and tying the bow on her dress, vowed silently to herself to be more sensible in future. Miss Tilney hinted that they should hurry, so they ran downstairs together to

Northanger Abbey

find General Tilney pacing the drawing room, watch in hand.

They went in to dinner, and he scolded Eleanor for rushing their guest. Catherine was a little frightened by his strictness. But her own healthy appetite soon restored her peace of mind.

The wind had gradually picked up throughout the evening and by the time they were going to bed, there was quite a storm outside. As Catherine crossed the hall, the wind howled and a door slammed shut, and she really felt she was in an ancient building which had perhaps witnessed some horrifying scenes in its past. *She* had nothing to fear, of course, she told herself as she went up the stairs. Henry Tilney had just been joking. She saw with relief that Miss Tilney's bedroom was only two doors away from her own. In her own bedroom, she was even more reassured by the blazing log fire that a maid had lit in the fireplace.

But then she noticed the curtains moving by themselves. It must be the wind, blowing through the old panes, she thought. She went over, humming a determinedly careless tune, and put her hand against the window to feel the draught.

She was in her nightdress, the fire dying down, when she noticed a strange black and gold cabinet. It was just like the one Henry Tilney had described… what a coincidence!

She took her candle and went to examine it. There was a key in the door, but it was stuck. Outside, the wind roared and the rain beat in torrents against the windows. She jiggled the key in the lock, and suddenly it turned. Inside were lots of small drawers. She searched one after the other, but they were all empty. There was one last little door with a key in it… At last – there was something inside! It was a small roll of paper, pushed to the back as if someone had tried to hide it. Her heart fluttered, her knees trembled, her cheeks grew pale. It was all happening almost exactly as Henry Tilney had described.

Catherine's knees trembled... It was all happening almost exactly as Henry Tilney had described.

Northanger Abbey

She eyed her candle in alarm, but it still had some hours left before it burned out. However, the wick was long, and the light dim. Catherine went to trim the wick, so the flame would burn more brightly, and she could read the manuscript. But in her haste, she extinguished the candle. She stood there in the pitch blackness, motionless with horror. A violent gust of wind howled outside, adding fresh horror to the moment. Catherine trembled from head to foot. She thought she heard distant footsteps, and then there was silence. A cold sweat broke out on her forehead, the manuscript dropped from her hand, and she dived into bed and hid under the covers. She lay there, tormented by the thought of what the manuscript might contain. She vowed to lie awake, until the sun's first rays enabled her to read it…

The storm raged; the house made terrifying noises; the curtains waved; and it seemed someone was trying the lock of her door. The blood chilled in her veins. Hour after hour passed, until, with the clocks striking three, Catherine finally fell into an exhausted sleep.

Catherine awoke at eight o'clock the next morning to a bright, sunny day, which had replaced the stormy night. At once, she remembered the manuscript. She sprang out of bed, gathered the scattered sheets, and leaped back into bed to examine them in luxury. But as she leafed greedily through the pages, she saw lists of words – shirts, stockings, waistcoats…

It was nothing but a list of laundry!

Was this all she had spent a sleepless night for? She had let her imagination run away with her again. She ought to have learned her lesson from her experience with the chest. How could she have been so foolish? Heaven forbid Henry Tilney should ever know, even though it was partly his fault for telling that silly story in the first place. She folded the papers up and stuffed them back into the cabinet. Then she got dressed and hurried down to breakfast.

Northanger Abbey

Henry was alone in the breakfast room. He said he hoped she had slept well, undisturbed by the terrible storm, especially considering they were in an abbey… She found this rather distressing, but could not lie and admitted the wind had kept her awake a little. "But we have a lovely morning after it," she added, eager to change the subject. "Oh, what lovely hyacinths…"

Fortunately, at that moment the General entered, and he was smiling. He was even happier when Catherine complimented him on the breakfast set.

When breakfast was over, Henry left for his house in Woodston, where he had business to attend to for two or three days.

"Is it pretty, his house at Woodston?" Catherine asked as they walked back inside after seeing him off.

"It is a lovely family home, standing among meadows," the General said. "Even if Henry only had this property, without his inherited fortune from me, he would be well off. You might wonder why he works at all, being from such a wealthy family. Well, I believe every young man should have some employment."

He then offered to show her around the Abbey. He said he could see she would rather be outside in such fine weather, so they would look at the gardens first. Catherine was dying to see the house and could not care less about the gardens, but did not feel able to object, so she, the General and Eleanor went outside.

From the lawn, Catherine was impressed by the Abbey's grandeur. The whole building enclosed a large court, and two sides of the quadrangle were visible to view, complete with their Gothic features, like something from a novel. Wooded hills rose up behind, framing the Abbey beautifully, even in the leafless month of March. Catherine burst forth in praise and delight. The General was flattered. He said he supposed Mr. Allen's garden was just as grand. When Catherine said that it was not, he smiled in triumph.

Northanger Abbey

After walking around looking at every wall and flowerbed, the General said he wanted to check some alterations, and suggested Eleanor take Catherine back to the house. But when they started off down a shady path, he said they ought not to go that way, as it was too damp. Catherine liked the look of the narrow, winding path so much that she set off down it anyway, as if she had not heard.

"I am so fond of this path," Eleanor told her. "My mother loved it. I used to walk here with her."

"In that case," Catherine wondered to herself, "the General ought to love it too, for the same reason." But aloud, she said, "Your mother's death must be so sad for you."

"Yes," Eleanor answered. "I was only thirteen when she died. But I miss her even now. If I had a mother, perhaps I would not feel so lonely when Henry is away."

Eleanor told Catherine that she had a portrait of her mother hanging in her bedroom. "My father did not like the painting. But after my mother's death, I hung it in my room. I would be happy to show it to you. It is very like her."

More proof, Catherine thought, that the General had not loved his wife. First the walk and now the painting. She no longer tried to repress her feelings for the General. He must be a cruel, odious man through and through!

She had just settled this in her mind, when the end of the path brought her face to face with the General himself! In spite of all her indignation, she had to smile and be polite to him.

A whole hour went by before they at last began the tour of the house. After ordering tea for their return, the General led them through the drawing room into a much larger, grander room kept for important visitors. Next, he showed her the vast library. Catherine praised it all, anxious to move on. Where were the secret, dark chambers and cobweb-draped corridors? They must be somewhere. It was all so unlike the Abbey she had imagined!

They returned through some less-used rooms and looked into the central courtyard to see traces of the former cloister, which soothed her a little. Then the General showed her the modernized kitchen. She was led past an astonishing number of curtseying maids and bowing footmen, and they arrived back at the main staircase. Upstairs, he showed her room after room, listing people who had stayed there, adding that he hoped the next people to stay might be Catherine's family. They came to a pair of doors which Miss Tilney threw open. But the General said sternly, "What are you doing? There is no more to be seen here."

Miss Tilney closed the doors again, but not before Catherine had managed to glimpse the narrow, winding corridors beyond. Reluctantly, she followed the General back down for tea. Why did he not want her to see beyond those doors? Something must be hidden there!

As they went downstairs, Miss Tilney quietly explained, "I was going to show you my mother's room, where she died."

No wonder the General did not want to visit those rooms, Catherine thought: because of the stings of his conscience!

"When did your mother die?" she asked Eleanor later.

"Nine years ago," Eleanor replied. "Unfortunately I was away. Her illness was quite sudden. When I arrived, it was all over."

Catherine's blood ran cold. Could it be possible? Could Henry's father have…?

That evening, which dragged by without Henry, she was glad when it was time for bed. The General said he had business to finish, and would stay up a little longer. Catherine wondered what he could be doing while the household slept, as she climbed the shadowed staircase. Then a terrible thought occurred to her. What

Northanger Abbey

if Mrs. Tilney was not dead, but imprisoned in some part of the Abbey? The suddenness of her death, the absence of her daughter – probably of all her children – pointed towards this conclusion.

Getting undressed in her room, Catherine shivered. What was to say that, in her tour of the Abbey, she had not passed the very room where poor Mrs. Tilney was kept?

Catherine's extreme imaginings surprised even herself, but she did not think them unreasonable. She peered out of her window, thinking she might catch a glimpse of the General's lamplight as he walked to his wife's prison. But she saw nothing. Too early, Catherine thought; she would check again at midnight…

But, when midnight came, she was sound asleep.

There was no chance the next day of investigating the mysterious rooms, as it was Sunday and they had to go to church. And she did not dare explore them after dinner, when the light was fading. So the day passed without anything interesting happening.

The following morning was more promising. General Tilney went for a walk, and Eleanor took Catherine to see the room. But first she showed Catherine the portrait of her mother in her bedroom. It showed a woman with a mild, thoughtful face. Catherine had to search to find a family resemblance to Eleanor and Henry, or, for that matter, any trace of tragedy.

Next, they approached Mrs. Tilney's room. Eleanor had her hand on the lock of the door, Catherine could barely breathe in anticipation, when there came a sharp, "Eleanor!" It was the General at the other end of the gallery. As her friend, with an apologetic look, rushed to join the General, Catherine, terrified, darted for safety to her own room and locked herself in. She stayed there for at least an hour, expecting any moment for the General to summon her. When a carriage drew up outside, and visitors went into the Abbey, Catherine plucked up enough courage to go downstairs. The General introduced her as a friend of his daughter, and so she felt secure of her life at least for the time being. Eleanor seemed impressively calm. After a while, Catherine began to wonder if perhaps the General had not seen her.

She had better go alone next time, she thought. She could not very well search for proof of the General's cruelty in front of Eleanor, and she did not want to confide her suspicions until there was proof. She might find a fragment of a journal, written almost at the moment of the poor woman's last gasp…

She wanted to get it over with before Henry's return the following day. So at four o'clock, the day still bright and her courage high, Catherine went upstairs half an hour earlier than usual to dress for dinner.

She found herself alone in the gallery before the clocks had finished striking the hour. The handle turned beneath her hand, and she tiptoed into the room, and then stood there, rooted to the spot. The room before her was large and sunny, with mahogany wardrobes and hand-painted chairs. First, Catherine felt astonished, and then a ray of common sense led to a bitter feeling of shame. She had been grossly mistaken. Instead of being awful and cell-like, the room was large, well-lit and modern. She had no inclination to search its wardrobes for a journal. Whatever the General's crimes had been, he had left no trace of them here.

She was about to retreat to her own room when she heard footsteps approaching. To be caught here would be terrible! She darted out of the room and closed the door. The footsteps continued – they were coming up the stairs in front of her, closing off her escape. She fixed her eyes on the staircase in terror, and in a few moments Henry Tilney appeared at the top.

"Mr. Tilney!" Catherine cried, then she blushed and fell silent.

"Miss Morland! What are you doing here?" he asked.

Catherine looked down. "I have been," she admitted, "to see your mother's room."

"My mother's room! Is there anything extraordinary in it?"

"No, no... I did not think you were coming until tomorrow."

"I did not either, but then I found I could come sooner. You look pale. Did I frighten you by running up the stairs?"

"No, it is nothing. It must have been a good day for a ride," Catherine said feebly.

"It was – but does Eleanor leave you to wander around the house by yourself?" Henry persisted.

"No, she showed me most of it on Saturday. We were about to come in here but..." she whispered, "your father was with us."

"And that stopped you?" Henry was looking at her earnestly.

"It must be late," Catherine said desperately. "I must go and dress for dinner."

"It is only quarter past four," said Henry, glancing at his watch.

For the first time ever, Catherine felt she would rather not be with him at this very moment, but she could not excuse herself, so they walked along the corridor together. "So what did you think of my mother's room? Eleanor sent you to look, I suppose?"

"No," Catherine admitted.

"It is completely your own doing?" Henry said thoughtfully. As he received no reply, he went on. "There is nothing in the room itself to raise your curiosity, so it must be from some idea Eleanor gave you of my mother... Has Eleanor talked of her a lot?"

"Yes – no – not so much, but what she said was interesting. About her dying so suddenly," Catherine said slowly and hesitatingly, "and none of you being home – and your father, I thought – perhaps had not been very fond of her."

Henry's quick eye fixed on hers. "You thought there had been neglect—"

Despite herself, she shook her head.

Northanger Abbey

"—Something worse?" Henry's eyes widened. "My mother's death," he said firmly, "was the result of an illness she often suffered. Three very good doctors attended her. Frederick and I – who were *both* at home – saw her throughout her illness, and she received every possible attention."

"Was your father saddened by her death?" Catherine asked.

"Very much," Henry said. "You are mistaken in thinking he did not care about her. I cannot say that his temper never caused her sorrow, but he loved her and was very affected by her death."

"I am glad!" burst Catherine. "It would be shocking if—"

Henry looked at her sternly. "If I understand you rightly, you have come to a conclusion of such horror I can hardly put it into words. Consider how dreadful your suspicions are. Consider the time and place in which we live. Could you really have thought such horrors probable? My dear Miss Morland, what *have* you been thinking?"

They had reached the end of the corridor and, bursting into tears of shame, Catherine ran off to her room.

All visions of romance were over. Henry's words had finally opened Catherine's eyes to how silly her imaginings had been. She cried bitterly. How could Henry ever forgive her, now he knew? She hated herself more than she could say.

She made herself as miserable as possible for half an hour, and when the clock struck five, went down for dinner with red eyes and a broken heart. When Eleanor asked if she was ill, she could barely answer. Henry, however, seemed to be paying her more, not less, kind attention. Catherine had never wanted comfort more, and it seemed as though he was aware of it.

As the evening wore on, all the usual politenesses calmed Catherine. She began to hope that her behaviour would not cause Henry to think badly of her forever. She realized now that since

Northanger Abbey

entering the Abbey, she had been craving to be frightened and had bent everything to fit that purpose.

The Gothic novels she read were enthralling, but they were perhaps not the best place to learn about human nature, particularly that of people in the English midlands. Murder, slaves, poison and the like were not often come across there. Moreover, while people were not perfect, they must be allowed to have both good and bad in them. Even Henry and Eleanor Tilney might have some imperfections, she was now prepared to admit. And while their father certainly had some flaws in his character, it was no reason to suppose him a murderer.

She vowed to herself that in future she would only act with the greatest good sense. All that remained was for her to forgive herself. The lenient hand of time did much to help her, in the course of the following days. Henry's astonishing generosity also did wonders – he never referred in the slightest way to what had happened. Sooner than she had expected, Catherine felt comfortable again.

A few days after this incident, a letter appeared for her at breakfast. It was James's handwriting, and sent from Oxford. She opened it and read:

Dear Catherine,

I am writing to tell you that everything is at an end between Miss Thorpe and me. I left her and Bath yesterday, never to see either again. I was foolish to think that she returned my love. Thank God I know the truth in time. She has made me miserable for ever.

I hope you have left Northanger before Captain Tilney announces their engagement, or you will be in an embarrassing

Northanger Abbey

position. It is her deception that hurts more than anything. Until the very end, she said she loved me as much as ever and laughed at my fears. I am ashamed to think how long my delusion lasted, but if any man ever had a reason to believe himself loved, I was that man.

We parted at last by mutual agreement – I wish we had never met. Dearest Catherine, beware how you give your heart.

Believe me, your loving brother,

James

Catherine had not read three lines before her face and her exclamations of sorrow showed the letter contained bad news. Henry, watching her earnestly, saw that it ended no better than it had begun. But before he had a chance to say anything, his father swept into the room and they sat down to breakfast. Catherine could not eat a thing. Tears filled her eyes and spilled down her cheeks. The General, hidden behind his newspaper, did not notice, but the other two saw how distressed she was.

As soon as she could, she excused herself and went up to her room. But the housemaids were busy in it, and she had to come back down. She hid in the drawing room, sobbing and thinking, for half an hour. After that, she emerged, and found Henry and Eleanor in the breakfast room, "There is no bad news from home I hope?" Eleanor asked anxiously. "Your family – I hope nobody is ill?"

"No, thank you," Catherine sighed, "they are all well. The letter was from my brother… Oh, it is terrible. Poor James is so unhappy!"

"To have such a loving sister must be a comfort," said Henry.

Northanger Abbey

"I have a favour to beg," said Catherine. "If your brother is coming here, could you let me know so that I can go away?"

"Our brother – Frederick?" Henry said in surprise.

"Yes. I would be sorry to leave so soon, but I could not be in the same house as Captain Tilney."

Eleanor gazed in astonishment, but Henry had begun to suspect the truth, and told Catherine what he thought it might be.

"How quick you are!" Catherine exclaimed. "You have guessed it. Isabella has deserted my brother and is to marry yours!"

"I hope my brother did not have a hand in your brother's disappointment," Henry said. "I am sorry that anyone you love should be unhappy. But I would be more surprised than anything if Frederick married Miss Thorpe."

"It is true. Read it for yourself," Catherine insisted. She blushed as she gave it to him, remembering the letter's last words.

Henry read the letter carefully, and returned it, saying, "If it is true, I am sorry about that too. I do not envy his situation."

Catherine handed the letter to Eleanor, who read it and asked about Isabella's family. "Her father is a lawyer. I do not think Isabella has any fortune to offer," Catherine told her, "but I do not suppose that will matter – your father said to me that he only valued money as far as it could make his children happy."

Eleanor and Henry exchanged doubtful glances at this.

"But," Eleanor hesitated, "will this girl make Frederick happy? She has behaved very badly to your brother."

"Perhaps she will behave better to yours," Catherine said. "Now she has the man she likes, she might be faithful to him."

"Until a better offer comes along…" Henry remarked.

"You think it is all for ambition then?" Catherine said, wide-eyed. "I must admit there are some things that make it seem so. I remember when she first learned how much money my father could give them to live on, she seemed disappointed that it was not more." Catherine sighed. "I have never been so deceived about anyone's character in my life. I so feel for my poor brother!"

"But what about yourself?" Henry asked. "You must feel that you have lost a close friend you could talk to about anything and everything. Balls must seem a dismal prospect without her…?"

Catherine thought for a moment, and then said, not without a note of surprise, "No. As a matter of fact, I do not feel that. I am hurt that I cannot still love her, and that I am never to see her again. But I do not feel as bad as I might have thought."

Henry looked at her warmly. "You feel, as you always do, something which shows human nature at its best."

Over the next few days, the three of them discussed the subject further. To Catherine's surprise, Henry and Eleanor were certain their father would forbid the marriage due to Isabella's lack of fortune. She felt alarmed for herself, to find the General's opinion so based on money. She had no fortune, and fewer connections than Isabella and yet the General had always seemed to think so highly of her… Perhaps they were wrong about him.

They assured her, at any rate, that their brother had never been less likely to turn up at Northanger, so Catherine felt sure that she would not have to leave suddenly.

A day or so later, the General said to Henry, "Let us all have dinner at your house one day. How about Wednesday next week?"

Henry went to Woodston a few days ahead of their visit. He joked that he would have to terrify his housekeeper into making a fine enough dinner for his father. Wednesday came, and Catherine was treading on air in anticipation. At ten o'clock the carriage and horses took her, the General and Eleanor from the Abbey to Woodston. Catherine thought the village very pretty, admiring all the neat little houses and shops they passed. At the far end of the village stood the vicarage, Henry's house. It was a large, new, stone

Northanger Abbey

house with green gates. They swept up the driveway to see Henry waiting outside to greet them.

"It is nothing compared to Northanger, but quite habitable," Henry said as he led them inside to a large, comfortable dining room, where some tea things were laid out. After tea, he showed them around the house. They went through a drawing room, which, though it was as yet unfurnished, delighted Catherine. It had long windows reaching down to the ground, looking out over green meadows. "Why do you not furnish this room, Mr. Tilney? It is the prettiest room I have ever seen," she said with honest enthusiasm. "If it were mine, I would never sit anywhere else. What a sweet little cottage you can see among the apple trees!"

"I am sure it could be fitted up for a lady. And make a note to your man, Henry – the cottage stays," said the General.

This comment made Catherine very self-conscious and she fell silent. But as they strolled around the meadow, her embarrassment melted away. After walking all around, and stopping to watch a litter of puppies playing in the barn, it was already time for dinner. Catherine thought never a day had passed more quickly!

By the time the General had called for their carriage after dinner, the hints he had dropped made it clear that he expected Catherine and his son to get married. If she were only so sure of his son's thoughts on the matter, Catherine would have left Woodston without worrying about when she might return.

The next morning brought the following very unexpected letter from Isabella:

My dearest Catherine,

A thousand apologies for not replying sooner. I meant to write every day, but have been distracted. I am leaving this vile place for home tomorrow.

Northanger Abbey

I am a little uneasy about your brother. I have not heard from him since he left, and am worried of a misunderstanding. He is the only man I ever loved.

The man I hate has left Bath. You will know I mean Captain Tilney. You may remember him following me around, before you went away. He spent his last two days in Bath following some other woman around. I avoided him after that. Now he has gone away with his regiment and I hope he will never plague me again. Such a difference between him and your brother!

I am worried about him. I would write myself but I have mislaid his address. Please can you explain everything to him? Convince him I love him, and let him know to write or visit me in Putney.

Lose no time, my dear, sweet Catherine, in writing to him and to me,

Your dearest friend,

Isabella

Catherine was not in the least taken in by the letter. She felt ashamed of Isabella, and ashamed of ever having loved her. When Henry came back from Woodston, she congratulated him and Eleanor on their brother being free of Isabella.

"She must think me an idiot to write this to me. I see now what she is about. She is a vain flirt, and her tricks have failed. I do not think she ever really cared for James or me. I wish I had never known her!"

"It will soon be as if you never did," Henry reassured her.

Northanger Abbey

Soon after this, the General had to go to London for a week. He urged Henry and Eleanor to look after Catherine in his absence. While he was gone, the three spent their time happily, doing what they liked with much laughter and merriness. It made Catherine realize how much the General dampened everyone's spirits by his very presence. She loved the place and the people she was with more every day. But she had stayed for four weeks already, and thought, with dread, that she ought not to outstay her welcome.

She mentioned as much to Eleanor. But Eleanor put the idea out of her mind, by begging her sweetly not even to think of leaving so soon. And Henry's warm smile too convinced Catherine that they loved her, and wished her to belong to them…

Henry was called away again to Woodston, and the girls lingered over dinner after he left, talking. It was eleven o'clock before they were heading to bed. They had just reached the top of the stairs, when a carriage drew up outside. Eleanor said it was probably her eldest brother, and she went back down to see him. Catherine carried on to her room, thinking perhaps she could see Captain Tilney now, as long as they never mentioned Isabella.

About half an hour later, she heard footsteps, and the noise of someone outside her door. The lock moved – someone's hand must be on it. Catherine trembled but, determined not to be ruled by her imagination this time, she went to the door and opened it. It was Eleanor, only Eleanor, standing there.

But Eleanor's cheeks were pale. "I come with such a message – I cannot bear it. Oh, how shall I tell you?" she cried.

Catherine stared in horror. "Is something wrong with Henry?"

"No," Eleanor said. Her voice faltered. "I hope you will not think the worse of me for what I have to say. My father has remembered that we have to take a trip on Monday, to Lord Longtown's near Hereford. And so we must part…"

"My dear Eleanor," Catherine said, "do not be upset. I am sad but I am not offended. I can visit another time – or you can come to Fullerton! I can leave on Monday, just before you. The General will send a servant with me for the journey, I suppose…"

"Catherine," Eleanor said, looking distraught. "He says you must leave early tomorrow, at seven o'clock. He is sending no servant with you. The carriage is ordered – you are to go alone."

Catherine sat down in shock. "Have I offended the General in some way?" she asked quietly.

"I cannot imagine how," Eleanor said. "All I can say is that he is very out of sorts. Something has ruffled him to an unusual degree – some disappointment or other. I have no idea what."

Catherine felt her friend's distress at having to tell her this, and made herself answer, "Do not be unhappy, Eleanor. I wish I had known sooner, so I could have let my mother and father know I was coming, but it does not matter."

"But a journey of seventy miles, at your age, alone…"

"It is nothing," said Catherine. "I will be ready for seven."

Unable to say anything to improve the situation, Eleanor left her with, "I shall see you in the morning."

As soon as she was alone, Catherine burst into torrents of tears. To be turned out of the house, and in such a way! Without any reason or apology from the General, and without a chance to say goodbye to Henry! Who could say when they would meet again? And the General had seemed so fond of her too. She was mortified. She could not understand it.

After a sleepless night, Catherine went down to breakfast with Eleanor. She tried to eat, but could not. The two friends sat in silence, until the carriage drew up outside. "Oh, Catherine," Eleanor burst out, "please write and let me know you have arrived safely home. Direct it to Lord Longtown's – address it to 'Alice' and I will be sure to get it."

Northanger Abbey

"You are not allowed even to have a letter from me? Then I will not write!" Catherine said. But Eleanor's look of sorrow melted her pride, and she said instantly, "Oh Eleanor, I *will* write to you."

The carriage was ready. A long hug replaced anything they could say to one another. As she turned to leave, Catherine's lip quivered. "Say goodbye to your brother for me," she managed to say. Then, hiding her face in her handkerchief, she darted across the hall, jumped into the carriage, and was driven away.

Catherine felt too wretched to be afraid of travelling alone. Leaning back in the carriage, she burst into tears. By the time she looked up again, she was far from the Abbey. As she passed Woodston, she thought mournfully of Henry. The day spent there had been the happiest of her life. And that was when the General had made it plain that he expected – wanted – Henry to marry her. And now – what had she done to merit such a change?

Stopping only to change horses, Catherine travelled for eleven hours, her worried thoughts churning all the way until, after six o'clock in the evening, she finally arrived in Fullerton.

A heroine returning in glory and triumph to her home village is an event on which any author would delight to dwell. However, my affair is very different. I bring my heroine back alone and ashamed.

The carriage attracted a lot of delight in her village. Catherine's family were at the window when it stopped, and tumbled out to welcome her. In their warm embraces, she felt soothed and cheered. Soon they were all gathered at the tea table to hear her news.

After hearing the manner of her departure from the Abbey, Catherine's mother dismissed the episode with: "What a strange business, and he must be a very strange man!" and very sensibly told Catherine not to let it worry her any more.

After breakfast the next morning, Catherine wrote a brief but affectionate letter to Eleanor, to let her know she was safely home.

Northanger Abbey

"What a strange acquaintance that was," remarked her mother, as she finished, "soon made and soon ended – I am sorry. Mrs. Allen thought a lot of them. And you were sadly out of luck with your friend Isabella, too. Poor James. Ah well, we must live and learn."

"No friend can be more worth keeping than Eleanor," Catherine said sadly.

"Perhaps you will meet again in a few years," her mother said in an attempt to console her. Catherine's eyes filled with tears.

Mrs. Morland quickly suggested they call on the Allens, to try to cheer her up. The Allens were kind in their welcome, and indignant at her treatment by General Tilney. Mrs. Allen reminded her of the fun they had had in Bath, and Catherine's eyes brightened at the memory of it all.

But on the way home, Catherine's thoughts were elsewhere. She could only think, silently, that Henry must now have arrived at Northanger, and have heard of her departure, and now, perhaps, they were all setting off for Hereford.

Catherine, not usually prone to sitting still for long, was even more restless than usual. This, added to her pale face, silence and obvious sadness, made her quite different from before.

"I am afraid you are fretting about General Tilney. It will not do – particularly as you never need see him again," her mother said to her at last. "Or is it that, after your experiences, you have grown into too fine a lady for sewing and sitting at home?"

Catherine's mother went to see if she could find a book on the subject. By the time she came back, a visitor had arrived. It was a young man, who rose respectfully as she entered, and whom Catherine introduced, self-consciously, as, "Mr. Henry Tilney."

With an embarrassment that showed real sensitivity, Henry apologized for his father's treatment of Catherine, saying he knew he had no right to expect any welcome at Fullerton, but he had

Northanger Abbey

wanted to know that Miss Morland had reached home safely.

Mrs. Morland thanked him, and kindly assured him that friends of her children were always welcome at Fullerton.

There was a little embarrassed silence, and then their guest turned to Catherine and asked if the Allens were home. When she said they were, he asked, with colour rising in his face, whether she might show him the way there so that he could call on them.

Although the Allens' property was visible from the window, Mrs. Morland urged Catherine to go, thinking Mr. Tilney might want to explain more about his father in private.

She was not entirely mistaken. But, in fact, his first wish was to explain himself. Before they had reached the Allens' house he had done so, and so well that Catherine did not think it could be repeated too often. He was in love with her, and wanted her hand in marriage. Catherine promised him her heart in return, although it was perfectly clear to both of them that it was already his.

After a very short visit to the Allens, where Henry talked at random and Catherine, wrapped in unutterable happiness, scarcely opened her lips, they walked home, and he explained everything.

It turned out that the only thing Catherine had done to offend the General was to have been less rich than he had supposed. He had invited her to Northanger, and approved of a marriage between her and his son, all because of his conversation with John Thorpe in Bath. John, who intended to marry Catherine himself, had boasted to the General that she was extremely rich.

While in London, General Tilney had heard a very different story, told to him by a now-rejected John Thorpe. Thorpe had said, spitefully, that Catherine's family was large and needy, and looking to marry into money. The General had ordered Henry to forget about Catherine. But Henry had said he was going to visit her at once, to offer his hand in marriage.

Northanger Abbey

Mr. and Mrs. Morland were surprised when Mr. Tilney asked their permission for their daughter's hand. But they soon got used to the idea and were proud and pleased. There was one problem, however: the General. Catherine's parents said that until he consented to the match, they could not agree to it either. They did not want his money, merely his consent.

The young couple parted, hoping the General would change his mind soon. Henry returned to Woodston to tend to his house, and Catherine remained at Fullerton to cry. However, it is useless to try to portray their prolonged anxiety, as you can see by how little is left of this story that we are hastening to a happy end.

But what could possibly have changed the General's mind? As it happened, it was the happy marriage of his daughter, Eleanor, to a rich, important man, a viscount no less, which took place that summer. This put him in such a good mood that he forgave Henry, and allowed him to marry Catherine.

Eleanor had been fond of the gentleman for a long time, but he had only recently inherited a title and a fortune, making their marriage possible. He has not appeared in this story so far, but in fact, it was his servant who had left behind the laundry list that had so alarmed Catherine...

The General welcomed his son and Catherine back to Northanger Abbey, having learned that not only had he been misled by John Thorpe's first account of her extreme wealth, but he had also been misled by his second account of her extreme poverty. Catherine's family were not poor or needy at all.

Soon afterwards, Catherine and Henry were married, the bells rang and everybody smiled; and, as this took place within a year of their first meeting, they did not have to wait so dreadfully long after all. To begin perfect happiness at the ages of twenty-six and eighteen is, all in all, to do pretty well.

Emma

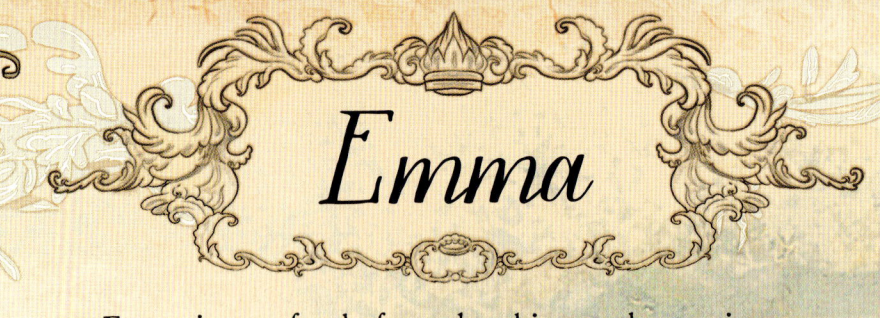

Emma is very fond of matchmaking, and sometimes gets carried away. When some of her matchmaking goes wrong, people get hurt. Is Emma really clever enough to know when her own match is made?

Emma Woodhouse
The lively, fun and rather spoiled daughter of the wealthiest man in Highbury. Spends her time meddling in the love lives of others.

Mr. Woodhouse
Emma's sweet, frail elderly father.

Harriet Smith
A naive, pretty girl, whom Emma takes under her wing, determined to find her a good husband.

Mr. Knightley
A close family friend, and Emma's only critic. But does he think as badly of her as he makes out?

Mr. Martin
A kind, well-spoken farmer, and an admirer of Harriet's. Emma discourages the match, thinking Harriet can do better.

Mr. Elton
The elegant, unmarried vicar of Highbury, whom Emma hopes to pair up with Harriet.

Mr. & Mrs. Weston

Emma's beloved governess, and a local widower, recently married as a result of Emma's matchmaking skills.

Frank Churchill

Mr. Weston's son, who has been brought up by his late mother's rich brother and wife. Emma imagines she will end up with him, but is he quite what she was expecting?

Jane Fairfax

An elegant, quiet orphan with no fortune, who comes to stay with her aunt, Miss Bates, in Highbury. She knows Frank Churchill, but their relationship is unclear…

Miss & Mrs. Bates

Jane Fairfax's kind, chatty aunt and her elderly mother, who live in Highbury. Less wealthy friends of Mr. Woodhouse, whom Emma finds a little tiresome.

*E*MMA WOODHOUSE, BEAUTIFUL, CLEVER, RICH, WITH A comfortable home and happy nature, seemed to unite some of the best blessings of existence. She had lived for twenty-one years with very little to upset her.

She was the younger of two daughters of a loving father, and since her sister Isabella's marriage, she had ruled the house. Her mother was no more than a memory of caresses; her place had been taken by a governess, Miss Taylor, who loved Emma with almost a mother's love.

Miss Taylor had been in Mr. Woodhouse's family for sixteen years and was more a friend than a governess. She was very fond of both daughters, but particularly of Emma. The mildness of Miss Taylor's nature hardly allowed her to restrain Emma, however, and since Emma grew up, she had done just what she liked. The real evils of Emma's situation were the power of having her own way rather too much, and a tendency to think a little too highly of herself.

Sorrow came – a gentle sorrow. Miss Taylor married. The marriage brought Emma's friend every happiness; her husband, Mr. Weston, was a man of excellent character, suitable age and wealth. But how was Emma herself to bear it?

The wedding was over; the couple had gone; she and her father were alone. Her father dozed off after dinner, as usual, while Emma thought of what she had lost.

Mrs. Weston was moving to a house only half a mile from them, but Emma knew that the difference between Miss Taylor living in the house with them and Mrs. Weston living half a mile away would be great. She would miss her every hour of the day. She dearly loved her father, but he was no match for her in conversation – playful or serious. She was in danger of being bored and lonely.

Her sister lived in London, about sixteen miles away, and so could not be seen very often. Emma knew most of the people in Highbury, the village to which her home, Hartfield, belonged, despite the estate's vast lawns separating the two. But everyone in the village looked up to the Woodhouses. No one there was a substitute for Miss Taylor.

Emma sighed about it until her father awoke, and then forced herself to cheer up on his account.

He was a nervous old man, not fond of change. "Poor Miss Taylor," he said at tea, exactly as he had said at dinner. "What a pity it is that Mr. Weston ever thought of her."

"I cannot agree with you, Papa. Mr. Weston is an excellent man, and deserves a good wife, and you would not want Miss Taylor to live here for ever, when she could have a house of her own."

"What is the advantage of a house of her own? Our house is three times as large as theirs."

"We shall see them very often!" said Emma. "We must pay our first visit very soon."

"But how shall I get there? I cannot walk so far."

"No, Papa, nobody thought you should walk. We will go in the carriage."

"Where can we put the horses while we are paying our visit?"

"In Mr. Weston's stable, Papa. It is already settled."

Emma hoped, by bringing out the backgammon table, to get him through the evening. But a visitor walked in just then, making it unnecessary.

Emma

Mr. Knightley was not only a family friend, but more closely connected as the elder brother of Isabella's husband. He lived at Donwell Abbey, about a mile from Highbury.

"Did the wedding go well?" asked Mr. Knightley. "Who cried the most?"

"Ah, poor Miss Taylor! It is a sad business," Mr. Woodhouse lamented.

"I cannot say 'poor Miss Taylor'. She is independent; and she now has only one person to please instead of two," Mr. Knightley said with a smile.

"Especially when one of those two is such a fanciful, troublesome creature," said Emma playfully. "I know that is what you meant."

"Very true, my dear," Mr. Woodhouse sighed. "I am very fanciful and troublesome."

"Dearest Papa! I did not mean you!" Emma cried. "Oh, no, I only meant myself. Mr. Knightley loves to find fault with me, you know – in a joke – it is all a joke. We always say what we like to one another."

Mr. Knightley, in fact, was the only person who could see faults in Emma Woodhouse, and the only one who ever told her of them.

"Well," said Emma, eager to let the moment pass, "everyone behaved charmingly. And you have forgotten one matter of joy to me: I made the match."

Mr. Knightley shook his head and Mr. Woodhouse said fondly, "Ah my dear, pray do not make any more matches."

"But it is the most fun in the world. Everybody said Mr. Weston would never marry again. Oh dear no! Some people even talked of a deathbed promise to his wife, or of his son not letting him. But I believed none of it. Ever since the day when Miss Taylor and I met him in the rain and he darted away for an umbrella, I planned it."

"What are you proud of?" asked Mr. Knightley. "You made a lucky guess."

"Have you never known the triumph of a lucky guess?" Emma said. "It is never merely luck. There is always some talent in it."

"No more matches, my dear," repeated Mr. Woodhouse.

"One more, Papa, for Mr. Elton. He has been our vicar for a year, and is all alone. I shall find him a wife."

"Much better invite him here, Emma," said Mr. Knightley, "and choose his dinner. But I think you should let him choose his own wife."

Mr. Weston had been born in Highbury. He had married a Miss Churchill, who was from a Yorkshire family so full of pride and importance that her brother and his wife were shocked at the match. They had cut her off, and the marriage had not been altogether a happy one because of it. Mrs. Weston had died three years later, leaving a little boy, Frank. Mr. and Mrs. Churchill, who had no children of their own, had offered to take Frank, and give him the name of Churchill. His father was reluctant, of course, but his feelings were overcome by other considerations. He was not so very wealthy, and would have struggled to make his way with a child; this way, Frank would be his uncle's heir, and have good prospects. And he could see him once or twice a year.

Mr. Frank Churchill, now an adult, had never been to Highbury. His visits were often discussed but never achieved. But he did write a very proper letter to the new Mrs. Weston after the wedding, proof, Mrs. Weston believed, of his good intentions.

The Westons, Mr. Knightley and Mr. Elton were Mr. Woodhouse's closest friends. After these was a second set, consisting of Mrs. and Miss Bates and Miss Goddard. Mrs. Bates, the widow of a former vicar of Highbury, was a very old lady, past almost everything but tea. Her daughter, Miss Bates,

Emma

was not clever, rich, beautiful or married. Her youth had passed, and now she was middle-aged she spent her time caring for a failing mother, and trying to make a small income go far. Yet she was a happy woman with a contented nature, and was a great talker.

Mrs. Goddard was a motherly kind of woman who kept a boarding school, in which about twenty girls scrambled their way into a little education without any danger of becoming prodigies.

Emma, having arranged an evening's entertainment for her father with these ladies, received a note from Mrs. Goddard asking if she might bring Harriet Smith. Emma immediately replied with a gracious invitation. She knew Miss Smith by sight on account of her beauty, and she no longer dreaded the evening.

Harriet Smith was the illegitimate daughter of somebody. That somebody had placed her in Miss Goddard's school, paid her fees, and that was all people knew of her background. She had just returned from paying a visit to some schoolfellows. She was very pretty, small, plump and fair, with blue eyes and a very sweet expression. She was neither shy, nor pushy, and before the evening was over, Emma had decided to become friends with her.

Emma knew the family Harriet had been staying with. The Martins rented one of Mr. Knightley's farms. She knew Mr. Knightley respected them, but she supposed they must be coarse and unpolished: unfit companions for a girl who needed only a little more knowledge and elegance to be perfect. She would improve Harriet; she would detach her from her inferior friends and introduce her to good society. It would be a kind deed, and an interesting project for someone with her talents.

Harriet's friendship with Emma was soon established. At first Harriet talked much of the Martin family and Abbey-Mill Farm, its eight cows, one a little Welsh cow, which they had called *her* cow. Emma had supposed there to be two Martin girls, and a mother and father, but it appeared she was wrong. The Mr. Martin who appeared so often in Harriet's conversation was a single man, the brother of the two girls.

"Have you never seen him in Highbury?" asked Harriet.

"Perhaps. A young farmer, whether on horseback or on foot, is the very last sort of person to raise my curiosity. Farmers are precisely the order of people with whom I feel I can have nothing to do. A degree or two lower and a decent appearance might interest me. But a farmer needs none of my help, and in that way is as much above my notice as in every other way he is below it."

They met Mr. Martin the very next day on their walk. Emma's quick eye took in his neat appearance, as she walked a few yards away while he and Harriet talked. They were only a few minutes together, as they thought that Miss Woodhouse must not be kept waiting. Then Harriet came running to her in a flutter of spirits which Emma hoped soon to quell.

"Miss Woodhouse, what do you think of him?"

"He is plain, undoubtedly, but that is nothing compared with his entire want of gentility. I had no idea he could be so clownish, so very far from being a gentleman."

"To be sure," said Harriet in a mortified voice, "he is not a real gentleman."

"Since you have been acquainted with me, Harriet, you have met such very real gentlemen that you must be struck by the difference between them and Mr. Martin. Do you begin to feel that now? His awkward look, his abrupt manner? His tone of voice?"

"He has not such a fine way of walking and talking as Mr. Knightley," Harriet admitted.

"Mr. Knightley is so remarkable that it is unfair to compare Mr. Martin with him. But he is not the only gentleman you have met lately. What about Mr. Weston or Mr. Elton? Compare

Mr. Martin with either of them."

"But Mr. Weston is almost old!"

"The older a person grows, Harriet, the more important it is that their manners should be good. Mr. Martin is now awkward and abrupt; what will he be at Mr. Weston's age?"

"There is no saying, indeed," replied Harriet rather solemnly.

Emma thought she might safely leave Harriet to herself. She waited a little before beginning again.

"Mr. Elton is good-tempered and gentle. I think he has become even more gentle of late. It must be to please you. Did you hear what he said about you the other day?"

She repeated some praise which she had extracted from Mr. Elton, and Harriet blushed and smiled.

Mr. Elton was the person fixed on by Emma to drive Mr. Martin out of Harriet's head. He was a gentleman, but without any family who could object to Harriet's doubtful birth. He had a comfortable home, and probably a good income. He was just the man for Harriet.

"What do you think of this friendship between Emma and Harriet Smith?" Mr. Knightley asked Mrs. Weston. "I think it is a bad thing."

"Why?"

Mr. Knightley frowned. "Neither will do the other any good."

"But Emma will do Harriet good," Mrs. Weston said, "and by giving her a new interest, Harriet will do Emma good. I agree Harriet is not the refined young woman which Emma's friend ought to be. But Emma wants to see her better educated, which will encourage Emma herself. They will read together."

"Emma has been meaning to read more ever since she was small," Mr. Knightley laughed. "I have seen the lists she drew up – very good lists, sometimes alphabetical, impressively arranged.

Emma

But she will never do anything that requires hard work. Emma is spoiled by being the cleverest in her family. She was always quick and confident. Harriet Smith knows nothing and thinks Emma knows everything. How can Emma imagine she is anything other than perfect when Harriet admires everything she says?"

"Emma has good sense, Mr. Knightley. Did she not look lovely last night? So pretty, with such bright, hazel eyes."

"I confess I have never seen a face or figure that pleases me more. I love to look at her, and considering how beautiful she is, she is not vain. Her vanity lies elsewhere. But I think her friendship with Harriet will do them both harm."

"Surely not. Even with Emma's faults, where shall we ever find a better daughter, a kinder sister, or a truer friend?"

"Very well. Emma is an angel," said Mr. Knightley. "But I feel anxious for her. I wonder what will become of her."

"I too," said Mrs. Weston.

"She says she will never marry, which means nothing at all. I think she has not yet seen a man she could love." Mr. Knightley frowned. "I should like to see Emma in love, and in some doubt of a return; it would do her good. But there is no one around here to attract her."

Emma was in no doubt at all that Mr. Elton was falling in love with Harriet.

"You have given Miss Smith everything she needed," Mr. Elton said to her. "She was always beautiful, but you have made her graceful too."

"She has a naturally sweet temper. I have done very little," Emma replied.

"If it were possible to contradict a lady..." Mr. Elton protested gallantly.

Emma was even more convinced when she suggested she draw

Harriet's portrait. "I used to have a passion for drawing portraits, but I gave it all up. But what an exquisite thing a good portrait of her would be."

"I beg you, do make one!" cried Mr. Elton. "I know your talents! The walls of Hartfield are covered with your landscapes!"

"Yes, but what has that to do with Harriet's face?" thought Emma. "Keep your raptures for that."

Emma produced her portfolio, to choose the best size for her portrait. Out tumbled her many beginnings. Miniatures, half lengths, whole lengths, pencil, crayon, watercolours had all been tried in turn. She had always wanted to do everything, but had finished little.

The portrait was to be full length, in watercolours. The painting began, and Harriet, blushing and afraid of not keeping still, presented a very sweet expression. But Emma could do nothing with Mr. Elton fidgeting behind her. She ordered him to read aloud to them both, to keep him out of her way.

Everyone approved of the picture.

"It appears to me a perfect resemblance," said Mr. Elton.

"You have made her too tall, Emma," said Mr. Knightley.

Emma knew she had, but would not admit it, and Mr. Elton warmly added, "Oh no, it gives one exactly the idea of Miss Smith's height…"

"It is very pretty," said Mr. Woodhouse. "The only thing I do not like is that she seems to be outdoors and it makes one think she must catch cold."

"But, Papa, it is supposed to be summer. Look at the tree," Emma protested.

"But it is never safe to linger out of doors, my dear."

"It is a happy thought, placing Miss Smith out of doors!" said Mr. Elton. "The naivety of Miss Smith's manner – oh, it is admirable. I cannot keep my eyes from it!"

The painting began, and Harriet, blushing and afraid of not keeping still, presented a very sweet expression.

Emma

The next thing was to get the picture framed. It must be done immediately; it would be best done in London, and through the hands of an intelligent person with good taste, Emma suggested. Of course, Mr. Elton offered to take it himself.

"He is almost too gallant," thought Emma. "He sighs and languishes, and offers so many compliments – even to me. I expect that is out of gratitude on account of Harriet."

The day that Mr. Elton went to London, Harriet arrived at Hartfield soon after breakfast, with a letter she had just received from Mr. Martin. It was a proposal of marriage.

"Who would have thought it?" said Harriet. "He writes as if he really loved me. Please advise me, Miss Woodhouse. It is a very good letter, do you not think? Pray, read it."

Emma was glad to do so. She was surprised. The style was above her expectations: there were no grammatical errors, and the language, though plain, was warm, sensitive and strong.

"Well," said the still-waiting Harriet, "What shall I do?"

"You must answer it."

"But what shall I say?"

"You must write it yourself. You must make your meaning plain, showing gratitude, and conscious of the pain you are inflicting."

"Should I refuse him, then?" said Harriet, looking down.

"Refuse him? My dear Harriet, I thought you were asking me about the wording of your reply. Have I misunderstood?"

Harriet was silent. For a little while Emma allowed it, but realizing that the bewitching flattery of the letter might be too powerful, she said, "Generally, Harriet, if a woman doubts whether to accept a man's proposal, she should certainly refuse it. But do not imagine that I want to influence you."

"Perhaps it would be safer to say 'No'," Harriet said hesitantly.

Emma waited, not without strong hopes.

"Miss Woodhouse, I have quite decided to refuse Mr. Martin. Do you think I am right?"

"Perfectly, perfectly right, my dearest Harriet. I am glad for myself too. I would have lost you. I could never have visited Mrs. Robert Martin of Abbey-Mill Farm. You would have thrown yourself out of good society."

"I never thought of that. How could I have borne it? It would have killed me never to come to Hartfield again."

"Dear creature! You, banished to the illiterate and vulgar all your life. How could he have asked it of you? You must reply at once, Harriet."

"What shall I say?"

Looking at his letter again had such a softening effect on Harriet that Emma believed he would, if he had appeared in person, have been accepted at once. Harriet's letter was, in the end, made up of Emma's thoughts and Emma's words.

"I shall never be invited to Abbey-Mill again," said Harriet in rather a sorrowful tone, when the letter was signed and sealed.

"Think of more cheerful things, my dear, modest little Harriet," said Emma. At this very moment, Mr. Elton has just left Bond Street. He is thinking how much more beautiful you are than the picture. He is looking at it. It is his companion all this evening, his solace, his delight."

Harriet was smiling once more, and her smiles grew stronger.

It was settled that Harriet should stay at Hartfield for a few days. She had gone for a walk, to collect some belongings from Mrs. Goddard when Mr. Knightley called upon Emma. He began to speak of Harriet.

"You have improved her, Emma. Her schoolgirl giggle has gone. You are expecting her back soon?"

Emma

"Any moment."

"Perhaps something has happened to delay her," Mr. Knightley said. "My tenant, Robert Martin – an excellent man – wants to marry her. He is desperately in love. He came to Donwell Abbey two nights ago to discuss it with me. He was worried that your making so much of her might have put her out of his reach. I reassured him and he went away happy. He may be proposing to her this very minute."

"Robert Martin," said Emma, "spoke yesterday – that is, he wrote, and was refused."

Mr. Knightley turned red with indignation. "Harriet Smith refuses Robert Martin! Madness! I hope you are wrong."

"I saw her answer."

"You saw her answer! You wrote her answer too. Emma, this is your fault. You persuaded her to refuse him."

"If I did, I did right. He is not Harriet's equal."

"Not her equal?" Mr. Knightley cried warmly. "You are blind, Emma. She is pretty and good-tempered, and that is all. What are her claims to any connection higher than Robert Martin? She is the illegitimate daughter of nobody knows whom, young, simple, inexperienced. She is below Robert Martin, but with a man so in love, the match would be bound to turn out well."

"Her father must be a gentleman. Why should she marry her inferior in rank?"

"Her father left her with Mrs. Goddard. Till you turned her into a friend, she had no further ambition. She was perfectly happy with the Martins in the summer. She had no sense of superiority then. If she has now, you have given it to her. You have been no friend to her, Emma."

"Oh, Harriet may pick and choose. She knows now what real gentlemen are. No one but a gentleman has a chance with Harriet."

"Such errant nonsense!" cried Mr. Knightley. "You would be

better without any sense than misuse it as you do."

Emma tried to look cheerfully unconcerned, but was really feeling uncomfortable and wanting him to be gone. However, he continued, "As you make no secret of your love of matchmaking, I shall just hint to you that if you are thinking of Elton for Harriet, your efforts will be in vain."

Emma laughed and denied it.

"Elton is a good man, but he will not throw himself away, Emma. I have heard him speak warmly of some young ladies his sisters know who have twenty thousand pounds apiece."

"I am done with matchmaking," said Emma, laughing again.

Mr. Knightley walked off with an abrupt, "Good morning." He was very disturbed. He felt Robert Martin's disappointment keenly, and the part he was convinced Emma had played in it infuriated him.

Emma was also disturbed. He had frightened her a little about Mr. Elton, but she thought Mr. Knightley could not have watched him as closely as she had. If he were really in love, his interest in money would be laid to one side. Mr. Knightley had made no allowance for passion.

Mr. Knightley might quarrel with her, but Emma could not quarrel with herself. It was longer than usual before he came back to Hartfield, and when Emma saw him again, his grave looks showed she was not forgiven. She was sorry they had disagreed, but, believing herself to be right, she could not repent.

Mr. Elton brought the picture back, and his raptures were all Emma could want. As for Harriet's feelings, they were rapidly forming themselves into a strong and steady attachment.

Emma's aim to improve Harriet's mind had faltered. It was much easier to chat than to study. The only literary pursuit enjoyed by Harriet was the collection of riddles that she copied

Emma

into her scrap book and illustrated.

Mr. Elton was invited to share his knowledge of any really good riddles, charades or conundrums.

The very next day, he called, offering a piece of paper to Emma. "I do not offer it for Miss Smith's collection," he said to Emma, "but perhaps you may like to look at it."

He was gone the next moment.

"Take it," Emma smiled, pushing it towards Harriet. "It is for you, after all."

But Harriet was trembling too much to take it, and so Emma read it herself.

Charade

My first displays the wealth of kings,
Their luxury and ease;
Another view my second brings:
The monarch of the seas!

United, what reverse we see!
Man's power and might are flown;
To woman, now, he bends a knee,
And woman reigns alone.

Emma pondered, understood, murmured, "I see: Courtship. Very good," and passed it to Harriet.

"It is so hard," said Harriet, puzzling over it. "Can 'the monarch of the seas' mean Neptune? Or could it be a mermaid? Or a shark?"

"Mermaids and sharks! Nonsense. Take the first two lines. They mean 'court' — like the king's court. The monarch of the seas is 'ship'. So the whole thing together means 'Courtship'. And the last part means that the woman has all the power over the man in the matter. It is a very proper compliment, and there can be no doubt that he wrote it for you. You are his object, and soon you will know it. This will be soon followed by a declaration of love."

Harriet could not speak at first. "Dear Miss Woodhouse," she managed at last. "That Mr. Elton should really be in love with me. I can scarcely believe it!"

The next day, Emma had a charitable visit to pay to a poor, sick family in Highbury. Harriet accompanied her, and as they passed the vicarage, Emma remarked, "Look. There go you and your riddle book one day."

"Oh Miss Woodhouse, whatever you say is always right. I do wonder…" Harriet ventured, "…that you are not married yourself, charming as you are."

Emma laughed and replied, "Being charming is not enough for me to get married. I must find others charming too – one other person in particular! I do not intend to marry. Why should I? Were I to fall in love, it would be different. But I never have – it is not in my nature – and I do not think I ever shall. And without love I would be a fool to change my situation. I am not in need of money, employment or importance."

"But then, to be an old maid, like Miss Bates!"

"If I thought I should be like Miss Bates, so silly, so satisfied, so smiling, so talkative, so gossiping, so dull, I would marry tomorrow. There is no likeness between us, except that we are both unmarried."

"But still, you will be an old maid – and that is so dreadful."

"Never mind, Harriet. I shall not be a poor old maid. A single woman with a very small income becomes a ridiculous, disagreeable old maid – that boys and girls make fun of – but a

Emma

single woman with a good fortune is always respectable. Miss Bates of course, is good-natured, not disagreeable... but still silly."

"But how would you occupy yourself as you grow older?"

"Isabella's children. I shall often have a niece with me."

"Like Miss Bates. Do you know Miss Bates's niece?"

"Oh yes. Jane Fairfax. That is almost enough to put one off nieces altogether. I am sick of the very name of Jane Fairfax. If she knits a pair of gloves for her grandmother, one hears of nothing else for a month. Every letter from her is read forty times over. Jane Fairfax tires me to death."

They were now approaching the cottage. Emma was very compassionate to its inhabitants. She understood their distress, their deprivation, and she entered into their troubles and gave her help with as much intelligence as goodwill.

"These are sights that do one good, Harriet," she said, as they walked away. "How trifling they make everything else appear."

As they rounded a bend in the path, Mr. Elton came into view, on his way to visit the same family.

"To meet on the same charitable errand," thought Emma. "What a piece of luck. This will increase their love on both sides."

Anxious to separate herself from them, she stepped onto a narrow raised part of the footpath, leaving them by themselves, but Harriet's habit of dependence made her follow Emma. This would not do. Emma stopped and tugged at her bootlaces, managing to break one.

"My lace is broken," she said. "May we go to your house, Mr. Elton and ask your housekeeper for a piece of string?"

Mr. Elton looked all happiness as he led them inside. Emma went off with the housekeeper, leaving the lovers alone. Ten minutes, she hoped, would do the trick.

He had not made any declaration of love, according to Harriet on the way home. But he had told her he saw them go by, and decided to follow them, which gave Emma hope. "He is very cautious," thought Emma. "He must be waiting to be sure of her feelings before declaring his love." She flattered herself on her ingenuity in leading them both forward to the great event.

On Christmas Eve, Emma and her father, Harriet, Mr. Elton and Mr. Knightley were all invited to dinner at Mr. and Mrs. Weston's house, Randalls. It was most unusual for Mr. Woodhouse to dine out so late, especially when the weather looked like snow. Harriet at the last moment was unable to attend. She was ill with a feverish cold, and was being nursed by Mrs. Goddard.

Emma met Mr. Elton on her way back from visiting Harriet.

"Are you still going tonight, Mr. Elton? In your case, I would excuse myself. Your voice sounds a little hoarse already, and when you think what demands tomorrow will bring… And the snow…"

But Mr. Elton insisted he would attend. Never had his smile been stronger, nor his eyes more exulting.

"Very strange, wanting to go out when Harriet is ill, when I gave him such a good excuse to refuse," thought Emma. "What a strange thing love is!"

Mr. Elton was already at Randalls when Emma and her father arrived. Harriet seemed quite forgotten. To Emma's surprise, he came and sat very close to her. He began to admire her drawings, hanging upon Mrs. Weston's wall, with so much zeal and so little knowledge that he seemed like a would-be lover. Emma found it hard to preserve her good manners. She was polite, for Harriet's sake, but she was longing to join in the conversation in another part of the room.

She could hear Mr. Weston saying the words "my son" and "Frank" and "a visit" and her spirits lifted. It appeared that Frank Churchill would soon be amongst them, if Mrs. Churchill could spare him.

In spite of Emma's resolution never to marry, there was something about the idea of Frank Churchill that had always interested her. She had frequently thought, especially since his father's marriage to Miss Taylor, that if she *were* to marry, he was the very person to suit her in age, character and standing in society. He seemed, by this connection between the families, to belong to her.

With such sensations, Mr. Elton's civilities were dreadfully ill-timed, but she had the comfort of appearing very polite while feeling very cross.

After dinner, Mr. Woodhouse was soon ready for his tea, and when he had drunk his tea, he was quite ready to go home. Mr. Elton was thus interrupted from his entreaties, begging Emma to promise not to visit Harriet, so as to escape the infection. Emma tried to laugh it off, but she was puzzled. It did appear exactly like the protestations of someone in love with her, not with Harriet, an inconstancy which, if real, was most abominable!

Mr. Knightley informed the company that the snow had begun in good earnest. Mr. Woodhouse became very anxious indeed. He looked to Emma for comfort.

"What is to be done, my dear?"

"We will order the carriages at once," said Mr. Knightley. "And I will accompany you, Mr. Woodhouse, with Emma."

The sight of the snow increased Mr. Woodhouse's alarm. Mr. Knightley escorted him into the carriage, with Emma following, but to her surprise, she found herself being helped into the second carriage by Mr. Elton, and the door shut upon them. It was, then, to be a drive with just the two of them. She would not usually have minded this – she could have talked about Harriet and the journey would have passed quickly. But tonight she believed that Mr. Elton had been drinking too much of Mr. Weston's wine, and would start talking nonsense.

To stop him, she began to talk about the weather, but scarcely had she started than her hand was seized, and Mr. Elton actually began to declare that he was passionately in love with her – as well she must know – hoping, fearing, adoring – ready to die if she refused him, but flattering himself that his feelings had not gone unnoticed; in short being very much certain of being accepted as soon as possible.

She hoped a mixture of the serious and the playful would quieten him. "I am very much astonished, Mr. Elton. You forget yourself – you take me for Miss Smith – I shall be happy to take any message you have for her...?"

"Message for Miss Smith?" repeated Mr. Elton. He had drunk enough wine to lift his spirits, not to confuse his mind. He knew perfectly well what he meant to say. "I never thought of Miss Smith in my life, never cared if she were alive or dead except that she is your friend. If her own fancies have misled her, I am very sorry. But, oh Miss Woodhouse, who can think of Miss Smith when Miss Woodhouse is near? Everything I have said or done over the past weeks was for you."

"I have completely mistaken your feelings!" cried Emma. "Am I to believe you have never thought seriously of Miss Smith?"

"Never!" he cried angrily. "I wish her well, and no doubt there are men who might not object to... Everyone has their level, but I myself do not sink so low. No, my visits to Hartfield were for you, and the encouragement you gave me—"

"I gave you encouragement? Sir, you have been entirely mistaken," said Emma. "I only saw you as the admirer of my friend. I am very sorry, but the mistake has to end here. I have no thoughts of marriage at present."

He was too angry to say another word, and in this state of mutual mortification, the carriage conveyed the one to Hartfield and the other to the vicarage.

Her hair was curled, and the maid sent away, and Emma sat down the following morning to think and be miserable. What a wretched business. Such an overthrow of all she had wished. Such a blow for Harriet – that was the worst part. Every part of it brought pain and humiliation, but Harriet would suffer the most.

"I was the one to talk her into being in love with him," she thought. "She never would have thought of it but for me. Oh, poor Harriet!"

How could she have been so wrong. The picture! He had been so eager about the picture. And the charade! Who could have seen through it to know he meant her not Harriet? Gradually, she realized that she had come up with the idea of the match first, and had then bent everything to fit it. Mr. Knightley had warned her that Mr. Elton would never marry below his station. She blushed to think that his judgement of character had been so much better than hers.

Mr. Elton's proposal had made her think worse of him. He only wanted to marry well, and was arrogant enough to raise his eyes to *her*. He had only pretended to be in love; there was no real affection in his language or manners. He only wanted to become rich, and if Miss Woodhouse, the heiress of thirty thousand pounds, were not available, then he would try for Miss Somebody with twenty, or ten.

"I am resolved," thought Emma, "never again to take an active part in bringing two people together. Oh, if only I had been satisfied with persuading her to refuse young Martin. I was quite right there. If she were not to feel the disappointment too much, then perhaps William Coxe... no, I could not endure William Coxe, a pert young lawyer... "

She stopped to blush at her own relapse into matchmaking.

Emma

The weather was helpful. It snowed, and she was unable to go to church on Christmas Day, or to visit Harriet. Mr. Knightley called; no bad weather stopped his visits. He had got over his bad temper with Emma, and was agreeable and kind. But despite the comfort of delay, she so dreaded the hour when she would have to explain everything to Harriet, that she could not be at ease.

A note from Mr. Elton arrived for Mr. Woodhouse. It sent his best compliments and said that he was going to Bath for a few weeks to stay with some friends.

Emma now resolved to go and tell Harriet. It was a difficult conversation. She had to undo everything she had so industriously built up. The confession renewed her shame, which was deepened by Harriet's tears. Harriet bore it very well. She had not deserved Mr. Elton, she assured Emma, and no one but so kind a friend as Miss Woodhouse would have thought it possible. Such modesty and innocence proved her sweetness, thought Emma. She herself would do well to be more like Harriet – warm and sweet instead of clever. But it was rather too late in the day for Emma to begin to be sweet and ignorant. She decided instead to become humble and stop her imagination from running away with her, and to help Harriet in some better way than matchmaking. So she took Harriet to Hartfield, to help drive away all thoughts of Mr. Elton.

Mr. Frank Churchill did not come. He wrote a letter of excuse, a very fine letter, explaining that Mrs. Churchill, his aunt, wanted him to accompany her to Weymouth. Mrs. Weston was even more disappointed than Mr. Weston, who, after the initial disappointment, said that perhaps a later visit would be better, with better weather, and perhaps a longer stay. A cheerful nature soon flies over a disappointment and begins to hope again.

Emma felt so low from recent events that she did not really care about him not coming, except for her sympathy with Mrs. Weston.

Emma

She wanted a quiet time. She told Mr. Knightley the news, trying so hard to appear normal that she found herself arguing against the view she really held.

"I expect he could have come, if he had really wanted to," said Mr. Knightley coolly.

"How odd you are. Why would you think him so unnatural as not to want to visit his father?"

"I do not think it unnatural for a young man to be selfish if he has been brought up by selfish people. If he really wanted to see his father, he could have managed a visit by now. A man of his age – twenty-three or twenty-four – is surely able to do what he feels is right. He does not lack money or time. On the contrary, he has plenty of both, and we have heard of him going visiting, which proves he can get away from the Churchills, if he thinks it worth his while."

"He might not be able to get away any time he chooses."

"There is one thing, Emma, which a man can always do if he chooses, and that is his duty."

"If he has looked up to his aunt and uncle all his life, it could be more difficult than you think to burst forth into independence!"

"He must be a very weak young man. He should have stood up to their slights against his father before now."

"We shall never agree about him," said Emma. "I feel sure he is not weak."

"He is the sort of man who can write a fine, flourishing letter full of falsehoods, and persuade himself that this is the best way of keeping the peace at home in addition to leaving his father no cause to complain. If Mrs. Weston were a person of importance, he would have visited at once. His letters disgust me."

"You seem determined to think badly of him."

"Me! Not at all," replied Mr. Knightley, rather displeased.

"He will be the talk of Highbury when he does come."

Emma

"I shall be glad to talk to him if he turns out to be worth it. But if he is only a chattering coxcomb, I shall not bother."

"We are both prejudiced: you against him, and I for him!" cried Emma.

"I am not prejudiced at all. I never even think of him," said Mr. Knightley with annoyance, though Emma could not think why he should be angry. She had always admired his open mind, and had never thought he could be unjust to the merits of another man.

Emma and Harriet were walking together one morning and, in Emma's opinion, had talked quite enough about Mr. Elton. After speaking of the sufferings of the poor in winter, and receiving the plaintive reply, "Mr. Elton is so good to the poor," she felt something must be done. She decided to call on Mrs. and Miss Bates to seek safety in numbers.

Mrs. and Miss Bates loved to be called on, and Emma knew she was remiss in avoiding them. She had picked up many a hint from Mr. Knightley and some from her own heart about her negligence. But she usually found it a waste of time. They were tiresome women, and she had a horror of getting mixed up with the lower classes of Highbury, and so she seldom went near them. But suddenly, while passing their door, she decided to go in. It would help to take Harriet's mind off things. She only hoped they had not received another letter from Jane Fairfax.

Mrs. and Miss Bates rented a small, upper-floor apartment. Mrs. Bates, a neat old lady, sat knitting in the warmest corner, and immediately wanted to give it up to Emma. Her daughter was even more overpowering with care and kindness, thanks for their visit, concern for their shoes, anxious enquiries after Mr. Woodhouse's health and offers of cake.

Mrs. Bates began, to Emma's horror, to speak of Mr. Elton, saying they heard he had gone away, but then Miss Bates changed the subject – she had had a letter from her niece, Jane Fairfax.

Emma groaned inwardly, but said something polite about the excellence of Miss Fairfax's handwriting.

"You are extremely kind," replied Miss Bates, highly delighted. "There is no one whose praise could give us greater pleasure. My mother cannot hear; she is a little deaf. Mother, did you hear what Miss Woodhouse said about Jane's handwriting?"

And Emma heard her own silly remark repeated twice before the old lady took it in. She was pondering how, without seeming rude, she could escape from Jane Fairfax's letter, and had almost resolved on hurrying away under a quick excuse, when Miss Bates began to read it aloud.

It seemed that Jane was to arrive next week in Highbury, rather than going to Ireland with the family she lived with. Emma endured Miss Bates's raptures, until she felt able to say, glancing at Harriet and beginning to rise, "I am afraid we must be running away. My father will be expecting us. I had no intention of staying more than five minutes, but I have been so pleasantly detained."

Jane Fairfax was an orphan, the only child of Mrs. Bates's youngest daughter, who had married a Lieutenant Fairfax. When both of Jane's parents died, she became the charge of her doting grandmother and aunt. But the compassionate feelings of her father's friend had changed her destiny. Colonel Campbell was a married man with a daughter Jane's age. He took her to live with them, the plan being that she should be brought up to be a governess, and make a living educating others. The money she had been left was not enough for her to live on otherwise. The Campbells showed her nothing but kindness, but now Miss Campbell had become engaged to a rich and agreeable young man named Mr. Dixon, whom she had met on holiday. The Campbells were going away to Ireland, and it was time for Jane to find a position as a governess and earn a living. She had decided to pay a visit to Highbury first.

Emma was sorry – she was going to have to be polite to a person she did not like for three whole months. Why she did not like Jane Fairfax was a difficult question to answer. Mr. Knightley once told her it was because Jane was the accomplished young woman that Emma would like to be. But really, she found Jane cold and reserved. She could not get to know her, and then her aunt was such an eternal talker! Everybody made such a fuss of Jane. And everybody supposed that Jane and Emma should be fond of each other because their ages were the same. It was such an unjust dislike that she never saw Jane Fairfax without feeling that she had harmed her in some way.

When Jane arrived in Highbury, Emma dutifully visited, and was particularly struck by her appearance. Jane Fairfax was very elegant. Her height was pretty, just what everyone would think tall, but not too tall, her figure graceful, her face had a very pleasing beauty, with deep grey eyes, and dark lashes and brows. When Emma considered all this attractiveness and elegance, and considered how Jane would have to live from now on, it was impossible to feel anything but compassion and respect.

These were charming feelings, but did not last long. Jane spent an evening at Hartfield with her grandmother and aunt, and everything lapsed into its usual state. Miss Bates was as tiresome as ever. Emma had to listen to a description of exactly what they all ate at breakfast. They had music: Emma played, but Jane played better. Worst of all, Jane was so cold, so cautious in all she said. There was no getting at her real opinion. Wrapped in a cloak of politeness, Emma found her disgustingly, suspiciously reserved.

She had been at Weymouth at the same time as Frank Churchill, but would give Emma no information. "Was he handsome?" She

Emma

believed he was reckoned so. "Was he agreeable?" He was generally thought so. She believed everyone found his manners pleasing. Emma could not forgive her for revealing so little.

Mr. Knightley had been at Hartfield too, but had only seen Emma's politeness, not her hidden resentments. He had always thought her unjust to Jane, so he was pleased.

"A very pleasant evening," he said, when he called the following morning. "You and Miss Fairfax gave us some very good music. I was glad you made her play so much. Having no instrument at her grandmother's, it must have been a treat for her. I am sure she enjoyed the evening. You left nothing undone."

Emma smiled. "I hope I am not deficient in what is due to guests," she said.

"No, my dear," said Mr. Woodhouse. "If anything you are too attentive. For instance, I think you need only to have handed round the muffins once."

"I think Emma knows what I mean," said Mr. Knightley.

Emma only said, "Miss Fairfax is so reserved."

"I think it would soon be overcome. I think it comes from a natural shyness."

"You think her shy. I do not see it."

"I hope everyone had a pleasant evening," said Mr. Woodhouse in his mild way. "I did. Once, I felt the fire rather too warm, but then I moved back my chair a little, a very little, and it did not disturb me."

"Emma," said Mr. Knightley, "I have some news for you…"

But he had no time to say more, for just then, the door was thrown open and Miss Bates walked in with Jane Fairfax. "Have you heard the news?" Miss Bates exclaimed, "Mr. Elton is going to be married! To a Miss Hawkins of Bath."

Emma was so surprised that she started a little, and blushed.

Emma

In the ensuing flutter of conversation over the news, she had time to reflect. She found it an amusing and welcome piece of news. It proved Mr. Elton could not have suffered long. But she was sorry for Harriet. Harriet would feel it. She wanted to tell Harriet herself, before she heard it from anyone else.

When everyone had left, and her father gone to rest, in came Harriet, with just the heated, agitated look which a full heart was likely to give. And her, "Oh, Miss Woodhouse, what do you think has happened?" which burst forth showed some painful disturbance too.

But the disturbance was not what Emma had thought. Harriet had been shopping for ribbons in Ford's, in Highbury. "And who should come in but Elizabeth Martin and her brother! Only think! I nearly fainted! But she spoke to me so nicely, though not in the same way that she used to speak, and then he said not to go to Hartfield the nearest way because it was all flooded with rain. So I thanked him. I wish I had never seen him, and yet I was glad to see him behave so kindly. Oh, Miss Woodhouse, do make me feel comfortable again!"

Emma was not thoroughly comfortable herself. The Martins seemed to have shown genuine fondness for Harriet, and she found herself pitying them. But she had never said they were not good people, she told herself, so what difference did it make?

She said, "It is over, and that awkward first meeting can never happen again, and therefore you need not think about it."

Harriet said she would not, but she could talk of nothing else. However, Emma was rather glad of her having met Mr. Martin, in the end, as it deadened the shock of the news of Mr. Elton.

The next day brought a happy visit from Mr. and Mrs. Weston, with a letter from Mr. Frank Churchill. He was to arrive the following day, to stay at Randalls a whole fortnight.

Emma

"I shall bring him to Hartfield very soon," said Mr. Weston.

When Frank Churchill, so long talked of, was introduced to Emma, she found him a very good-looking young man. He had spirit and liveliness, and was pleasing in height, manner, and the way he spoke to her. She felt immediately she would like him.

He certainly knew how to be likable. He declared himself exceedingly pleased with Randalls, refused to consider it small, even calling it "home," which delighted his father; he praised Mrs. Weston's beauty, and wound it all up by admiring Highbury village.

When Mr. Weston rose to go, saying he had business to see to, his son rose too. "Then I will take the opportunity of paying a visit which may as well be done now. A Miss Fairfax is living here, with a family named Bates. Another day would do as well, but I knew her a little at Weymouth…"

"Go today, Frank. If you do not call early, it will be a slight. We are all fond of Mrs. and Miss Bates. I must give you a hint. At Weymouth, you saw Miss Fairfax with the Campbells, the equal of anybody. Here, she is with her grandmother, who has barely enough to live on, waiting for a position as a governess."

"A most elegant young woman," said Emma.

"Yes," he said. But his answer was so quiet that Emma doubted he really agreed.

The next morning brought Mr. Frank Churchill again, inviting Emma to show him the sights of Highbury. Their first pause was the Crown Inn. A large room had been added to it, built as a ballroom, but no balls had been held there now for many years.

"Why do you not revive the custom, Miss Woodhouse?" asked Frank. "You, who can do anything in Highbury."

Emma smiled. He spoke, she noted, as a man very much bent on dancing and pleasure.

"How did you find Miss Fairfax yesterday?" she asked.

"So pale and sickly looking," he replied.

Surprised, Emma pointed out Jane's delicacy and elegance.

Frank laughed. "I cannot separate Miss Fairfax from her looks."

"Do you know her well?"

At that moment, they were passing a shop. Frank stopped and exclaimed, "Oh, Ford's! I must go in. I hear this is the shop that everybody visits in Highbury. I must buy something. I daresay they sell gloves."

"Oh yes. Everyone in Highbury will adore you if you buy gloves at Ford's."

A pair of York Tans bought, Frank Churchill came back to the subject of Jane. "You asked how well I knew Jane Fairfax. I met her frequently at Weymouth. But only she could say how well she thinks we know each other. Do you know her well?"

"I have known her since childhood, but we were never friends. Perhaps it was wickedness on my side, resenting everyone adoring her so... but it was also her reserve. I could never be fond of someone so reserved."

"True. It is safe to be reserved, but never attractive. One could never love a reserved person. Did you ever hear her play?"

"She plays charmingly," Emma said.

"I know nothing about such matters myself," Frank said. "But I do know that Mr. Dixon, even though he was then engaged to Mrs. Dixon, would never ask her to play if Miss Fairfax was there. He preferred to listen to Miss Fairfax."

"Poor Mrs. Dixon!" said Emma. "Well, I am glad they have gone to settle in Ireland then!"

Emma's very good opinion of Frank Churchill was a little shaken the following day by hearing he had gone off to London, merely to get his hair cut. There was an air of foppery and nonsense about it of which she could not approve. His father called him a coxcomb and thought it a good story, but Mrs. Weston did not like it, only remarking, "All young people have their whims."

Everyone in Highbury spoke well of Mr. Frank Churchill – except for Mr. Knightley. Hearing of the haircut, he remarked to Emma, "Hum! Just the trifling, silly fellow I took him for."

She had half a mind to resent it, but decided he had only said it to relieve his feelings, not to provoke hers, and so she let it pass.

An invitation now arrived for all the families in Highbury, from the Coles. The Coles had lived in Highbury for some years, and were a very good sort of people, friendly, open and unpretentious, but they were of low birth, and not very genteel. The last year or two had seen them grow much richer. They had added to their house, to their number of servants, their style of living, and now, they were only second in importance to the Woodhouses.

When Emma's invitation arrived, at first she thought she would decline it. The Coles were rather beneath her. However, nobody else in Highbury seemed to think so. Mr. Knightley was going, and so was almost everyone else she knew. As Emma realized how many other people would be there, and how much she might be missing if she did not go, she became rather more inclined to accept.

Her father, disliking late hours, could not be persuaded. And when Emma said she would go, he wanted her to promise to leave early, and only allowed her to stay longer when she suggested that her leaving might insult the Coles.

"But promise me – if you come home cold, you must warm yourself, and your maid shall sit up for you, and the butler too…"

Emma promised everything, and arranged for Mrs. Goddard to visit him that evening so that he would not be by himself.

Mr. Frank Churchill returned, his hair cut, in good time for the party. It was a large one, comprising all the major families from

Emma

Highbury, as well as Miss Bates and Miss Smith.

Emma arrived at the same time as Mr. Knightley. Passing his carriage as they went inside, she said, "I am glad you came in your carriage instead of walking as you usually do. It befits your gentlemanly status!"

"Nonsensical girl!" was his reply, but not at all in anger.

Mrs. Cole was telling the company how she had called on Miss Bates, and had seen a new, very elegant-looking piano from Broadwood's, which had been delivered for Jane Fairfax the day before. Neither Miss Bates nor her niece knew who had sent it.

"Jane thinks it must be from Colonel Campbell, but it is unlike him to plan a surprise," said Mrs. Cole. "I am so glad for her, as she loves music. We hope that she, and Miss Woodhouse, may play for us tonight."

Emma agreed, but then turned to Frank Churchill, so as not to be trapped by Mrs. Cole.

"Why are you smiling?" she asked.

"No, why are you?"

"I am because you are. If Colonel Campbell did not send the piano, who did?"

"Oh, I suspect Mr. Dixon. I think that after proposing to her friend, he fell in love with *her*. Or he may have found she had feelings for him. Why else should she come to Highbury?"

"Indeed."

When dinner ended, the ladies went to sit in the drawing room. After a while the gentlemen joined them there, and Frank Churchill came to sit by Emma again. He seemed to be seeking her out. Emma thought everyone else must have noticed it too.

"Upon my word, Miss Fairfax has done her hair in a very odd way," he said. "Shall I ask her if it is an Irish fashion? Shall we see if she blushes?"

He rose, and his seat was taken by Mrs. Weston. "Do you know,

Emma

Emma, how Jane got here this evening?" she said. "Mr. Knightley sent his carriage for her. He must be concerned for her health. The more I think about it, the more I am convinced of a match between those two."

"Mr. Knightley and Jane Fairfax!" cried Emma in shock. "Oh no, no; every feeling revolts against the idea. Mr. Knightley does not want to get married! He is happy unmarried. He does not love Jane Fairfax! And how could he bear to have Miss Bates belonging to his family?"

"Hush, Emma," Mrs. Weston scolded.

At that point, Mrs. Cole asked Emma to sing. To her surprise, when she sat down at the piano, she found Frank Churchill by her side again, ready to accompany her. Twice they sang together and then it was Jane's turn. Frank Churchill accompanied her too. Her voice wavered, and Frank persuaded her to sing one more song, causing Mr. Knightley to growl, "That fellow thinks of nothing but his own voice. Can he not see that she should sing no more?"

He mentioned his worry to Miss Bates, who immediately bustled over to stop Jane from straining her voice.

When the concert part of the evening was over, the dancing began. Mrs. Weston played an irresistible waltz, and Frank Churchill gallantly asked Emma for her hand and led her to start the dancing.

She found herself well matched. She looked anxiously at Mr. Knightley; if he were very quick, he could ask Jane, which might reveal some feelings for her, but no, he was talking to Mrs. Cole and Jane was asked by someone else.

It was growing late. Two dances were all that there was time for.

"Perhaps it is just as well," said Frank Churchill, as he helped Emma into her carriage. "I must otherwise have asked Miss Fairfax, and her languid dancing would not have suited me, after yours."

Emma

The Coles' party left Emma with one regret – that she could not play the piano as well as Jane. She practised vigorously for an hour and a half before Harriet arrived the following day, and they went shopping together in Ford's.

Peering out of the window as Harriet changed her mind yet again over muslins – Harriet was always very long buying anything – she saw Mrs. Weston and Frank Churchill hurrying by.

Mrs. Weston caught her eye and came in. "We are going to the Bates' to hear the new instrument. Frank says I promised to do so, though I have no memory of it. Come with us, Emma."

"We will, when Harriet has finished here."

When Emma and Harriet arrived, Miss Bates greeted them with her usual torrent of words. "How is Mr. Woodhouse? My mother is delightfully well, and Jane caught no cold last night. Mr. Churchill is here, would you believe it, very obliging, mending my mother's spectacles. Everyone ought to have two pairs of spectacles, Jane says. Mr. Knightley has just sent a large basket of apples, so very good of him, as Jane likes nothing so well as baked apples, and dear Jane – at present she really eats nothing, has such a shockingly small breakfast, I dare not let my mother know how little she eats. Pray take care, Miss Woodhouse. Ours is rather a narrow staircase, and darker than one could wish. I should not like you to trip…"

Emma let her talk on and joined Frank Churchill by the window where he was busy with the spectacles. Jane sat down at the new piano, beginning feebly, but quickly flowing into the full force of the instrument.

"She is playing Mr. Dixon's favourite piece," Frank Churchill whispered into Emma's ear.

"Hush. She will hear you. You will distress her."

But Emma could not help being amused and when, on glancing at Jane, she saw that Jane was smiling a smile of secret delight, she

Emma

was less concerned for her. This upright, perfect Jane Fairfax was apparently capable of hiding some very disgraceful feelings.

Mr. Frank Churchill, having danced at Highbury, longed to dance again. He made plans to open the ballroom at the Crown. One room could be used for supper; another for cards; nothing could be better. He asked Emma to save the first two dances for him. But no sooner was the day of the ball fixed, than it had to be given up. A letter arrived from Mr. Churchill, urging his nephew's instant return. Mrs. Churchill was unwell. Frank must be gone within a few hours.

He called to say goodbye to Emma. His sorrowful look and total lack of spirits told all. "If I can come again, we must still have our ball. Such a fortnight this has been! In short, Miss Woodhouse, I think you cannot be without suspicion…"

He stopped, seeming embarrassed. He looked at her, as if wanting to read her thoughts.

He must be more in love with her than she had supposed! And after he left – a very friendly shake of the hand, a very earnest "Goodbye," she could not doubt his admiration.

Their time together had been short; Emma was sorry to part from him, and thought she would miss him a little too much for comfort. This added to her feeling that he warmly admired her, made her think that *she* must be a little in love with *him*.

"Why else," she thought, "would I have this feeling of weariness and stupidity, this feeling of everything being dull? I must be in love!"

She did not doubt that she was in love; her ideas only varied as to how much. At first, she had thought very much, but as time passed she thought it was only a little.

She found that although she was eager for news of how he was, she was not unhappy in his absence. As she sat drawing or working, she imagined their conversations and letters, but the conclusion of his every imagined declaration of love was that she refused him. Their affection always subsided into friendship.

He was in love, undoubtedly, but, she concluded, she was not.

"I do not altogether trust his constancy," she thought. "His feelings are warm, but I can imagine them rather changeable. It will be a good thing once it is over; for they say everybody is in love once in their lives, and I shall have been let off lightly."

His letter to Mrs. Weston, which Emma was given to read, contained all that was proper: regret, thanks, respect and affection. Her name was mentioned several times, but she found it gave her no feeling of lasting warmth. He mentioned Harriet: "I had not a moment to spare to say farewell to Miss Woodhouse's beautiful little friend." That gave Emma an idea. Why should not Harriet replace her in his affections? Was it impossible? It would be delightful for Harriet!

All Highbury was now fixed on the return of Mr. Elton and his bride. Emma grew sick at the sound of their names. She had enjoyed Mr. Elton's absence, hoping Harriet's heartache was growing less. But curing Harriet was still hard work.

At last Emma said, "Your unhappiness, Harriet, is the strongest reproach to me. It was all my doing. The pain goes deep."

The idea of hurting Miss Woodhouse had more effect on Harriet than anything else. "You are the best friend I ever had in my life. Hurt you! Oh no! Nobody is equal to you. I owe you everything!"

Such expressions made Emma appreciate Harriet more than she had ever done before. "She has tenderness of heart. So has my father, which is why people love him so. I do not have it, but I do know how to prize and respect it."

Mrs. Elton was first seen at church. But there Emma could

not judge; she would have to visit. She did, accompanied by Harriet, and it brought back painful memories. Into that house they had gone, only three months ago, with the broken shoelace. Compliments, horrible blunders and charades had followed.

She did not really like Mrs. Elton. She was too familiar and easy in her manner, without enough elegance. As for Mr. Elton, he seemed awkward. But then, when she considered how peculiarly unlucky poor Mr. Elton was in being in the same room at once with the woman he had just married, the woman he had wanted to marry, and the woman whom he had been expected to marry, she had to admit he had the right to look as awkward as could be.

When the visit was returned, Emma made up her mind. Mrs. Elton was vain, ignorant and extremely pleased with herself. All she seemed to talk about was her brother's house, Maple Grove – Hartfield reminded her of it so much in the size of the rooms, the grand entrance hall... "When you are transplanted like me, Miss Woodhouse, you will understand how very delightful it is to meet with anything like what one has left behind. I always say having to move away is one of the evils of matrimony."

Emma made some slight reply, which was quite enough for Mrs. Elton, who only wanted to talk about herself.

"My brother and sister-in-law will be enchanted with Hartfield. People with extensive grounds themselves are always pleased with anything in the same style."

Emma doubted this. She thought that people with extensive grounds themselves cared very little for the extensive grounds of anyone else, but it was not worthwhile saying so. Anyway, the grounds of Hartfield, though pretty, were small. But Mrs. Elton was now talking about forming a music club with Emma. "I hope we shall arrange many sweet little concerts together."

Emma's reply was non-committal and Mrs. Elton rattled on.

Emma

"We have been calling at Randalls. Mr. Weston is quite a favourite with me already. And Mrs. Weston – she was your governess, I think? I was rather astonished to find her so ladylike. But she is really quite the gentlewoman. And who do you think came in while we were there? Knightley! I knew he was a particular friend of Mr. E's so I was really impatient to see him, and I told my dear husband he need not be ashamed of his friend. Yes, Knightley is quite the gentleman."

Thankfully, she left, and Emma could breathe.

"Insufferable woman!" she fumed. "She is even worse than I thought! Knightley! She has never seen him in her life, and she calls him Knightley! And wanting to form a music club, as if we were friends. And for her to be actually astonished that the person who brought me up should be a gentlewoman! She is a pretentious little upstart."

Praise of Mrs. Elton passed from mouth to mouth in Highbury, and Emma did not voice her opinion. However, Mrs. Elton's feelings towards Emma changed. She became cold and distant. And both she and Mr. Elton were sneering and unpleasant to Harriet.

She took a great fancy, however, to Jane Fairfax. Before she stopped confiding in Emma, she said, "I quite rave about Jane Fairfax. And her situation – to be just a governess – is so sad. I shall have her at my house very often, for musical parties, so she can play, and I shall look out, amongst my extensive acquaintance, for a suitable position for her."

"Poor Jane," thought Emma. "You may have done wrong with Mr. Dixon, but you certainly do not deserve Mrs. Elton's attentions." Her only surprise was that Jane accepted them.

Jane had come to Highbury for three months, while the Campbells were in Ireland, and now they pressed her most invitingly to join them there – they said they would send servants, provide money, and would overcome any difficulty in her travelling there, but Jane refused to go.

"She may not want to be with the Dixons," thought Emma, "but why go about with the Eltons?"

"Perhaps," said Mr. Knightley, when she presented him with this conundrum, "Miss Fairfax awes Mrs. Elton with her brilliant mind, and in private Mrs. Elton treats her with the respect she clearly deserves."

"I know how highly you think of Jane Fairfax," said Emma.

"Anyone may know that."

"Perhaps...?" ventured Emma.

"No, Emma, I am not thinking of asking her to be my wife," said Mr. Knightley firmly. "She is a very charming young woman, but not even Jane Fairfax is perfect. She has a fault. She does not have the openness a man could wish for in a wife."

Emma rejoiced. Mr. Knightley had admitted that Jane Fairfax had a fault.

Mr. and Mrs. Weston brought Frank Churchill's latest letter for Emma to read. He would, she learned, often be in Highbury now. Mrs. Churchill had decided that Yorkshire was too cold for her, and she, Mr. Churchill and their nephew were moving to Richmond, only nine miles from Highbury.

As soon as he could, Mr. Frank Churchill held the ball at the Crown. The evening proceeded with elegance apart from Mrs. Elton's fishing for compliments – it was: "How do you like my hair? My dress?..." She was convinced that the ball was being given for her, as a tribute to the bride.

"How awkward," Mrs. Weston whispered to Emma. "She will expect to open the ball, with Frank. And Frank wanted to have this ball for you."

"My first dance is indeed with Miss Woodhouse," said Frank.

Emma

"We arranged it long ago."

It was true, although since then Emma's feelings had changed. And, now she saw Frank, she felt certain that his had too. He was as ready to laugh as ever, but he did not seem as tender, thankfully. Also, he was in an odd humour tonight: restless and dissatisfied.

In the end, Mrs. Elton opened the dancing with Mr. Weston, and Emma had to stand in second place even though the ball had been for her. It was almost enough to make her think of marrying.

Emma was more disturbed by Mr. Knightley's not dancing at all. She wished he loved a ballroom more; he looked so very gentlemanly, his figure tall and upright. She tried to catch his eye while dancing with Frank, but he looked grave. But if he was feeling critical of her, she was not worried. There was no flirtation between her and Frank; they were just friends.

Harriet was the only young lady without a partner. As she sat, Mr. Elton sauntered past her.

"Will you not dance, Mr. Elton?" asked Mrs. Weston.

"With you, Mrs. Weston? Delighted!"

"I am no dancer, Mr. Elton. No, I mean with Miss Smith."

"Then I must beg to decline."

Poor Harriet! Such mortification! So public! Emma could hardly bear it. In another minute, a happier sight met her eyes. Mr. Knightley was leading Harriet to dance, Harriet all smiles, and Mr. Knightley dancing as well as any man she had seen.

After the dance was finished, her eyes invited him irresistibly to come to her. He was warm in his condemnation of Mr. Elton's rudeness. "He wished to hurt you, Emma, as well as Harriet, and so does Mrs. Elton. Why are they your enemies?"

"Because I wanted him to marry Harriet and they cannot forgive me. I admit I was mistaken in Mr. Elton. There is a meanness in him, which you discovered, and I did not. I thought he was in love with Harriet."

Emma

"And in return for your confession, I too confess that you were right about Harriet. She is a sweet, unpretentious girl, infinitely preferable to a woman like Mrs. Elton, as any man of sense and taste would agree."

They were interrupted by a call for the dancing to begin again.

"I am ready," said Emma.

"Who are you going to dance with?" asked Mr. Knightley.

"With you, if you will," said Emma. "Though my sister is married to your brother, that does not make us brother and sister."

"Brother and sister? Certainly not!" he said, offering his arm. "Will you?"

The thought of the conversation with Mr. Knightley was one of the pleasant memories of the ball that she dwelled on over the next few days. Another was the fact that Harriet seemed to have been cured of her infatuation with Mr. Elton. Before they had left, Harriet had told her that Mr. Elton was not the superior gentleman she had believed him to be. Her eyes had been opened.

Mr. Knightley had agreed with her about the Eltons, and about Harriet; he did not want to quarrel with her; Frank Churchill was not in love with her… How very happy a summer she had to look forward to! Emma was strolling in the garden, thinking about all of this, when Harriet appeared, arm-in-arm with Frank Churchill, looking white and frightened. She sank onto a seat and fainted.

As soon as she recovered, her story was told. She had been out walking and had been set upon by a gang of ruffians, shrieking for her purse, when Frank Churchill, fortunately passing by, had rescued her. His first thought was to bring her to Hartfield.

Emma's mind immediately set to work. It could not be better; a fine young man and a lovely girl thrown together like this…

Her imagination was further fuelled when Harriet, a few days

*Mr. Knightley offered Emma
his arm to join the dancing.*

later, came to her solemnly with a little parcel. It was full of things she had treasured from Mr. Elton. Shavings from his pencil and a handkerchief he had touched… Emma was torn between awe and amusement. She never would have considered treasuring anything like this from Frank Churchill.

Harriet had brought them solemnly to burn. "There they go," she said, watching them turn to ashes. "I shall never marry now."

"Never marry? My dear Harriet!"

Emma did not catch Harriet's reply, only the last muttered phrase "… so superior to Mr. Elton…"

Ah, that was it: Harriet was in love again.

"You mean the person whom you might prefer is above you in station?" Emma asked.

"Oh yes," said Harriet.

It had to be Frank Churchill.

"I am not surprised, Harriet," Emma said. "What he did for you was enough to warm your heart."

"Oh!" cried Harriet. "In one moment he changed my utter wretchedness to perfect happiness."

"Consider carefully, Harriet. Do not trust your feelings till you are sure of them being returned," said Emma. "I will not interfere. No name will pass our lips. We were very wrong before. Yet there have been marriages of greater disparity…"

Harriet nodded in gratitude, while Emma was very certain that the attachment would be an excellent thing for her friend.

Mr. Knightley's early dislike of Frank Churchill increased. He began to suspect him of double-dealing with Emma. There was no doubt that Emma was the object of his affections. Everything declared it; his attentions, words, and behaviour. But Mr. Knightley also suspected him of trifling with Jane Fairfax. There seemed to be a private understanding between them, he had seen

Emma

them exchange meaningful looks which seemed out of place. "Have you ever thought that he admired her or she admired him?" he asked Emma.

"Never!" she cried. "Never for one twentieth part of a moment! I know for certain on his side, at any rate. He is indifferent to her."

She spoke with a confidence and satisfaction that silenced Mr. Knightley. She asked him merrily to describe the looks he had seen. But he was in no mood, and soon went home.

It was now the middle of June and the weather was fine. Mrs. Elton arranged a picnic-party at Box Hill for them all. Mr. Knightley, the Eltons, Emma and Harriet, Miss Bates and Jane Fairfax, Frank Churchill and Mr. Weston were all to come. Mrs. Weston kindly volunteered to stay home with Mr. Woodhouse, who was too frail and worried about the damp grass for picnics.

It was a fine, sunny day. Carriages took the ladies, the servants and the picnic, and the gentlemen went on horseback. Nothing else was needed but to be happy when they got there.

But everyone seemed languid and dull, and it was difficult to get a conversation going. When they sat down for the picnic, however, Frank paid Emma every attention. To amuse her, and be agreeable in her eyes seemed to be all he cared for.

Emma, glad to be enlivened, and not sorry to be flattered, encouraged him. It meant nothing to her, but no other word than 'flirtation' would have described the way they were talking to one another. Not that Emma meant to flirt. She liked his attention, but she still only meant him to be her friend. She noticed that no one else was talking, and said as much to him.

"What shall we do to make them?" whispered Frank mischievously. "Ladies and gentlemen, I am ordered by Miss Woodhouse (who is in charge wherever she goes) to say that she desires to know what you are all thinking of."

Emma

Mrs. Elton swelled with indignation at the idea of Emma being in charge.

Mr. Knightley asked pointedly, "Is Miss Woodhouse sure she would really like to know our thoughts?"

"They are all offended! I will attack them again," whispered Frank. "Ladies and gentlemen, Miss Woodhouse waives her right to know what you are thinking. Instead, she demands from each of you either one thing very clever, or two things moderately clever, or three things very dull indeed."

"Oh," exclaimed Miss Bates. "Three things very dull indeed. That will do for me. I shall be sure to say three dull things as soon as I open my mouth," she said, looking round good-temperedly.

Emma could not resist. "Ah, but you may find it difficult: you are limited as to the number – only three at once."

Miss Bates blushed, deeply pained, as she caught her meaning. "I see what she means," she faltered as she turned to Mr. Knightley. "I must be very disagreeable or she would not have said such a thing to an old friend."

"I have a great deal of vivacity, Mr. Churchill," said Mrs. Elton, "but I cannot be ordered how to speak."

"Yes," said Mr. Elton with a sneer. "I have nothing to say that can entertain Miss Woodhouse."

The Eltons walked off arm in arm.

"What a happy couple!" said Frank Churchill. "How well they suit one another. Very lucky, considering they only knew each other a short time before they married. How many a man has thus committed himself and regretted it all his life."

Jane Fairfax spoke up, for the first time. "Such things do occur," she said, "but there is usually time to rectify it. I think only a weak, indecisive person, whose happiness depends on chance, would regret something like that all his life."

Frank made no answer, merely bowed. Then he said cheerfully

to Emma, "I would like you to choose my wife for me. Will you? Find her? Adopt her? Educate her?"

He must mean Harriet!

Eventually Emma grew tired of his merriment, however, and was glad to see the carriages arrive to take them home. She was walking along to her carriage, when she found Mr. Knightley at her side. Looking round and finding no one in earshot, he said, "Emma, I cannot see you acting wrongly without saying so. How could you behave like that to Miss Bates?"

Emma blushed and was sorry, but tried to laugh it off. "How could I help it? It was not so very bad. And besides, she did not really understand me."

"She felt your full meaning. She has talked of it since; you would be sorry to see with how much generosity."

"I know she is kind, but she is rather silly," Emma protested.

"But she is poor. She has sunk from the luxuries she was born to, luxuries which you have. She requires your compassion, Emma. It was badly done, indeed," Mr. Knightley said.

He helped her into her carriage. She turned her face away and could not say a word. Never had she felt so mortified, agitated, grieved. How could she have been so brutal to Miss Bates? She sank back, overcome, as the horses began to move. To Mr. Knightley, her silence would seem like sullenness. She looked up, to show him it was not true, but too late. He was turning away. She felt tears running down her cheeks all the way home.

Time did not compose her. The more she reflected, the more deeply she seemed to feel it. Her wretchedness haunted her all evening. She played backgammon with her father – there lay real pleasure, in giving up time to his comfort. She knew she had always been scornful and ungracious to Miss Bates. But it would be so no more. Truly sorry and eager to make amends, she decided to begin the very next morning, with a regular, sincere, kindly friendship.

To liven up a dull picnc, Emma could not resist making a witty comment at the expense of poor Miss Bates.

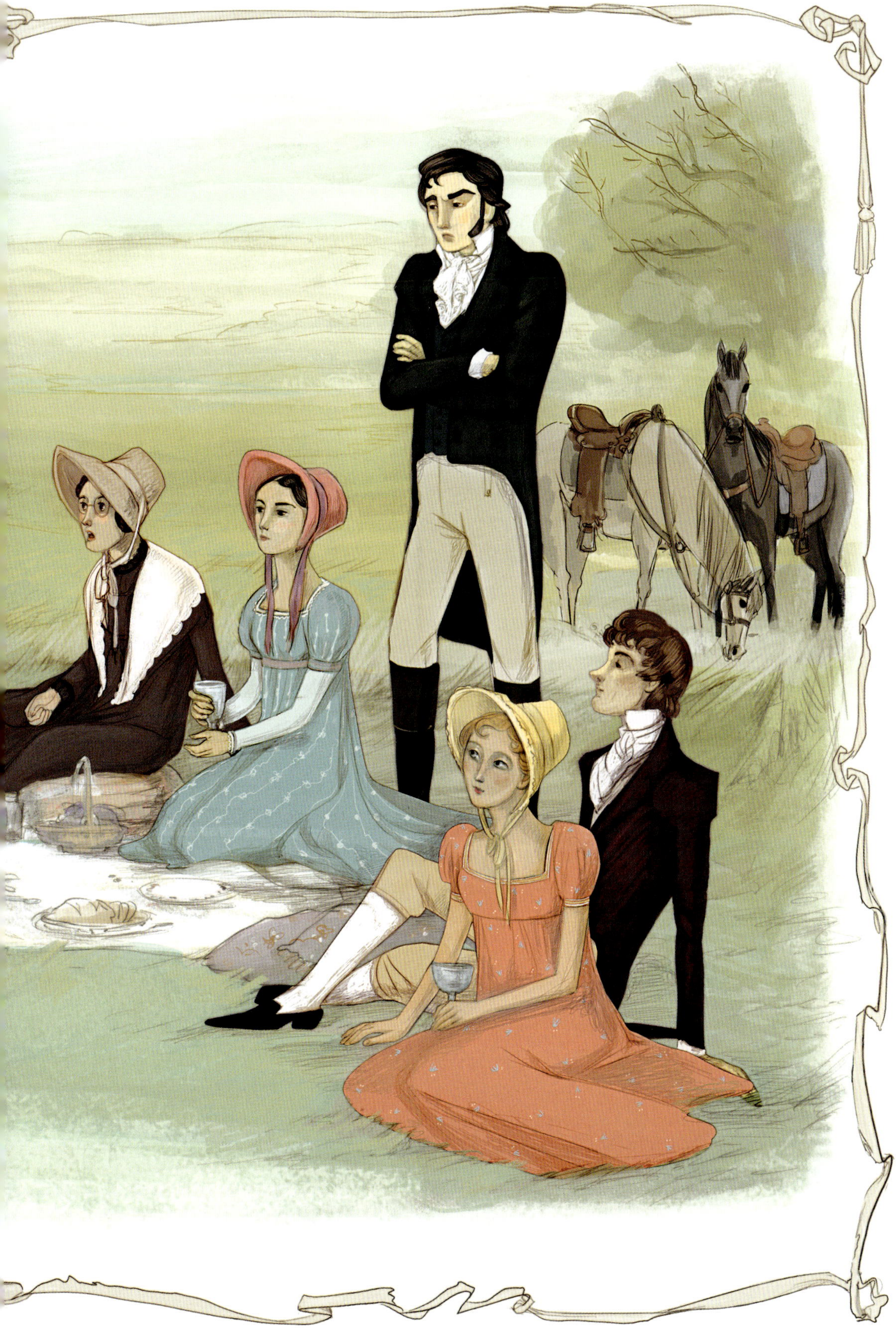

Emma

But when she arrived at the Bateses' door the next morning, she overheard Jane saying that she would see no one, and Miss Bates's manner was awkward. Emma asked after Jane, expressing her concern, and hoping for a return to old feelings.

The effect was immediate. "Oh, Miss Woodhouse, how kind you are, but then you are always kind. Perhaps you have come to wish us joy, though we feel little of that. Jane is going to be a governess to friends of Mrs. Elton, very near Maple Grove. We went to the Eltons' after Box Hill, and Mrs. Elton told her about it again, and said she must accept. Jane has told her many times before that she was not ready for such a position. But she accepted it this time, right after we heard that Mr. Frank Churchill had left and gone to his aunt in Richmond…"

All the way home, Emma mused on the difference between the destiny of a man like Frank Churchill, who had everything, and a woman like Jane Fairfax, who had nothing. She found Mr. Knightley and Harriet sitting with her father.

"I would not go away without seeing you," Mr. Knightley told her. "I am going to London to see my brother and your sister."

Emma was sure she had not been forgiven.

"Dear Emma has been to see Mrs. and Miss Bates," said Mr. Woodhouse. "She is always so kind to them."

Emma blushed and shook her head at the unjust compliment, and instantly perceived a change in Mr. Knightley. He looked at her with a glow of warmth. He took her hand, pressed it – and was gone. It was an unusually gallant action which, she realized, suited him, although the way he left seemed unusually abrupt.

The following day brought news. The great Mrs. Churchill was no more. She had died. After being generally disliked for years, she was now spoken of with compassion. Certainly, death is to be recommended to cleanse a bad reputation.

Emma wondered how her death would affect Frank. It might grant him more freedom, and it might ease Harriet's path to him.

About ten days later, Mr. Weston, agitated and disturbed, called at Hartfield, asking Emma to come at once to Randalls.

When Emma arrived, she found Mrs. Weston as agitated as her husband. "Frank was here this morning," Mrs. Weston began, "to inform his father of an attachment…"

Emma thought of herself and then of Harriet.

"Or rather, an engagement," Mrs. Weston continued. "Emma, Frank Churchill is engaged to Miss Fairfax!"

Emma was horror-struck. "Good God! You cannot mean it?"

"Yes, it was a secret engagement, since October, when they met at Weymouth. I can hardly believe it myself," Mrs. Weston said. "It has hurt me… but you, Emma…" Mrs. Weston's eyes were full of apprehension.

Emma understood. "I did, at one time, like him very much," she said, "but I assure you I care nothing about him now."

Mrs. Weston kissed her with relief. "We have been wretched with worry about you. It was our wish that you and Frank might be attached to each other…"

"But what right did he have to act the way he did?" Emma said. "He acted so freely, not like a man engaged. How could he know he might not be making me fall in love with him? He was wrong, very wrong indeed. And Jane was actually on the point of taking the job as a governess! What could he mean by it all?"

"He told me there were misunderstandings between them, which they have since resolved," Mrs. Weston told her.

"And how has Mr. Churchill taken the news?"

"He happily gave his consent. While Mrs. Churchill lived, there could have been no hope; what a blessing it is when undue influence does not survive the grave! Now, dearest Emma, we must forgive them both, and be thankful that Frank is attached to a steady woman."

"Indeed!" cried Emma, and as Mr. Weston came in, she congratulated him so heartily that he soon recovered his usual cheerful smile.

Poor Harriet! The thought of her tormented Emma. But Harriet, learning the news, showed no disappointment. Emma was confused. "But your feelings… are not they disturbed?" she asked.

"You thought I cared for Frank Churchill?"

"But you did!"

"Never! How could you so mistake me? I know we agreed never to name him, but I thought you had guessed. He who is so infinitely superior! And you said there have been marriages of greater disparity – your very words."

Emma was silent a moment. Then she said slowly, "Harriet, are you speaking of Mr. Knightley?"

"I am."

Emma stared at her in consternation. "And have you any idea of Mr. Knightley returning your affection?"

"Yes," said Harriet modestly. "I have."

Emma sat down. Why did she feel so terrible? And why was the evil increased by Harriet's hope of affection returned? Then it darted through her, with the speed of an arrow: Mr. Knightley must marry no one but herself!

How long had he been dear to her? She looked back and saw that there had never been a time when she had not wanted him to think well of her. She had been totally ignorant of her own heart. With unpardonable arrogance, she had made so many mistakes. Worse still, he never would have known Harriet but for her. Oh, she should have left Harriet be, as Mr. Knightley had once advised. Mr. Knightley and Harriet Smith! But then who had given Harriet such ideas? It was all her own fault.

Until she was threatened with its loss, Emma had never known how much of her happiness depended on being *first* with Mr. Knightley, first in his interest and his affection. Loneliness and melancholy reigned in the next few days. Emma decided to be out of doors as much as possible, in the soothing calm of nature. She was walking in the garden alone, when she saw Mr. Knightley coming towards her through the garden gate.

They walked together, but he was silent. Perhaps he wanted to speak of Harriet. But he began instead to speak of Frank Churchill: "Time, dearest Emma, will heal your wound…"

"You are very kind, but I am not in want of that sort of compassion," Emma assured him. "He is no object of regret."

"In marrying Jane Fairfax, he is a fortunate man. He behaves like a scoundrel and everyone forgives him. I envy him… Are you not curious as to why?"

"No!" cried Emma. Any moment now he would mention Harriet, and she could not bear to hear it.

He looked pained, and she regretted being the cause of it. "It was not kind of me to stop you," she said. "If you wish to tell me anything at all, I will listen as a friend."

"As a friend?" said Mr. Knightley. "Have I no chance then of your love?"

He stopped in his earnestness, and the expression in his eyes overpowered her.

"I cannot make speeches," he continued. "If I loved you less, I might be able to talk about it more. But you know what I am. I have criticized and lectured you, and you have borne it as no other woman in England. God knows, I am no great romantic speaker. But dearest Emma, I think you understand me. What do you say?"

Emma understood him, and with extraordinary velocity, they

Emma

both managed to pass from a thoroughly distressed state of mind to perfect happiness.

Poor Harriet! Emma felt for her with some sorrow once again, as her own feelings took flight. On Mr. Knightley's side, he had been in love with Emma and jealous of Frank Churchill for about the same period of time. He had come anxiously to see how Emma had taken the news of Frank's engagement, and her declaration of indifference had given birth to his hopes.

Emma wrote to Harriet, anxious to avoid a meeting. Harriet, it seemed, would rather avoid her too. But, not long afterwards, Mr. Knightley came to her and said, "I have news for you, Emma… Harriet Smith is engaged to Robert Martin."

"Are you sure?" Emma said.

"I have just spoken to him – he asked and she accepted."

Mr. Martin had seen Harriet again, and, when she had realized that he still loved her, had removed all thoughts of Mr. Knightley from her mind. She was happy, very happy, to accept the man she had first thought of, before all of Emma's plans.

"I most sincerely wish them well!" cried Emma. The joy, the gratitude, the exquisite delight of her sensations may be imagined, and she was now really in danger of becoming too happy.

It was to be a season of weddings: Harriet and Robert Martin's wedding came first; Emma and Mr. Knightley's next, and Jane and Frank's was planned for a few months' time.

Jane seemed happier and much more open-hearted, now that she was not hiding her engagement to Frank. It was he who had sent her the piano, she told Emma and, looking at the light in her eyes and the flush in her cheeks, Emma felt sure they would be friends.

Neither Emma nor Mr. Knightley enjoyed finery or parade, and their wedding was described by Mrs. Elton as "a pitiful business."

Emma

But, despite its simplicity, the hopes and wishes of the small band of true friends who witnessed the ceremony were fully answered in the perfect happiness of the union.

Sense and Sensibility

On the death of their father, the Dashwood sisters and their mother are forced to leave their home. The move throws love in the way of the eldest two sisters, who have very different personalities. Will either of them be able to find true happiness?

Mrs. Dashwood
Elinor, Marianne and Margaret's mother. Like Marianne, her emotion often clouds her judgement.

John & Fanny Dashwood
The Dashwood sisters' half-brother and his wife. They are both obsessed with money and very selfish.

Margaret Dashwood
The youngest Dashwood sister.

Elinor Dashwood
The eldest Dashwood sister. Sensible, reserved and kind, she puts others before herself.

Edward Ferrars
The shy elder brother of Fanny and Robert Ferrars, who seems to have feelings for Elinor.

Sir John & Lady Middleton

Sir John is a distant relative of the Dashwoods. He loves entertaining, while his wife, Lady Middleton, dotes on her children.

Mrs. Jennings

Lady Middleton's widowed mother. She loves to gossip, but is also warm, friendly and caring.

John Willoughby

Dashingly handsome, he seems to be the man of Marianne's dreams, but is he all he appears?

Marianne Dashwood

The lively, passionate and romantic middle Dashwood sister. She believes in being led by her emotions.

Colonel Brandon

A friend of Sir John's, who seems enchanted by Marianne from the start.

Lucy Steele

A distant relative of Mrs. Jennings. Clever, spiteful and manipulative.

Robert Ferrars

Edward's younger brother.

When old Mr. Dashwood died and did not leave his grand house, Norland Park, to his nephew, Henry, everyone was shocked and surprised. The elderly man had, some time ago, invited Henry Dashwood and his family to live with him at Norland Park, and there had been an understanding that Henry would inherit his fortune. But on his death, it turned out that he had left almost everything to Henry's son from his first marriage, John, and John's four-year-old son. Norland would still belong to Henry as long as he lived, but that was all.

Henry was disappointed, but resolved to live modestly and save money to provide for his wife and his daughters – Elinor, aged nineteen, Marianne, aged fifteen and Margaret, aged thirteen. Alas, within a year, he became very ill. Before he died, he begged his son John to be generous with his stepmother and sisters.

John was already wealthy. He had inherited a large sum from his mother, and had married well: his wife, Fanny, was wealthy in her own right. So he readily agreed to his father's request, and decided to give his sisters a thousand pounds each.

And so everything might have gone well for Elinor, Marianne, Margaret and their mother after all, had it not been for Fanny Dashwood. Within the short space of a conversation, Fanny had whittled down a "thousand pounds each" to a single gift of fifty pounds, to a mere intention, then right down to a vague thought that her husband might offer them kindness and assistance – very occasionally – should they desperately need it. For how, as Fanny pointed out, could John rob *their* poor son of three thousand pounds by giving it to someone else? And after all, his father had not said *exactly* how much his half-sisters should have. And, indeed, they were only *half*-sisters. And surely they did not *need* much money to live on anyway.

In this way, Fanny argued away the Dashwood sisters' financial security. It would not be unfair to say that Fanny Dashwood was a selfish woman, or that her husband was easy to persuade when his own interests were at stake.

As soon as Henry's funeral was over, John and Fanny moved into Norland with their little boy, without so much as letting Mrs. Dashwood know that they were coming. Fanny had never been a favourite with her husband's family, but until this point she had not revealed quite how little she cared for their feelings.

Mrs. Dashwood was so offended by her insensitivity that she would have taken her three daughters and left the house immediately, without a suitable place to go, were it not for the advice of her eldest daughter.

Elinor, although only nineteen, was sensitive, intelligent and level-headed. Her mother respected her advice, and, on more than one occasion, Elinor had stopped her from acting unwisely in the heat of the moment. For while Elinor had strong feelings, she knew how to control them – something her mother had yet to learn, and her middle sister, Marianne, had resolved never to be taught.

Marianne, like Elinor, was also sensitive and clever, but perhaps a little too eager in everything. Her feelings tended to be extreme. She either passionately liked something or passionately disliked it. While she was generous, friendly and interesting, she was rarely careful. She was, in fact, remarkably similar to her mother, and although Marianne's emotional, romantic approach to life worried Elinor, their mother valued and cherished it.

Sense and Sensibility

Mrs. Dashwood had another reason for staying at Norland. Since John and Fanny had moved in, Fanny's brother, Edward, had often visited, and a close friendship seemed to have developed between him and Elinor.

It was Elinor who pointed out to her that Edward Ferrars was quite unlike his sister Fanny. "That is enough to make me love him already!" Mrs. Dashwood declared.

"I think you *will* like him when you get to know him," was Elinor's more cautious reply.

Edward was a quiet, shy young man, but he seemed warm and affectionate. No sooner had Mrs. Dashwood seen a hint of warmth in his behaviour to Elinor than she pronounced to Marianne that they would be married in a few months. "How we will miss her! But at least we know she will be happy."

"Perhaps Elinor will be," Marianne replied. "But as much as I love Edward, *I* require so much more…" Marianne sighed. "The more I know of the world, the more I am convinced that I shall never see a man whom I can really love."

"Remember, my love, you are not yet seventeen. It is too early to despair of finding happiness!" her mother reminded her.

The problem with Edward, in Marianne's view, was that he was a little too mild. He did not enthuse about writers, he did not draw, or seem interested in music. In view of this, how could Elinor possibly be interested in him?

"He is good and intelligent, and handsome," Elinor told her.

"Do not worry, I shall love him as a brother, as soon as you tell me to!" her sister declared.

Elinor was shocked, and tried to set her straight. "I do not deny that I – I like him…"

"How can you be so cold-hearted, Elinor! You only *like* him?"

Elinor laughed. "Very well, believe that my feelings are

stronger, if you like. But go no further than that. I am by no means certain of how he feels towards me. Sometimes he seems to care for me, and other times I think we are only friends."

Elinor's mother and sister were not the only ones to have noticed that Elinor and Edward seemed attracted to one another. Fanny had seen it too, and as far as she was concerned it simply would not do. She informed Mrs. Dashwood that she and her mother intended Edward to marry well: "We are particularly alert to the dangers of just *any* young woman *drawing him in.*" Well, the implications of this were clear: to marry Elinor would *not* be to marry well. This insult was the final straw. Mrs. Dashwood could no longer remain in the same house as Fanny. When she received a letter from a distant cousin, Sir John Middleton, offering her a cottage on his estate in Devonshire, she gladly accepted.

It was with much sadness that the Dashwoods left their beloved Norwood, but when they arrived at their new home, they were immediately charmed. Barton Cottage was much smaller than they were used to, and had its faults, but these could soon be overcome, and in the meantime, it was comfortable. After all, they only had three servants now, so there was room enough. They were busy unpacking, when their new landlord arrived to welcome them.

Sir John Middleton was a friendly, good-looking man of forty. By the end of his visit, he had invited the Dashwoods for dinner at Barton Park every day until they were settled. And before the day was out, he had sent them a basket of fruit and vegetables, some meat and a promise of newspapers every day. With such a warm welcome, the Dashwoods felt very happy with their new home.

The Middletons, it soon became apparent, entertained very often. In fact, they did very little else. Sir John liked to go hunting, and his wife doted on their children, but mainly they liked having

Sense and Sensibility

guests and throwing parties, and they were very good at it.

When the Dashwoods visited Barton Park the next day, there were two guests staying. One was Lady Middleton's mother, Mrs. Jennings, a merry, chatty old lady who liked to tease. The other was Colonel Brandon: a not bad-looking gentleman of around thirty-five years which, to Marianne, seemed terribly *old*. He was a friend of Sir John's, but seemed as unlike him as Mrs. Jennings was her daughter. There was no one in the party whom the Dashwoods thought they might be friends with. While Mrs. Jennings spent the evening teasing the girls and trying to make them blush, Lady Middleton was dull, and preoccupied with her noisy, spoiled children. Sir John was boisterous, while Colonel Brandon was serious and quiet.

When Marianne was discovered to be musical, she was invited to play the piano. Marianne played and sang well, but her audience was less satisfactory. Sir John was almost as noisy in his applause at the end of each piece, as he was in talking to the others while she was playing. Lady Middleton requested songs already sung. Only the Colonel gave her his full attention. Marianne noticed, with growing respect for him, that although he did not burst into raptures, he paid her the compliment of truly listening to her.

A few days later, Mrs. Jennings declared that Colonel Brandon was clearly in love with Marianne. For had he not listened carefully when she had sung that first evening? And had he not listened equally carefully at Barton Cottage the following day? It must be so. She was convinced of it. It would be an excellent match, for *he* was rich, and *she* was pretty. And from then on, she teased the pair relentlessly about it.

Marianne hardly knew whether to laugh or be angry. "How could Mrs. Jennings be so cruel as to taunt the Colonel in this way!" she said to her mother and Elinor. "He is so old! Far too old to be in love. It is too ridiculous! Thirty-five has nothing to do with marriage!"

Her mother laughed, "It is not so very old, Marianne!"

"You only think he is so past anything because you heard him mention rheumatism in his shoulder yesterday," Elinor said.

"*And* flannel waistcoats!" Marianne shuddered. "Only *old, ill* people wear flannel!"

"Admit it, you would not mind the illness so much if it were something more romantic," Elinor teased. "Perhaps something that gave him flushed cheeks and a pounding heart...?"

The Dashwoods soon settled into their new life. The countryside around the cottage was beautiful, and they often went for long walks. One morning, after days of rain, the sun finally broke through the clouds, and Marianne and Margaret decided to go out. It was a windy day, but they laughed as they battled against it, enjoying the fresh air. After twenty minutes, however, the sky darkened, and it began to pour with rain. There was nowhere to shelter, so they raced back down towards the cottage. Marianne was in the lead, but tripped and fell, and the hill was so steep, that Margaret was unable to stop to help her. When she looked back, there was a man stooping over her sister. He had run to Marianne as soon as he saw her fall, and was now trying to help her to her feet. Marianne's ankle was too badly twisted for her to stand, so the man gathered her up in his arms and carried her down the hill all the way to the cottage.

The young man took Marianne straight into the parlour, where he was greeted by a surprised Mrs. Dashwood and Elinor. He introduced himself as Mr. Willoughby. He was so charming, polite and handsome, that he soon won their admiration. And Marianne? Well to her, he was just as good as any storybook hero.

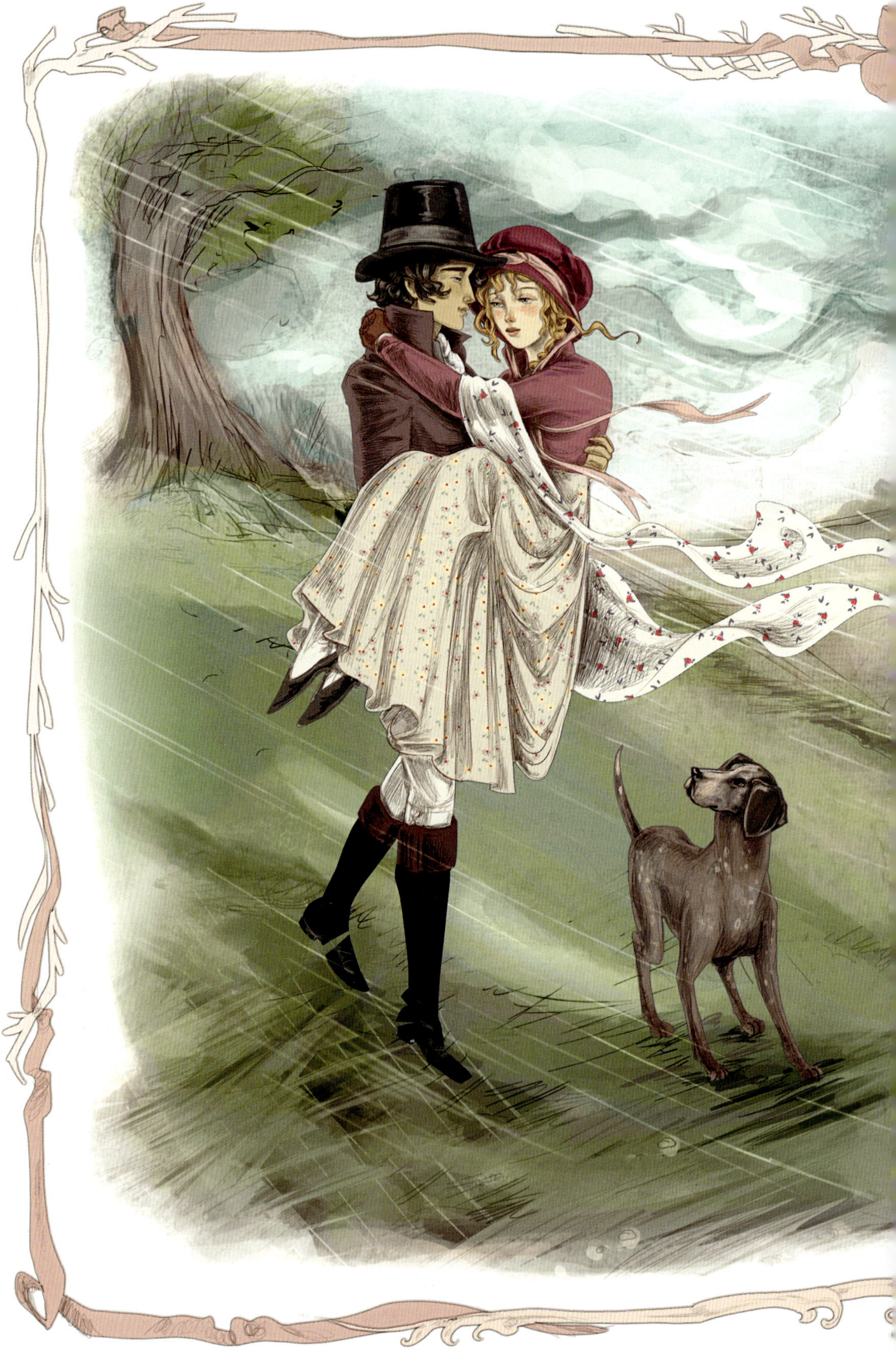

Marianne's ankle was too badly twisted for her to stand, so the man gathered her up in his arms and carried her down the hill to the cottage.

Sense and Sensibility

Everything about him was interesting. His name, where he was staying, his clothes… Her imagination was soon so busy that the pain of her ankle was quite forgotten. As he left, he asked gallantly if he might visit the following day. Of course, she readily agreed.

A visit from Sir John provided a few more details about this attractive young man. Mr. Willoughby was the heir of an elderly lady who lived in a nearby mansion. He owned a small estate, and was an enthusiastic dancer. Just like Marianne…

Willoughby returned the next day. He liked the Dashwoods as much as they liked him. He found Elinor pretty, but Marianne more strikingly beautiful. He discovered that she shared his love of music and dancing, that their tastes in literature were remarkably similar, and wherever they differed, he was soon infected by her enthusiasm. By the end of the morning, it felt as if they had known one another for years.

Willoughby visited every day after that. He was a lively young man with a quick imagination and an open, affectionate manner. He sang with emotion and read aloud with spirit. It seemed as if he had been made to capture Marianne's heart. Her fear of never meeting a man who measured up to her ideas of perfection, she realized, had been unjustified. By the end of the week, her mother not only hoped for a marriage, but expected it.

As soon as Marianne's ankle was better, Sir John began to hold parties and balls to which the Dashwoods – and Willoughby – were always invited. This gave Willoughby and Marianne the chance to get to know one another even better. Elinor was pleased, but it worried her that her sister was so openly affectionate towards Willoughby. Whenever he was present, she had no eyes for anyone else. Everything he did was right. Everything he said was clever. He, meanwhile, cheated at cards to let her win, danced with her and only her, and hardly talked to anyone else. Marianne floated on a cloud of happiness. Her heart belonged to Willoughby.

They seemed so intimate, so close, that Elinor wondered if they had made promises of marriage to one another in private. And then one day Margaret told her she had seen Willoughby cut a lock of Marianne's hair, kiss it, and put it in his wallet! To Elinor, this seemed like proof.

One morning, they had all arranged to visit a grand house a few miles away. They were about to set off, when a letter arrived for Colonel Brandon. He took one look at it, turned pale and left the room. Five minutes later, he returned to tell everyone that he was urgently needed in London, and must go immediately. He could not say how long he would be gone, nor why.

Mrs. Jennings's curiosity was raised. "I wonder what it could be," she said, when the Colonel had left. Mrs. Jennings was a great wonderer, and left to her own devices could wonder, often out loud, for days at a time. "I bet it is Miss Williams!" she declared, then whispered in Elinor's ear, "His daughter, so people say," and gave her a meaningful look. "I suppose it *could* be his brother that has called him away. Or his estate. But I bet it is Miss Williams…"

In the end, the party set off as planned. Marianne went with Willoughby in his carriage. They shot off before the others could get started, and did not return until after the others did. When quizzed on where they had been, Marianne replied, "Oh just up and down the lanes."

But Mrs. Jennings later found out that she and Willoughby had visited the house of Willoughby's elderly relative – the house that he would one day inherit. The implication of this was clear (to Mrs. Jennings at least). Willoughby intended to marry Marianne! He had been showing her around her future home.

Yet again, Elinor could not help but feel concerned. It was not proper for her to have gone there with Willoughby – just look at the conclusion Mrs. Jennings had jumped to – and especially not to have gone with him on her own. But when she challenged her sister later, Marianne did not seem to care. She had had a lovely time and that was all that mattered, as far as she was concerned.

The way the pair was behaving preyed on Elinor's mind. They certainly acted as if they were engaged. Willoughby spent most of his time with Marianne. He *seemed* to be in love with her. Yet they said nothing. Then one day something happened that seemed to change everything.

Mrs. Dashwood, Margaret and Elinor had been at Barton Park all morning, and on their return saw that Willoughby's carriage was outside their cottage. They went inside to see Marianne rushing out of the sitting room, a handkerchief at her eyes, and a look of dreadful distress on her face as she wordlessly dashed up the stairs. They found Willoughby in the parlour, a look of deep discomfort on his face.

"Whatever is the matter?" Mrs. Dashwood cried. "Is she ill?"

"I hope not," Willoughby said, trying to look cheerful, but failing. "In fact, it should rather be *me* who is ill. I am suffering from a great disappointment, ladies. Mrs. Smith, my relative, is sending me to London, and I shall not be back for at least a year."

"A year!" Mrs. Dashwood said, shocked. "What a shame, Willoughby! Can you not come and visit us?"

Willoughby looked at the floor and turned red. "I fear my commitments in London are such that I may not…" There was a silence. Then: "I am torturing myself by staying any longer. I must go." And with that, he left. Surely this was not the act of a man in love. Had he *never* been serious? Had the two quarrelled? Elinor was keen to get to the bottom of it, but Mrs. Dashwood refused to allow Marianne to be questioned. She said they must wait until she volunteered the information herself.

Sense and Sensibility

They saw nothing of her until dinner, when, without a word and avoiding all eye contact, she sat down at the table. Her eyes were red and swollen, and she was clearly struggling not to cry. She refused to eat or speak, and when her mother took her hand, she burst into tears and ran upstairs.

Marianne would have been ashamed of herself if she had been able to sleep that night. But it turned out there was no danger of that. She wept for hours and came down the next morning with a headache, still unable to talk or eat. A little later, she walked to the village where Willoughby had stayed, and wept over how wonderful it had all been. In the evening, she sang the songs they had sung together. Over the next few days, she read the books they had read together, and sobbed over her lost happiness. She fed her grief and refused all consolation. But this could not last forever, and eventually she settled into a gentler sadness.

No letter came from Willoughby in the days that followed.

"We should ask her what happened," Elinor said.

"No!" cried her mother. "It will only upset her more!"

About a week later, Elinor and Marianne were out for a walk when they saw a man on horseback in the distance.

"It is him! Willoughby!" Marianne cried excitedly. Elinor was sure it was not. The man was not tall enough, and carried himself differently. But Marianne could not be dissuaded until the man was close enough for them to see that it was, in fact, Edward Ferrars!

Edward was, perhaps, the only person in the world whom Marianne could forgive for not being Willoughby. In her happiness for her sister, for a moment she forgot her own sadness. But as they walked back to the cottage, Marianne noticed that Elinor seemed cool toward Edward, and Edward seemed distant. *This* was not how reunited lovers behaved! And then, Edward told them that he had already been in the area for two weeks. Two weeks! And he had

Sense and Sensibility

only just come to see Elinor! *Willoughby* would never do such a thing. And Elinor did not even seem to care!

In fact, Elinor *did* care. She was upset at Edward's coolness, but had decided not to let her feelings show.

Mrs. Dashwood's warm welcome when they arrived at the cottage made Edward a little more like his old self. She pressed him to stay with them and he accepted with a smile. But in the days that followed, it was clear to Elinor that he was unhappy. The way he behaved made her even more uncertain about his feelings for her. One moment he looked warmly at her, the next he was reserved and distant, and she began to fear that he no longer cared for her.

He was taking a cup of tea from their mother, when Marianne noticed a ring on his finger which had a lock of hair set into it. "Oh, is that your sister's hair?" she blurted out.

Edward blushed and muttered that yes, it was his sister's hair. But the hair looked exactly like Elinor's. Elinor met his eye and blushed too. She had never given Edward such a gift, so how *could* it be? Edward seemed embarrassed and eager to change the subject. What on earth did it mean?

Edward seemed happier and happier the more time he spent with them, and sighed whenever he mentioned leaving. And yet, at the end of a week, he announced that he must go. His departure left Elinor feeling unhappy and worried. But unlike Marianne, rather than shutting herself away to dwell on her feelings, she sat down at the drawing room table and kept herself busy. Marianne could not understand it. How could someone who was in love behave like this… unless, of course, she was not in love at all…

A few days later, Sir John dashed over to the cottage to tell them about two new visitors at Barton Park. Miss Anne and Miss Lucy Steele were distant relatives of Mrs. Jennings. "The Miss Steeles are the sweetest girls in the world," he gushed. This was not very informative, Elinor thought, as "the sweetest girls in the world" could be found in every part of England. "You simply must come and meet them!" he continued. "You cannot imagine how much you will like them. They are both so pretty, and *so* agreeable! They long to meet you more than anything, as they have heard you are the most beautiful creatures in the world. And you will be delighted with them!"

A couple of days later, the Dashwoods met the new visitors at Barton Park. They found Anne, a lady of about thirty, to be plain and sensible-looking, rather than the ravishing creature Sir John had led them to expect. Her younger sister, Lucy, was pretty and seemed intelligent, if not very well educated. They both clearly had enough sense to compliment Lady Middleton's children and lavish them with attention and praise, even though, arguably, they deserved to be told off. And anyone who praised Lady Middleton's children automatically earned her approval.

"I suspect you think the little Middletons are rather spoiled," Lucy said to Elinor when they were out of their hostess's hearing. "But I love to see children full of life. I cannot bear them if they are quiet and tame."

"I confess," replied Elinor, "that while I am at Barton Park, I really do not mind the idea of tame and quiet children."

There was then a short, uncomfortable silence.

"Do you miss Norland Park, Miss Dashwood?" Anne suddenly asked. "I imagine there were many smart young men there. I do hope Devonshire is not lacking in them. But then perhaps you do not care for them. I can do as well without them as with them. But if they dress smartly and are polite they can be most agreeable."

"Anne, can you talk of nothing but young men?" Lucy interrupted before her sister could continue. "Miss Dashwood will believe you think of nothing else!"

Sense and Sensibility

This introduction to the Steele sisters was enough to give Elinor an accurate impression of them. The elder was foolish, and the younger lacked elegance, in spite of her prettiness and shrewdness. Elinor left the house with no desire to get to know them better. Unfortunately, the feeling was not mutual. The Miss Steeles were *very* eager to get to know the Dashwoods, and Elinor soon found herself in their company again. Sir John, keen to promote the friendship, told the Miss Steeles absolutely everything he knew about the Dashwoods, and the next time they met, Anne congratulated Elinor on her sister's luck in having made a conquest of a *very* smart young man so soon after moving to Barton.

"It will be a fine thing to have her married so young," she commented. "And I do hope you will have such luck yourself before too long. But perhaps you already have someone…?"

Elinor would not be drawn on this, of course, but later on, she heard Sir John tell the Miss Steeles in a very loud whisper: "His name is *Ferrars*. But, pray, do not tell, for it is a secret."

"Ferrars! What? Your sister-in-law's brother, Miss Dashwood?" Anne cried. "I know him well. A very agreeable young man."

"How can you say that!" Lucy glared at her. "You only met him once or twice at our uncle's."

They had *met* him? How? Who was this uncle? These questions ran through Elinor's mind, but she said nothing.

Marianne, who had no tolerance for bad taste or even tastes that differed from her own, was cold towards the Miss Steeles. This, Elinor thought, must be why Lucy Steele went to such lengths to befriend her over the next few days. Lucy was clever and could be amusing, but she was also ignorant. After half an hour of her company, Elinor had usually had enough. She found it hard to warm to her, especially as she was forever flattering the Middletons. She could not enjoy the company of a person who was so insincere.

Sense and Sensibility

Then one day, they were out walking when Lucy suddenly said, "Do you know your sister-in-law's mother, Mrs. Ferrars?"

Elinor replied that she had not met the lady.

Lucy was quiet for a moment, then said, "I hope you did not think my question nosy. I would hate *you*, of all people, to think that of me. I am sorry you do not know her, though, as I wanted advice on an uncomfortable issue regarding her."

"I am sorry I cannot help you," Elinor replied cautiously. "But I am perplexed as to what connection you have to the family, and why Mrs. Ferrars so concerns you."

Lucy sighed. "Well, she does not concern me at the moment, but may do soon. How soon depends on her…" Lucy looked down bashfully, but then shot a sideways glance at Elinor to see what impact this statement had on her.

"Good heavens!" Elinor said. "What can you mean?" In fact, Elinor could only conclude that what Lucy meant was that she was to marry into the family. And there was only one man she could possibly marry. "You know Mr. Robert Ferrars?" she asked.

"Oh no! Not *Robert* Ferrars!" Lucy replied. "I have never met *him*." Then fixing her eyes on Elinor: "His brother, Edward."

Elinor was shocked. She found it impossible to believe what Lucy had just said, and simply turned to her in astonished silence.

"You may well be surprised," Lucy continued, "for it is a secret from everyone but Anne. I would never have told *you*, but I thought if I did not, you might think my question about Mrs. Ferrars odd. And, of course, I know I can trust you to keep our secret. I am sure Edward will not be cross, because I know he has the highest respect for your family, and looks on you as a sister."

After a few seconds, Elinor forced herself to speak, managing to conceal her surprise and discomfort really rather well, she thought. "May I ask if you have been engaged for long?"

"Four years. And goodness knows how much longer we may

have to wait, poor Edward." She took a miniature portrait out of her pocket and handed it to Elinor. There was no doubt that it was of Edward. Elinor hastily gave it back.

"Dear Edward spent four years studying under my uncle. That is how we met. We have been engaged for four years, but secretly. I would hate the news to get back to Mrs. Ferrars, as I am certain she would disapprove. I am not wealthy enough for her."

"Of course I will keep your secret," Elinor replied. "But I am surprised that you felt the need to tell it to me." She looked Lucy in the eye, hoping to detect some sign of falsehood in her, but Lucy's expression did not change.

"Although we have not known each other long," Lucy replied, "it feels as if we have, and I have no one else to confide in but Anne. How I have suffered, having to keep quiet for Edward's sake." Lucy dabbed a tear from her eye, but Elinor was not feeling particularly sympathetic. "Sometimes I think I should break the whole thing off," Lucy continued, "but I could not *bear* to make Edward so miserable. What do *you* think I should do, Miss Dashwood?"

"I really cannot advise you," Elinor replied. "Did he come from your uncle's when he visited here last week?"

"Yes. Did he seem sad? I told him he must take care to hide his feelings," Lucy said. "He was so sad to leave me. And he is sad still – he says so in this letter." Lucy wafted a letter in front of Elinor.

Elinor could believe that Lucy might have acquired the picture from some other source than Edward – he might not have given it to her himself – but a *letter*… only Edward could have given her that. Her heart sank.

"At least we can write," Lucy went on. "It pains me that he has no picture of me. But at least he has my hair in a ring. Did you see it?" Lucy asked, the picture of innocence.

"I did," Elinor replied, her voice steady, but hiding distress the strength of which she had never felt before. She was horrified, confused and utterly shocked. Fortunately, at this point, they reached Barton Cottage and the conversation came to an end.

On reflection, Elinor could not doubt that Lucy had told the truth, and at first she felt a little sorry for herself, and indignant that she had been fooled. But when she looked back on how things had been between her and Edward at Norland, she found she could not stop believing that he loved her. Whatever Edward's engagement had meant, she was sure he did *not* love Lucy now. His affection was all her own. Her mother and sisters and even Fanny had seen it. She was not deceiving herself about that. If he had done anything wrong, it was in continuing to visit Norland once he began to develop feelings for her. But if her case was pitiable, then his was even worse – to be engaged to someone he did not love and to be in love with someone else! Elinor doubted that Edward could ever be happy with Lucy. How could he be when she was so manipulative and selfish? She was totally unsuited to him.

Elinor decided not to tell her mother and sisters. It would only upset them. Besides, their knowing would not make her feel any better. And so she was able to join her family for dinner a mere two hours after the destruction of all her dearest hopes, without any of them guessing how much she suffered. Marianne, meanwhile, was having equally secret thoughts. In her case, about the man whose heart she felt wholly belonged to her, and whom she expected to see in every carriage which came near their house.

Painful as the subject was, Elinor was anxious to speak to Lucy about it again. Partly to clarify just how she and Edward had become engaged, partly to try to gauge Lucy's real feelings for him and partly to make it clear to Lucy that she had no feelings for Edward herself. It seemed likely that Lucy was jealous of her – she was sure that was why Lucy had told her. It was her way of warning Elinor off Edward. And while Elinor fully intended to do the right thing and see as little of Edward as possible from now on, she would not deny herself the comfort of convincing Lucy that her heart was unwounded, and that Lucy's words had no effect.

It was a few days before she had a chance to talk to Lucy again. Then at Barton Park one evening, a game of cards was proposed. Lucy was sewing a gift for Lady Middleton's daughter, and chose not to take part, and Elinor, seeing an opportunity, offered to help her. Thus the two fair rivals sat side by side, out of earshot of the others, as if they were the best of friends. It was Elinor who first raised the subject she so wanted to hear about.
"I am truly sorry you and Edward are in such a predicament," she said carefully. "I gather he is entirely dependent on his mother for an income."
"Indeed. And we dare not upset her. She has a terrible temper. If Edward upsets her, there is a danger she will give everything to his brother Robert. Without her, Edward only has two thousand pounds of his own, which *I* could easily live off, being used to so little," Lucy replied. "But I could not inflict such a small income on him. I love Edward far too much to force him to live in such poverty. So it may be many years before we marry. With any man but Edward, I would find this an alarming prospect."
"And indeed, were he not so fond of you, I am sure it would be alarming for him too."
Lucy looked sharply at Elinor to see if her words had a hidden meaning, but Elinor's expression betrayed nothing. "Edward's love has been put to the test," Lucy replied carefully, "and it would be indefensible of me to doubt him now."
Elinor knew hardly whether to smile or sigh at this statement.
"I confess I have a jealous streak," Lucy continued, "and if there had been the slightest change in his feelings for me, I would

have been instantly aware of it."

"So what will you do?" Elinor asked.

"Well," Lucy said, lowering her voice, "I had thought that you might use your influence with your brother to gain Edward a position as a clergyman. That way he would have another income."

"I would be happy to," Elinor replied, "but surely his own sister is in a better position to help you than I am."

"Oh, but I think his sister would not approve of such a plan."

"In that case, I fear my influence would be very little."

There was a short silence, then Lucy said, "I know the wisest thing to do would be to call off the engagement. There are *so* many difficulties. It would make us both miserable for a time, but we would, perhaps, be happier in the end. What do you think?"

"I am afraid I cannot advise you." Elinor replied, "I imagine you would not act on my advice unless it agrees with what you already believe, and as an impartial observer I am hardly in a position to give you good advice."

"You do me an injustice, Miss Dashwood. I would do whatever you advised. It is because I know you *are* impartial, that I ask you. If you told me to break off the engagement, I would."

Elinor blushed. "Then I fear I *dare* not advise you."

Lucy was silent again for a moment, then asked, "Will you be going to London this winter, Miss Dashwood?"

"No, I will not."

"What a pity," Lucy replied, but her eyes lit up. "I only go for Edward, of course. It holds no other charms for me."

Elinor returned to the card table with a heavy heart. She did not have the impression that Lucy loved Edward, and she was sure that Edward did not love Lucy. Yet Lucy insisted on holding him to the engagement. From then on, Elinor avoided the subject. Whenever Lucy tried to talk about it, which she did often, Elinor changed the subject as quickly and politely as possible.

Sense and Sensibility

Two months later, after Christmas, Mrs. Jennings prepared to make her usual annual move to her London home, and invited Marianne and Elinor to go with her. At first, Elinor declined, saying they could not leave their mother, but on hearing this, Mrs. Dashwood insisted that they should go.

So in the first week of January, Elinor, Marianne and Mrs. Jennings set off on the long carriage ride to London. Marianne's joy was almost a degree beyond happiness. She was clearly convinced that she would see Willoughby in town. Elinor was less happy, but comforted herself that they would be back home before Edward arrived in London. She was also determined to find out as much as possible about Willoughby's intentions towards her sister while she was there, and keep a watchful eye on them, if they arranged to meet.

Marianne remained mostly silent throughout the three-day journey, leaving Elinor to listen to, laugh with and generally give Mrs. Jennings all the attention she deserved. By the time they arrived in London, Elinor was very relieved to be released from the confines of the carriage.

As soon as they had been shown to their room, she sat down to write to her mother. Marianne also sat down to write. She did not say to whom, but she said it was not to their mother, and Elinor realized that she must be writing to Willoughby. If this were so, then surely the two *must* be engaged!

Marianne was restless for the remainder of the day. She could barely eat dinner, and was constantly listening out for the sound of a carriage. Every noise had her jumping to her feet. When at last there *was* a knock at the door of the house, Elinor, too, was sure it must be Willoughby, and Marianne seemed almost ready to throw herself in his arms. In fact, it was Colonel Brandon, and Marianne, unable to bear the terrible disappointment, ran out of the room.

Sense and Sensibility

"Is your sister ill?" the Colonel asked, full of concern.

Elinor had to make excuses for her.

The next day, Mrs. Jennings's younger daughter, Charlotte Palmer, visited, and offered to take Marianne and Elinor out shopping. While they were out, Marianne was forever looking around, as if hoping to see someone, and when they returned home, the first thing she did was run to see if there was a letter for her. There was none. "How very odd!" she said in a low, disappointed voice. How very odd indeed, thought Elinor, for surely Marianne would not have written to Willoughby if he were not in town, and, if he *were* in town, why had he not replied?

Marianne was on edge and unable to concentrate for the rest of that day and the next, but gradually they managed to settle into a routine: visiting Mrs. Jennings's friends, going out to the shops and so on. Colonel Brandon visited them almost every day, and Elinor began to fear that Mrs. Jennings was right: the Colonel was interested in Marianne, and his interest seemed to be getting stronger rather than weaker. When he visited, he came to look at Marianne and talk to Elinor. Even so, Elinor often found their conversations were the best part of her day.

It was about a week after their arrival in London that a calling card was left while they were out. It was from Willoughby. Marianne was ecstatic and, convinced he would call again the next day, she stayed in all day. But he did not. The following morning, Elinor saw her write another letter. What on earth was going on?

Later that day when Colonel Brandon arrived, he looked even more serious than usual. And he wanted to speak to Elinor – alone. When he finally spoke, the question he asked was not one she had expected. "Am I to congratulate you on the gaining of a brother?"

Elinor was so taken aback, all she could say was, "Whatever do you mean?"

Sense and Sensibility

"Your sister's engagement to Mr. Willoughby is widely known," was his disconcerting reply.

"But – but it cannot be widely known," replied Elinor, "when her own family does not know it."

The Colonel looked surprised and apologized. Apparently, everyone knew that Marianne and Willoughby wrote to one another, and everyone was talking about their imminent marriage. "I might not have believed it myself, but as I was coming in, I could not help noticing a servant carrying a letter addressed to Willoughby in your sister's handwriting," he told Elinor. "I came to ask… Is there nothing that can be done to stop… I know I have no right and cannot hope to succeed… I should not have said so much, but I hardly know what to do, Miss Dashwood."

This was, it seemed to Elinor, an open declaration of the Colonel's love for Marianne, and for a moment she had no idea what to say. She knew so little herself. She did not want to give the Colonel false hope. In the end, she told him that the affection between Marianne and Willoughby was mutual, and that she was not surprised that they were writing to one another. Colonel Brandon listened in silence, and when she had finished, merely said, in a voice full of emotion, "I wish your sister all imaginable happiness, and hope that Willoughby will try to deserve her." He said goodbye, leaving her feeling very uneasy.

For the next three days, nothing was seen or heard of Willoughby. On the fourth day, Elinor and Marianne were invited to a party with Lady Middleton, who had come to town with Sir John. Almost as soon as they arrived, Elinor spotted Willoughby. He was in earnest conversation with a fashionable young woman, but when Elinor caught his eye, he merely bowed, and made no attempt to speak to either her or to Marianne.

Elinor turned to Marianne and saw her face light up with

delight as she too spotted him. Elinor was only just able to stop her sister from going over to him.

"Good heavens! Why does he not come over and speak to me!" Marianne gasped.

"Perhaps he has not seen you," Elinor offered, not believing this for a second.

Then, at last, Willoughby turned to look at them.

Marianne leaped to her feet and held out her hand, but when he came over, Willoughby spoke only to Elinor, avoiding even meeting Marianne's eye.

Elinor was speechless, but Marianne was not. "Willoughby, what is the meaning of this? Did you not receive my letters? Will you not even shake my hand?"

Her touch seemed painful to him, and he held her hand only briefly. He was clearly struggling to remain calm. "I did call upon your residence last week and leave my card," he said stiffly. "I hope it was not lost."

"For heaven's sake, what is the matter?" cried Marianne.

Willoughby looked embarrassed. Pretending to catch the eye of the young lady from before, he made his excuses and walked away.

Marianne turned as white as a sheet, and seemed on the verge of fainting. "Go to him Elinor," she said sinking into a chair. "Tell him I must to speak to him right now."

But Elinor would not, and had to restrain Marianne from following him herself, and not long after, she saw him leave. Marianne begged to go home, and once there, fled to her room, pleading to be left alone.

The next morning, Marianne refused to eat or speak. Then, after breakfast, a letter arrived for her. On reading it, she turned deathly pale and ran from the room.

Elinor rushed upstairs and found her sister lying on the bed,

Sense and Sensibility

almost choked with grief. She had the letter in her hand, and several others in her own handwriting scattered around her. Elinor sat down, kissed her, then burst into tears herself.

Unable to speak, Marianne pushed the letter into Elinor's hand. It was from Willoughby. With a pounding heart, Elinor read it.

My dear Madam,

I have just received your letter. I am very concerned to discover that you found something in the way I behaved last night that met your disapproval and, although I am quite at a loss as to what that might be, I beg your forgiveness. I assure you, it was perfectly unintentional. I shall always remember my acquaintance with your family with pleasure. My respect for your family is very sincere, but if I said anything that caused you to believe that I felt more than I do, then I am very sorry and wish I had been more careful. I am sure you understand that it cannot have meant anything - that would be impossible, given that my affections have been long engaged elsewhere. It will not be many weeks, I believe, before I shall be married. It is with great regret that I obey your request to return the letters you kindly sent to me, and the lock of hair you gave me.

I am, dear Madam, your most obedient, humble servant,

John Willoughby

Elinor was shocked. Not so much by what it revealed about the man's character, or because it meant that he and Marianne were to be forever separated, but that he could be so cruel. She was shocked that he could deny ever having felt anything for her sister.

*Marianne pushed the letter into
Elinor's hand... With a pounding heart,
Elinor read it.*

Sense and Sensibility

She was shocked that he did not admit he had done anything wrong. Every line was an insult; the author was a villain. She was so angry, she did not trust herself to speak. Marianne, who had been sobbing quietly, now began to wail.

"You must try, Marianne, for our mother's sake, if not for yours, to—" Elinor began.

"I *cannot* try," Marianne wept, "and if you had ever suffered as I do, you would understand. You cannot *know*, Elinor, you who are so happy."

"How can I be happy when you are like this?" Elinor replied.

"Forgive me," Marianne sobbed into her neck. "I know you suffer seeing me like this, but you have Edward who loves you, so you *must* be happy. What could take away that happiness?"

"Many things," Elinor said quietly.

"No! He loves you and only you," Marianne wailed. "You cannot be unhappy as I am. And I… I will never be happy again."

"Marianne, you must not talk so. At least your engagement did not carry on for months before—"

"Engagement! What engagement?"

"There was no engagement?"

"No, he has broken no promise. He is not as bad as you think."

"But he told you he loved you?"

"Yes – no – not in so many words. I *felt* as if we were engaged."

"But *he* did not," Elinor replied flatly.

"He did! He did! For weeks. I do not know what made him change his mind. You see this lock of hair? He begged and begged me for it. Oh Elinor, someone must have made him think badly of me. I cannot stay here any more. I must go home. Tomorrow!"

Elinor persuaded her to try to get some rest, but shortly after, Mrs. Jennings came into the room to ask how Marianne was. She had heard the news that "that good for nothing" Willoughby was to be married. "Well, all I can say is that I hope his new wife plagues him," she said. Then with, "Oh you poor thing," she left Marianne to her weeping.

Downstairs, a little later, Mrs. Jennings filled Elinor in with the details she had heard about Willoughby. He was to marry a Miss Grey, a wealthy heiress to a huge fortune. "At least this will be good news for Colonel Brandon," she said. "I bet he and Marianne will be married by midsummer! He is a much better match for her anyway – apart from having a daughter – but no matter. His home, Delaford, is such a nice place…"

Marianne woke the next day as miserable as ever. Elinor encouraged her to talk about how she felt. How Marianne felt veered from one extreme to the other, then back again. She wanted to avoid Mrs. Jennings at all costs. "All she wants is gossip," Marianne declared, "and she only likes me now because I can supply it." When Mrs. Jennings brought her a letter, which she said would make Marianne feel better, Marianne assumed it was from Willoughby, and would be followed by the man himself, full of tenderness and apologies. When it turned out to be from her mother, she thought Mrs. Jennings even more unkind. The letter brought her great pain. Mrs. Dashwood knew nothing of the situation with Willoughby, and mentioned him on every page.

Colonel Brandon called later that morning, causing Marianne to flee once again upstairs. But it was Elinor that he had come to speak to. He too had heard about Willoughby.

"Miss Dashwood, I have something to say about Willoughby which I hope might provide some comfort – no, not comfort, but…" he tailed off, looking uncomfortable.

"If you have something to say that will help Marianne, then please do tell me," Elinor said.

"I have, and I shall try to be brief," said the Colonel. "There

Sense and Sensibility

was a young lady, Miss Dashwood, whom your sister reminds me of. She was orphaned as a child and brought up by my father. I cannot remember a time when I did not love Eliza. As we grew up, my love changed and became as intense as your sister's was for Mr. Willoughby, I believe. But at seventeen, she married my brother – against her will. You see, she was wealthy, and my family was not, and my father… We were about to run away to get married, but were found out. I was sent away, and my father made her marry my brother. My brother did not deserve her. He did not love her. He was unkind to her and made her miserable. She was left with no one to advise her and, well, she was unfaithful to him, and became pregnant by another man. I was with my regiment in the West Indies at the time, and heard nothing of the divorce until two years later. I cannot tell you what a shock it was."

The Colonel paused, clearly upset.

"By the time I got back," he continued, "she had disappeared, but I tracked her down. She was living in poverty and debt. She had changed so much… she seemed faded and worn and was very, very ill. I moved her to comfortable lodgings, and visited her every day for what was left of her short life. I hope you are not offended by my comparing her with your sister, Miss Dashwood. But Eliza, with good advice and love, would not have come to what she did.

"She left her daughter in my care. I paid for little Eliza to go to school and told people she was a distant relative. She was the reason I was called away last year when we were to visit Whitwell Manor. She was fourteen, and I had left her with someone who I thought was a responsible person. But while in her care, Eliza was allowed to travel, unattended, with friends to Bath. She disappeared, and I could not find her for eight months. You can imagine what I feared. Then I received a letter, and those fears were confirmed. She had been seduced by a man you know. By…"

"Willoughby?" Elinor cried.

Sense and Sensibility

"Yes. She was pregnant," the Colonel went on, "and too afraid to go home. When he left her, she had nowhere to live, no friends, no help at all and he did not even give her his address. He promised to return, but he did not. Nor did he write, or help her in any way. When at last I found her, Eliza was almost ready to give birth to her child." Colonel Brandon sighed. "Now you see his true character, and now, perhaps, you can guess what I felt when I saw your sister so fond of him, so sure she would marry him. Compared to Eliza, however, your sister's situation is fortunate. She has done nothing wrong, unlike poor Eliza who loves Willoughby as much as your sister does, but who will regret her actions for the rest of her life. Please use your judgement to decide how much of this you tell Marianne. I have only inflicted it on you in the hope that it will do some good."

When Elinor repeated the whole story to Marianne later, she seemed to believe it. But the knowledge of her lucky escape did not make her any happier. Realizing that Willoughby was not the man she thought seemed even worse than losing his love.

Marianne was now even more anxious to return to Barton, but when Mrs. Dashwood heard about Willoughby, she wrote to say she thought it better if Marianne and Elinor remained where they were. Barton would only remind Marianne of Willoughby and, besides, their stepbrother would soon be in London. It would be good for them to see him again.

About two weeks after Marianne had received that fateful letter, Elinor heard that Willoughby was married, and had the painful task of informing her sister. Marianne received the news calmly, although later she burst into tears. Thankfully, the Willoughbys left London straight after the wedding.

Not long after that, the Miss Steeles arrived in town. Everyone

Sense and Sensibility

seemed delighted, except Elinor and, perhaps, Marianne. It was hard to react graciously to Lucy's professed delight at the Dashwoods *still* being in town. "I am so glad you are *still* here. I always thought you *would* stay longer than a *month*, even though you said you would *not*. I am glad you did not keep *your word*." Elinor smiled, but she knew exactly what Lucy really meant: she would really rather Elinor was *not* in town.

One morning, Elinor managed to persuade Marianne to go out with her. They were in a shop when Elinor spotted their half-brother, John Dashwood. John was not displeased to see his sisters, and promised to call on them the next day.

He kept his promise, although Fanny did not come. At the end of his visit, he asked Elinor to walk with him to the Middletons' house and introduce them. On the way, he quizzed her about the Colonel, whom he had met briefly at Mrs. Jennings's. He had somehow got it into his head that Colonel Brandon wanted to marry Elinor.

"You really should try for him, Elinor. You have no prior attachment. Or at least, you know that such an attachment is impossible. But a match with the Colonel would be of great satisfaction to all. Fanny will be particularly pleased. And Mrs. Ferrars. And it would be very amusing if Fanny should have a brother and a sister married at the same time," he told her.

"Is Edward Ferrars to be married?" Elinor asked, surprised.

"It is not settled, but such a thing is in the wind, so to speak. The lady's name is the Honourable Miss Morton. Her father, Lord Morton, has £30,000 a year. It is a very desirable match. Mrs. Ferrars will give them £1,000 a year too, when they marry. She is so very generous. Knowing how great our needs are in London, she gave Fanny £200 when we got here."

Elinor had to force herself to speak. "Your expenses must be considerable," she said, "but your income is large."

"Not so large as some, and I did feel obliged to buy a farm this year. These things cost a great deal of money, you know."

Elinor could do nothing but smile.

"And your father left quite a valuable collection of household items to your mother," John continued. "Obviously that was his right, but we have had to replace all the things she took, and so far not a stone has been laid for Fanny's new greenhouse, or even a plan made for the new garden. So after all of these expenses, we are really very far from being rich."

Having made his excessive poverty clear, John went on to talk about Marianne. What *was* the matter with her? "She has lost her bloom. Fanny always thought Marianne would marry before you, Elinor, but now it seems doubtful she will marry anyone with more than five or six hundred a year. But I am sure *you* might do better than that now…"

By this point they had reached the Middletons' house. Luckily, they were at home and John was introduced to them. The meeting was a success: Sir John was ready to like anyone, although he was a little disappointed that John Dashwood knew so little about horses; Lady Middleton decided that John might be worth knowing; and John was charmed by them both.

On hearing her husband's assessment of Mrs. Jennings and the Middletons, Fanny decided to call upon them both the next day. Fanny found Lady Middleton charming. Mrs. Middleton was likewise delighted with Fanny, who seemed to have so much in common with her. Mrs. Jennings, however, took an instant dislike to her, shocked by how cold her behaviour was towards Marianne and Elinor.

Elinor had wanted to ask Fanny if Edward was in town, but did not dare. However, the question was answered when Edward himself called at Mrs. Jennings's house while they were out, and left his card. Elinor was glad to know where Edward was, and glad he had called, but was even more glad to have missed him.

    Mr. and Mrs. John Dashwood were *so* taken by the Middletons that they invited them to dinner, along with Mrs. Jennings, Elinor, Marianne and Colonel Brandon. Mrs. Ferrars would be there, and the Miss Steeles, who had invited themselves to stay with the Middletons in London. Edward would *not* be there, much to Elinor's relief. She had no wish to see him in Lucy's company.
    Elinor arrived at her brother's house at the same time as Lucy.
    "Pity me," Lucy whispered as they went inside. "In a moment, I shall see the lady who will be my mother!"
    Elinor could have spared her some anxiety by telling her that the lady was about to become *Miss Morton's* mother, but instead assured her that she *did* pity her, much to Lucy's disappointment. She had rather been hoping that Elinor would be jealous.
    Mrs. Ferrars was a thin, proud-looking woman, with an upright posture and a sour expression. She was a woman of few ideas and equally few words. Of the few that did escape her, not one was directed at Elinor: having presumably heard of Edward's friendship with her, she seemed determined to dislike her at all costs. A few months ago, this would have hurt Elinor, but now Mrs. Ferrars had no power to upset her. Both Mrs. Ferrars and Fanny were pointedly friendly towards the Miss Steeles, particularly Lucy, clearly to snub Elinor. If only they knew of the secret engagement, Elinor thought with a smile. But while finding this amusing, she could not help but think how mean-spirited they were; nor could she observe the effort Lucy and Anne were making to gain Mrs. Ferrars' and Fanny's approval, without despising all four of them.
    It was a lavish dinner, and in spite of John's claims to be short of money, there was no sign of poverty, except in the conversation.

Sense and Sensibility

John had nothing to say worth hearing, and his wife even less.

Not only was the evening dull, but Mrs. Ferrars found every opportunity she could to belittle Elinor. When John invited Colonel Brandon to admire some screens that Elinor had painted, Mrs. Ferrars, not realizing who had made them, asked to see them. But as soon as she discovered they were Elinor's, she passed them on without even looking at them.

"Do you not think the style is similar to Miss Morton's?" Fanny said, as she took them back. "*She* paints delightfully!"

"Indeed!" her mother replied. "But *she* does everything well."

Marianne had, throughout the evening, noticed all the snubs, and this was the last straw. "What is Miss Morton to us?" she suddenly cried out. "Who knows or cares about her? It is Elinor we are talking about. Dear Elinor, do not mind them. Do not let them make you unhappy." And she burst into tears.

Elinor was far more upset by Marianne's outburst than by the snubs. But she was glad to see that the Colonel reacted with sympathy and concern: he jumped up and went over to Marianne when she began to cry.

"Poor Marianne!" she overheard her brother say to the Colonel, in a low voice later on. "Her health is not as good as her sister's, and, unlike Elinor, she is very nervous. It must be very trying for a young woman to lose her looks. You would not think it, but until a few months ago, she was as beautiful as Elinor."

After what seemed like an eternity, the evening ended. Elinor was grateful to have seen how very unpleasant Mrs. Ferrars was – how mean and full of pride; how determined to dislike her. Had she and Edward married, the obstacles would have been immense.

When Lucy visited the following day, she was delighted with the evening, but clearly oblivious to the fact that Mrs. Ferrars had only been nice to her simply because she was *not* Elinor. "I am *so* glad that Mrs. Ferrars likes me," she told Elinor. "She was so sweet and kind and charming, as was your sister-in-law, and they had no need to be. Are you unwell, Miss Dashwood? You are very quiet. I would hate you, my dearest friend, to be ill… I would have been *so* upset if Mrs. Ferrars had ignored me last night, and looked at me in that forbidding way – you know what I mean – for I know when she dislikes someone, she does so most violently…"

The next day, news came that Mrs. Jennings's younger daughter, Charlotte, had given birth to a son, and so from then on Mrs. Jennings was busy, visiting her every day. The Middletons invited Elinor and Marianne to spend most of their time at their house – with the Miss Steeles. No one was truly enthused by this arrangement. The Dashwoods were certainly not keen. The Steeles were jealous, not wanting to share the Middletons' generosity. Lady Middleton, although polite to Elinor and Marianne, did not really like them, as they never flattered her children, *and* they were so fond of reading.

A few days later, Fanny was obliged to take Elinor and Marianne to a musical party. The hostess had met them at Fanny's house, mistakenly thought that they must be staying with her, and had extended the invitation to them. It was most inconvenient, as Fanny would have to pretend to be pleasant to them. The events of the evening were unremarkable, with two exceptions.

The first was that Elinor was introduced to Edward's brother, Robert. She soon realized that the two brothers were as different as could be. Robert was vain and arrogant, and wholly unlikable. He began by telling her that Edward was so awkward because he had not had the right sort of education. He then prattled on about nothing until the music started. Elinor nodded at everything he said: she did not think him worth the bother of argument.

The second occurred when John Dashwood, bored by the music, had the idea of inviting his sisters to stay. When he told his wife, for one terrible moment she found herself struggling to come up with a valid objection. Luckily, she suddenly had the idea of inviting the delightful Miss Steeles to stay. Of course they did not have room for both the Miss Steeles *and* the Miss Dashwoods. The next day, rejoicing in her escape and at her own cleverness, Fanny invited the Miss Steeles, which made Lucy very happy indeed.

It was about a week later that Mrs. Jennings came back from her daughter Charlotte's with some shocking gossip. Fanny had found out that Lucy and Edward were engaged to be married!

"It was poor Anne, such a well-meaning creature, who told her," Mrs. Jennings said. "Seeing how much Fanny seemed to like Lucy, she had seen no reason not to tell. But when she let it drop, Fanny became hysterical. She screamed at Lucy with such violence that Lucy fainted. Apparently, it was only because Mr. Dashwood dropped to his knees and begged that his wife allowed the Miss Steeles to pack their things before being thrown out of the house! Mrs. Dashwood became so hysterical that her husband had to send for a doctor! I have no pity for her. I never understand why people make such a to-do about money and social standing…"

Eventually, Mrs. Jennings came to a stop, and Elinor realized she would have to tell Marianne about Edward before Mrs. Jennings repeated the story to her. It would not be a pleasant task, as Marianne clearly regarded Elinor's 'inevitable' marriage to Edward as consolation for her own disappointment. She did not want to damage Marianne's opinion of Edward either, and was determined to tell Marianne without dwelling on her own feelings or demanding pity.

Marianne listened in horror as Elinor gave her the news in as unemotional a manner as she could manage. In fact, she succeeded so well that it was Elinor who had to comfort Marianne, rather than the other way around.

Sense and Sensibility

"You have known for *four months*!" Marianne cried. "Why did you not say anything? Did you not love him?"

"I did," Elinor replied calmly. "But he is not the only one I loved. I wanted to spare you my suffering. I am suffering no longer. I firmly believe that Edward has done no wrong. He may regret this, but he has promised to marry Lucy, and so he must. It is not impossible that he may be happy with her, in time."

This way of thinking was alien to Marianne. Surely Elinor could only be so calm because she had never really had strong feelings for Edward in the first place, in which case she could not have suffered very deeply when she had heard about his engagement to Lucy. She did not quite say this, but Elinor knew her sister well enough to guess what she was thinking. At last her composure crumbled.

"I *did* feel, Marianne. For four months, I have had to keep this to myself, while all the time I had to listen to Lucy boasting about it over and over. And, as you know, this was not the only thing making me unhappy. If you think I am capable of feeling anything at all, surely you must believe that I have suffered *now*. I have not achieved my present state of calm as easily as you think, but only very slowly, by painful effort."

Marianne was quiet for a moment, then she flung her arms around her sister's neck. "Oh, Elinor," she sobbed, "how dreadfully I have behaved towards you! How ungrateful I have been!" Elinor hugged her back, and the two cried.

Elinor made her sister promise not to mention to anyone how she had once hoped to marry Edward, or how hurt she was, and not to behave any differently towards Edward or Lucy. These were difficult things for Marianne to promise, but she felt so guilty about how thoughtless she had been towards Elinor that she agreed, and did her best to keep her word.

John visited the next day to deliver the news about Lucy.

Sense and Sensibility

"Fanny was so terribly upset, but she has borne it with the strength of an angel," he told them. "Although she fears she will never think well of anyone again. And after all she has done for those girls! 'How I wish I had invited your sisters instead,' she said to me…" John paused to be thanked by his sisters, then continued. "And what poor Mrs. Ferrars has suffered! For Edward to go behind her back like this. She was *quite* in an agony. Edward was sent for, so that his mother could put an end to the engagement, but instead… I have never seen Edward so stubborn and unfeeling. Even after his mother explained what a generous settlement she would give him if he married Miss Morton, he *persisted* in saying he would make this *low* connection. Mrs. Ferrars vowed to give him nothing, said she would never see him again and that she would make sure he failed in any profession he attempted. Still he would not back down!"

"Well, it sounds as if he acted like an honest man, standing by his promise," Mrs. Jennings declared. "How did it end?"

"Not well, ma'am. He was dismissed by his mother, and left. Where he went, we do not know."

"The poor young man! What is to become of him!"

"Indeed. How is he to live on a mere two thousand? And his mother now intends to give his inheritance to his younger brother, Robert! I cannot imagine anything worse."

When he had left, all three ladies found it impossible to hold back their outrage at Mrs. Ferrars and Fanny. But only Elinor and Marianne knew just how much Edward was really sacrificing.

A few days later, Elinor and Mrs. Jennings went for a walk in Kensington Gardens. Mrs. Jennings was chatting to a friend she had bumped into, when Elinor was suddenly accosted by Anne Steele. "Get it all out of her," Mrs. Jennings whispered before going back to her own conversation. But Anne Steele was more than willing to talk without any encouragement whatsoever.

Sense and Sensibility

"I am so glad to see you. Is Mrs. Jennings angry with us? Is Lady Middleton? Goodness, I have had such a terrible time. Lucy was furious with me, but she has come round and we are friends again. Miss Dashwood, people can say what they want about Mr. Ferrars not wanting to marry Lucy any more, but it is not true."

"I never heard such a thing," Elinor replied.

"Oh, but Miss Godby told Miss Sparks who told me that Mr. Ferrars would never give up Miss Morton with her thirty thousand for Lucy with nothing. And my cousin said the same and then we did not see Edward for days. But he came yesterday and said he had told his mother he loved Lucy, although he said that as he now had almost nothing, it would be unkind to hold her to the engagement. He could not bear for her to have to live on so little. But of course Lucy would not hear a word of it, and spoke such words of love that I cannot possibly repeat. Edward was monstrously pleased and they decided they would wait to marry until he had a position as a vicar, and after that I heard no more because my cousin arrived, so I was forced to go into the room and interrupt them."

"Interrupt them! But were you not already in the same room?" Elinor asked.

"The same room? La! No. Do you really think they would have said all that, Miss Dashwood, if someone else were present? Surely you must know better than that!" Anne laughed. "Goodness, no! I was listening at the door."

"If I had known that, I would not have listened to what you had to say!" Elinor said, shocked. "How could you do such a thing to your sister?"

"Ah, that was *nothing*! She would do the same to me. Anyway, Edward plans to go to Oxford. Goodness, his mother is a nasty woman. And his sister! I was worried she would ask me to return the sewing kit she gave me, so I hid it! Ah! There is my cousin. I must go. Do tell Mrs. Jennings I am so glad she is not angry and that we would be happy to come and stay with her *any* time…"

On the way home, Mrs. Jennings was keen to hear all. Elinor kept her account to a bare minimum, but it did not stop Mrs. Jennings predicting their future with little money, no servants and a baby born every year.

The next day, Elinor received a letter from Lucy herself. In it, she said she had urged Edward to break off the engagement for his own sake, but he would not hear of it. He had told her she was far more important to him than his mother or money.

It was now almost two months since Elinor and Marianne had come to London, and they longed to return to Barton. Mrs. Jennings persuaded them to come and stay with her daughter Charlotte at her house in Somerset. The house was rather too close to the Willoughbys' country home, but it was also only a day from Barton. So they agreed to stay there for a week, and then go home.

Shortly before they left, Colonel Brandon came to visit one last time to talk to Elinor. What he had to say surprised her greatly.

"I have heard," he said, "how your friend Mr. Ferrars has been cast off because of his engagement to a young woman. Is this so?"

Elinor nodded.

"It is cruel to separate two young people who are in love… I have a proposal, Miss Dashwood. I understand Mr. Ferrars is to become a vicar. I can offer him a position in my village at Delaford. The salary is not large, but – would you tell him?"

Elinor agreed to do so. She was very grateful to the Colonel for the offer, although it pained her to be the one to tell Edward the news. If Edward accepted, it would mean he could marry Lucy sooner rather than later.

When the Colonel had gone, she sat down to write to Edward. No sooner had she started, than the doorbell rang, and Edward himself was shown into the room. After a short, embarrassed silence, Elinor told him of the Colonel's offer. "How is this possible?" Edward said, astonished. "I realize I must owe this to you, to your goodness. I wish I could express how very grateful I am, but – but you know I am not good with words…"

"No," Elinor said. "This is entirely Colonel Brandon's idea."

"Then I must go and give him the thanks which you will not allow me to give you," Edward said, clearly not quite believing her. "And reassure him that he has made me a very… happy man."

And with that, he left, leaving Elinor thinking sadly, "When I see him again, he will be Lucy's husband."

On her last day in London, Elinor decided she should visit John and Fanny. When she arrived, John was keen to speak to her before she saw Fanny. He had heard about the Colonel's offer to Edward. "Whatever you do, do not mention it to Fanny," he begged her. "It will only upset her." Then, "We are now thinking of marrying *Robert* to Miss Morton."

Elinor could not help but smile. "And the lady has no choice in the matter? You make it sound as if it is all the same to her whether she marries Robert or Edward."

"There is no difference between them," John sniffed. "She will still be marrying the richest son."

There was a short silence. Then he said, "You know, Elinor, Mrs. Ferrars has suggested that she might not have been *half* so angry had Edward proposed a certain *other* connection than the one he is now intent on."

Elinor, of course, knew full well what he meant: if Edward had wanted to marry *her*, it would have been the lesser of the two evils.

"Not that this can be of much concern to you now," John said. "Have you seen the Colonel lately?" he added.

Elinor was, perhaps thankfully, spared the need to respond by the arrival of Robert Ferrars. Robert had also heard of the

Sense and Sensibility

Colonel's offer to Edward, and seemed to find the idea of Edward becoming a vicar ridiculous. "The very idea of him saying his prayers all dressed in white," he guffawed. "It is such a joke!"

Elinor could not help looking at him with contempt as he spoke, but he did not notice.

"Oh, poor Edward," he drawled, after he had finally finished laughing. "He really does have a good heart. You do not know him well, Miss Dashwood, so you must not judge him harshly. We cannot *all* be born with good social skills. He is ruined forever, over a mere awkward country girl who has no style, elegance or beauty. I am shocked, but not at all surprised."

At that point, Fanny entered the room and the subject matter was hurriedly dropped.

It was early April when Mrs. Jennings, Charlotte and the Dashwoods left London to go and stay at Charlotte's house in Somerset. Colonel Brandon went too.

Marianne, delighted to be back in the countryside, enjoyed walking around the grounds of the house. Then one day, after an unwise walk in the rain, she came down with a terrible cold. The cold got worse and, when she developed a fever, they sent for the doctor. He was confident that the infection would pass in a few days, but there was now no question of going home as planned.

By the end of the fourth day, Marianne was worse than ever and woke in the night delirious. Elinor was very worried. She had not wanted to trouble her mother before, but now felt she should send for her. In the morning, to her immense relief, Colonel Brandon volunteered to take a message.

"Is Mama coming?" Marianne murmured feverishly as Elinor sat at her bedside. "I might not see her unless she comes soon."

"Soon," Elinor told her, her heart full of dread. What if she had not sent for her mother early enough?

Sense and Sensibility

When the doctor arrived, his confidence in Marianne's recovery comforted Elinor at first. But as the hours passed, Marianne still seemed no better, and a feeling of hopelessness came over her.

By noon, Marianne's pulse seemed a little stronger, and Elinor felt a cautious tendril of hope returning. She felt its anxious flutter as she bent over her sister to watch for she knew not what. Marianne gradually seemed to improve and, when the doctor returned later, he declared that she was out of danger. A strong and silent joy swelled Elinor's heart.

By evening, Elinor had only left Marianne's side once, and then only very briefly. She had not eaten all day, nor slept since the night before last, but she refused to leave her sister's side to rest.

At eight o'clock, she heard a carriage outside. How could the Colonel and her mother have got there so quickly? She rushed downstairs, her heart beating fast with joy at the prospect of seeing her mother. But when she burst into the drawing room, it was not her mother or the Colonel that stood there.

It was Willoughby.

A look of horror came over Elinor's face, and she turned to leave the room, but his voice stopped her.

"Miss Dashwood, I beg of you – half an hour – just ten minutes – I beg you to stay."

"No, sir," she replied firmly, "I shall *not*. Your business cannot be with *me*. I assume the servants forgot to tell you that Mr. Palmer who owns the house is not here."

"Had they told me that Mr. Palmer had gone to the devil, it would not have turned me away," Willoughby replied heatedly. "My business is with you, and only you."

Elinor considered what to do. But she was curious. "Please be quick, then. I have no time to spare."

"The servants said your sister is out of danger. Is it true?" Then, when Elinor said nothing, "For God's sake, tell me!"

Sense and Sensibility

"We hope so," Elinor replied coolly. "Why are you here, Mr. Willoughby?"

"If I can, to make you hate me less. To offer you an explanation. To convince you that, although I have always been a blockhead, I have not always been a scoundrel. And to gain forgiveness from your sister."

"Marianne has already long forgiven you."

"Then she has done so too soon, without knowing all the facts. Will you listen to me?"

Elinor nodded.

"When I first met your family, my intention was only to amuse myself while I stayed in Devonshire. Your lovely sister – well, I could not help but enjoy her company. I was flattered by her interest in me and, thinking only of my own amusement, I did everything in my power to make myself more pleasing to her. I had no intention of returning her affection."

Elinor flashed him a look of contempt, but he continued.

"My fortune is not large, Miss Dashwood, and my lifestyle is expensive. My debts have been mounting since I turned twenty-one, and I was depending on my relative Mrs. Smith's inheritance to clear them when she died. But the date of her death being uncertain, I decided in the meantime to marry a wealthy woman. So you see I could not *possibly* marry your sister. But in my defence, at that point, I could not *possibly* see how much I would hurt her. For at that point I did not know what it was to be in love. If I had, how could I have sacrificed my feelings or hers for wealth? But I *have* done it, to avoid poverty. I have chosen wealth which, I have discovered, is not enjoyable without her love."

"So you did love her, after all?" Elinor asked tentatively.

"How could I *not*? How could any man resist? I fell in love with her. The happiest hours of my life were the ones I spent with her. I intended to propose to her, but each day I was put off by the fear of the poverty it would result in. Then finally, I resolved to speak to her, but before I could, something happened. Someone told Mrs. Smith about an affair I had been involved in. Ah, I see I need not explain it," Willoughby said, seeing the look of disgust on Elinor's face. "You have heard the story."

"I have," Elinor replied coldly. Elinor's feelings towards him had begun to soften, but now they hardened again. "And I cannot see how you can possibly explain away your guilt in that affair."

"Can you have heard an unbiased account of it, given who must have told you? I admit, I should have respected Eliza more than I did. But I cannot let you think that because she was injured, she was blameless, or because I was a sinner, that she was a saint. I do not seek to justify or defend myself. I wish it had never been. I did not love her. And she is not the only one injured. Your sister is too, who, dare I say it, was far dearer, far superior…"

"And Mrs. Smith?" Elinor interrupted him abruptly.

"I could not hope to stand up for myself. With her high moral standards she was already disposed to think badly of me, and she was angry at how little time I had spent with her, so this was the final straw. She threatened to cut me out of her will, unless I married Eliza. I found that impossible, but if I could marry a *rich* woman… I spent the night trying to decide what to do. Marianne or wealth? The fear of poverty won out in the end, and I decided to marry my present wife. I persuaded myself it was the rational and right thing to do. I visited Marianne the next day, to tell her I was leaving for London. My intention was never to see her again. When I set off, I was glad that I had made my decision, but when I saw her, I almost changed my mind. To see her so miserable at my simply leaving Devonshire was a terrible thing. And then you and your mother arrived, and were so kind to me. It was torture. When I left, I left all whom I loved and went to those for whom I felt nothing!" Willoughby paused, full of melancholy.

Sense and Sensibility

"Well then, is that all? Have you finished?" Elinor felt some pity for him, but she was eager for him to leave.

"No! Have you forgotten the infamous letter in town? Did she show it to you?"

"Yes. I saw every letter you wrote to her."

"When I received her first letter in town, so full of affection, it was as if I had been struck by a thunderbolt! It was clear that I was still dear to her. Her faith in me filled me with remorse. I had talked myself into believing that I had not loved her, nor she me. That it had just been idle fun. But now, after her letter, I realized she was dearer to me than any woman in the world, and that I was mistreating her horribly. But it was too late. My marriage to Miss Grey was settled and could not be unsettled. So I decided to avoid you both. I thought of your sister all the time, and all the time I had to pretend to be the happy fiancé of another woman. It was unbearable. And then when we met at that party. To hear her voice, sweet as an angel, asking me what was wrong… Her bewitching eyes fixed on me, while Sophia looked on jealously. Then her face as white as death – She *is* going to be all right?"

"Yes, she is. But the *letter*, Mr. Willoughby."

"Ah yes. The letter. Marianne wrote to me. Her letter was forwarded to me at Sophia's. Sophia had heard of Marianne and was jealous. She snatched the letter from me and when she read it, was upset and furious. What do you think of my wife's style of letter writing? It was very feminine, did you not think?"

"*She* wrote it? But it was in your handwriting!"

"She wrote it, and I copied it. I had no choice. The wedding preparations were underway. Oh, who am I fooling? I needed her money. My wife then found your sister's other letters and the lock of her hair, and forced me to send them back."

"You were very wrong, Mr. Willoughby," Elinor said, but she could not conceal the sympathy she felt for him. "You made your

Sense and Sensibility

own choice. And you should not speak of your wife in this way. She deserves your compassion, or at least your respect."

"My wife knew I did not love her before we married. But has what I have said made any impression on you? Do you still think me just as guilty? Not *all* my motives were bad ones. Will you repeat this to your sister? Tell her I am miserable and sorry, and that I have never wavered in my love for her."

"I will tell her what is necessary," said Elinor, "but you still have not told me how you came to be here."

"I bumped into Sir John in London. He told me Marianne was dying of a fever, and I decided to come as soon as possible. So now you know everything, Miss Dashwood."

Elinor was silent. She was pondering how this man, who was naturally open, honest and affectionate, had been spoilt by acquiring money and independence at too young an age. The world had made him extravagant and vain, and extravagance and vanity had made him cold-hearted and selfish. His vanity had brought him close to Marianne, but his extravagance had taken him away from her. In the end, not only Marianne, but he too suffered.

"I shall leave now," Willoughby interrupted her train of thought. "And live in dread of one event: your sister's marriage."

"That will not make her more lost to you than she already is, Mr. Willoughby."

Willoughby shook his head. "Goodbye, and God bless you!" And with these words, he hurried out of the room.

Elinor's mind was a whirlwind of thoughts and emotions. She felt sad for Marianne, and found herself regretting that Willoughby could not be part of their lives. But she also realized she had been partly swayed by his personality, rather than by reason. When she returned to her sister, her heart was full, and her mind in turmoil.

When Mrs. Dashwood finally arrived, she was too overcome

with happiness to speak, at first, after hours of frantic worry. She was determined to sit up all night with Marianne, and Elinor was at last persuaded to go to bed. However Elinor was unable to sleep, in spite of her exhaustion. Her thoughts kept her awake. She dreaded having to tell Marianne what Willoughby had told her – dreaded what effect it might have. For a moment, she even wished Willoughby's wife might die, so that he could marry Marianne.

Marianne's health improved the next day, no doubt helped by Mrs. Dashwood's cheerful mood. Mrs. Dashwood's cheerful mood was, meanwhile, improved by Colonel Brandon telling her that he loved Marianne, and had done ever since the first moment he saw her. Mrs. Dashwood, who had once championed Willoughby, now declared the Colonel a most excellent, noble and sincere man. Willoughby… well, there had always been something in his eyes… Marianne could never have been truly happy with him.

Within a week, Marianne was well enough to go home. On the journey, she seemed calmer and more contented than she had been in a long while. But as they got closer to Barton, every tree and field seemed to bring back painful memories. At one point Marianne wept, but she did so without drawing attention to it as she would once have done. She seemed determined to be cheerful, and not to wallow in memories of Willoughby. She planned walks for when she was better, and resolved to study and devote her time to reading and music.

Just a few days later, Marianne was well enough to go for a short walk with Elinor, and it was she who raised the subject of Willoughby. "I no longer have any regrets," she began, as she spotted the place where she had first met him. "And I do not want to talk about how I felt, or how I feel now. But there is one thing that would make me happier. If I could believe that he was not always pretending, that he was not always deceiving me, and, above all, that he is not the wicked person I fear he is, after hearing stories about that poor girl. It is not just because I do not want to think of him as being bad, but also because of how it makes me think of myself. How foolish I must have been to fall in love with such a man."

"But if he is not wicked, then how else would you explain the way he behaved?" Elinor asked cautiously.

"I would suppose him… fickle. Very, very fickle," Marianne replied. Elinor was silent, unsure whether to say more or not.

"I am not wishing him too much good," Marianne continued with a sigh, "when I wish that his thoughts about what has happened may be no more painful than mine. He will suffer enough if they are as bad as mine."

"Do you compare your conduct to his?"

"No, I compare it to what it ought to have been. I compare it to yours. My illness has made me think, dearest Elinor. I see now that since I met him, my actions have shown a lack of wisdom with regard to myself, and a lack of kindness to others. My feelings paved the way for my emotional and physical suffering. In my emotional pain, I neglected my health, and if I had died it would have been my own fault. And when I look back, I see everyone injured by me in some way. I repaid the unceasing kindness of Mrs. Jennings with contempt. To the Middletons, Palmers and Steeles, I was rude and unfair. Even to John and Fanny, who deserve little, I gave less than they do deserve. But above all, I have wronged you. I knew you were unhappy, yet I did not try to comfort you. I was so wrapped up in my own misery that I could not believe anyone else could feel as bad as I did."

Elinor tried to comfort her, but Marianne would not allow it. "My feelings and temper will no longer be a trouble to others. From now on, I shall live solely for my family. I shall never forget Willoughby, of course, but my memory of him will be controlled." She paused, then said in a low voice, "But if I could only know what is in his heart, it would be so much easier."

Elinor decided to tell Marianne what Willoughby had told her. Marianne listened silently, holding Elinor's hand. Her face became paler than it had been when she was at her most ill, and tears streamed down her cheeks. But she listened without asking the questions she was bursting to ask. By the time Elinor had finished, they had arrived back at the cottage. Marianne simply kissed Elinor on the cheek and said, "Tell Mama," then walked slowly upstairs to her room.

That evening, Marianne raised the subject again: "I want you all to know that I now see I could never have been happy with Willoughby. I would have lost all self-esteem and confidence."

"Indeed," Elinor said. "Marriage to him would have brought problems which his love alone could not have solved. You would have had little money. He is extravagant and barely understands the concept of self-denial. I have no doubt you would have attempted to economize, but that would have had little impact on him and, in his selfishness, in time, he might have come to resent you.

"Selfishness…" Marianne's lips quivered. "Do you really think him selfish?"

"He has been selfish in all of this from start to finish," Elinor replied. "In encouraging you for his amusement, and then in putting off confessing his true feelings and motivations."

"It is true, my happiness was not his goal," Marianne conceded.

"He does regret what he has done," Elinor continued. "But only because it makes him unhappy. He is unhappy now because he is married to a wife who is less amiable than you. But if he *had* married you… he would have had to face different drawbacks. While he now thinks that having a loving wife is the most important thing, if he had married you, he would no doubt have thought that having a good income was the most important thing."

Sense and Sensibility

Life gradually began to return to normal, but in all this time, Elinor heard nothing of Edward. Then one day, while serving dinner, one of the servants casually said, "I suppose you have heard, ma'am, that Mr. Ferrars is married."

Elinor turned pale.

"I saw Mr. Ferrars himself," the servant continued. "With Miss Steele. She called me over and told me they were married."

Neither Elinor nor Mrs. Dashwood had any appetite after that. They sat in silence. Mrs. Dashwood was afraid of saying the wrong thing. She realized she had been wrong in thinking that Elinor was not deeply affected by Edward's engagement. She had been misled by Elinor's careful, considerate behaviour into believing that her feelings for Edward were not strong. She feared that she had been unjust – almost *unkind* – to her Elinor. Marianne's distress, because it was so obvious, had blinded her to the fact that Elinor had suffered as much, even if she did not show it.

Elinor, meanwhile, realized that, in the back of her mind, she must have held onto a hope that Edward might not marry Lucy. The pain of the reality was worse now this hope was destroyed. The couple would soon move to Delaford. She could see it all: Edward and Lucy in a little vicarage; Lucy trying to keep up appearances, while struggling with a lack of money, and trying to get into the good books of any wealthy friend she could make. And Edward… well, she tried not to imagine. It was just too painful.

Over the next few days, Elinor expected to hear official news of the wedding from her friends in London, but none came. All she could do was wait for the Colonel, who was due to visit soon. Surely *he* would bring some news. When she heard the sound of a horse's hooves outside one morning, she was certain it would be him. But when she looked out, the man dismounting from the horse did not look like him. It looked like Edward…

It *was* Edward!

The man dismounting from the horse looked like Edward... It was Edward!

Sense and Sensibility

Elinor moved away from the window and sat down. "I *will* be mistress of myself. I *will* be calm," she said to herself.

Her mother and Marianne had seen who it was too, and looked at her with concern. Elinor wanted to tell them to behave normally, but could not speak. The three sat in silence, hearing first Edward's feet crunch along the gravel, next his footsteps coming down the hallway, and then he was entering the room. He looked pale and unhappy, as if he feared an unkind reception.

He was not incorrect, at least with regard to Mrs. Dashwood, who received him coolly. Elinor meant to get up and shake hands with him, a friendly expression on her face, but she did not, and then it was too late, so instead she sat and talked about the weather. Then an awful silence fell.

"I trust you left Mrs. Ferrars well," Mrs. Dashwood finally said.

Edward replied with a hasty, "Yes," followed by another silence.

"And is Mrs. Ferrars at your uncle's?" Elinor asked.

"No." Edward looked surprised. "My mother is in town."

"I meant," Elinor replied, fixing her eyes on the table and trying to look composed, "Mrs. *Edward* Ferrars." She dared not look up, but both Marianne's and her mother's eyes were fixed on Edward.

Edward blushed, looked confused, then after some hesitation said, "Perhaps you mean my brother's wife, Mrs. Robert Ferrars."

"Mrs. *Robert* Ferrars!" Marianne and Mrs. Dashwood said at the same time. Elinor could not speak, but her eyes were now fixed on Edward in wonderment.

Edward walked over to the window, apparently not knowing what to say or do. "Perhaps you do not know, have not heard that lately, my brother has married Miss Lucy Steele," he said.

"Miss Lucy Steele!" echoed Marianne and her mother.

"Yes, they were married last week."

Elinor got up. She just about managed to stop herself from

running out of the door. Once she had walked through it and shut it, she burst into floods of tears. They were tears of joy, which she thought would never stop.

Edward became silent and thoughtful, and then also left the room. The Dashwoods were left at a loss as to what had happened, and why Edward had come to Barton. But one thing was evident – he was now free.

In fact, Edward's reason for coming to Barton was perfectly simple: to ask Elinor to marry him. How long it took him to summon up the courage to ask her, how an opportunity arose to do so, how he expressed himself when he did and how Elinor reacted need not be told in detail. Only this need be said: that when they all sat down together about three hours later, he had secured his lady, gained her mother's consent, and become one of the happiest men on earth.

Mrs. Dashwood was unbearably happy, Marianne was so happy she cried. As for Elinor, she was almost overwhelmed by her joy, and it took a good few hours for her to return to her usual state of calm.

They decided that Edward would stay at the cottage for at least a week. He and Elinor had so much to talk about. One of the first topics was, of course, how Lucy had come to marry Robert. Why would Robert have done such a thing? Apart from the fact that Lucy was engaged to his own brother, Robert had said that he did not even find Lucy attractive. Edward said that he could only suppose that the vanity of one (Robert) had been overwhelmed by the flattery of the other (Lucy). He had no idea how long it had been going on. Edward had gone to Oxford directly after the argument with his mother, and had not seen Lucy since. But she had continued to write to him with as much affection as ever. He had not had the slightest suspicion of anything having changed

Sense and Sensibility

until he received a letter from her, beginning, "Dear Sir" and ending, "Your sincere well-wisher, friend and sister, Lucy Ferrars." In this letter, she had claimed that she thought Edward no longer loved her, and so considered herself free to bestow her affections on someone else. She and Robert could not live without one another, and had married.

"Your mother must be as hurt by this as she would have been had you married Lucy," Elinor commented.

Edward nodded. "More hurt. She always preferred Robert to me. More hurt, but for the same reason, more quick to forgive."

On the matter of Edward's continued engagement to Lucy, Edward confirmed what Elinor had suspected. He had felt duty-bound to keep his promise to her, even though he did not love her. Until recently he had believed her to be good-natured, which had made him all the more reluctant to end the engagement.

The pair spent the week talking and filling in the gaps. But, there was, after all their talk, still one difficulty to overcome. They loved each other, their friends approved, and their happiness seemed certain apart from just one thing. If only they had enough to live on. Edward had just two thousand pounds, and Elinor only one. They would have a small income from the living at Delaford, but apart from that, nothing, and neither of them was quite enough in love to think that three hundred and fifty pounds a year would supply them with all the necessities of life.

About four days after Edward's arrival, Colonel Brandon joined them. He had spent three weeks at Delaford, during which he had had little to do other than dwell on the age difference between him and Marianne. But the improvement in Marianne's health and her kind welcome soon helped restore his mood. He had not heard about Lucy and Robert, but was now even more glad to have offered Edward the living, as it would also benefit Elinor.

Sense and Sensibility

Soon, letters began to arrive with news of Lucy and Robert's marriage. The first was from Mrs. Jennings, full of pity for "poor Edward," who she thought must be suffering from a broken heart. The next came from John Dashwood: Mrs. Ferrars was a poor, unfortunate woman, and Fanny had suffered *agonies*. Robert's crime was unpardonable, but Lucy's far, far worse. Neither were to be mentioned to Mrs. Ferrars and, even if she ever forgave Robert, Lucy would *never* be accepted as his wife. John suggested that if Edward were now to write a letter of "proper submission" to his mother, she might possibly forgive him.

"Proper submission!" Edward snorted.

"You could ask for forgiveness for offending her," Elinor suggested reasonably. "For entering into an engagement which you knew she would not approve of."

"I suppose so." Edward conceded.

"And perhaps later, when she has forgiven you, a little humility might not go amiss when you tell her about your *second* engagement, which she will not approve of either."

Edward agreed with this too, although instead of writing a letter, he decided to visit his mother in London.

In the end, after offering as much resistance as her dignity and fear of seeming amiable demanded, Mrs. Ferrars forgave Edward. When he told her of his engagement to Elinor, she listened calmly. She did try to dissuade him – Miss Morton had a higher rank and greater fortune – but in the end, gave her consent for him to marry Elinor. She would even give them ten thousand pounds on their marriage, as she had Fanny. This outcome was more than Edward and Elinor had expected.

Their marriage took place in the autumn, in Barton Church, and not long after, the happy couple moved into Delaford vicarage.

Mrs. Ferrars, in due course, forgave her other son, and by

her constant attention, flattery and apparent humility, Lucy managed to gain her acceptance. In fact, before long, Lucy went from tolerated, to someone regarded with affection, to someone of influence and, finally, to being even more indispensable than Fanny. Lucy was proof that ruthless and unceasing self-interest, even in the face of seemingly insurmountable obstacles, can yield a good result, with no other sacrifice than time and conscience!

It turned out that Robert had initially visited Lucy to try to persuade her to break off her engagement to Edward. By the end of the first meeting, Lucy had refused, but had given him hope that she might agree after a second meeting. The second meeting ended the same way, as did the third and the fourth… and eventually, rather than talking about Edward, they began to talk about Robert's most beloved topic – himself – until it became evident that Robert had in every way replaced Edward. Robert was proud of his conquest of Lucy: proud of tricking Edward and proud of marrying without his mother's consent. Once forgiven, he was given an ample income, and never showed any remorse at living off what would have been his brother's money.

Mrs. Dashwood and her other two daughters spent as much time as possible at Delaford, partly because Mrs. Dashwood enjoyed being there, and partly to allow Marianne to spend as much time with Colonel Brandon as possible. Elinor and Edward were keen for them to marry and, with so much stacked in this direction, what else could Marianne do?

Marianne Dashwood was born to an extraordinary fate. She was born to discover that some of her most dearly-held beliefs were wrong, and in the end to break her most treasured rules. She was born to overcome a love formed as late in life as seventeen years old and, with no feelings better than great respect and lively friendship, to agree voluntarily to marry another man. A man moreover who, two years before, she had considered too old to marry *anyone*, let alone *her*. And so instead of falling head over heels in love, or of staying with her mother for the rest of her life, she found herself, at nineteen, a wife, and the mistress of a very large house.

Colonel Brandon was at last as happy as his friends thought he deserved to be. Marianne was happy making him happy and, as she could not love by halves, in time, her whole heart became as devoted to her husband as it once had been to Willoughby.

And what of Willoughby? He could not think of Marianne's marriage without a pang. His punishment was soon after completed, when his relative, Mrs. Smith, told him that she might have forgiven him had he married Marianne – he might have been happy *and* rich after all. He could not for a long time think of the Colonel without envy, or Marianne without regret. But did this make him retreat from society or give up the pleasures of London life? It did not. He did not die of a broken heart, and his wife was not always unfriendly. His life was, in short, not unpleasant. Marianne did, however, become in his mind the standard by which all other women were judged and fell short. And ever after, many a rising beauty would be slighted by him as bearing no comparison to Mrs. Brandon.

Mansfield Park

As a little girl, Fanny Price is brought to live at her wealthy aunt and uncle's country mansion, and is treated little better than a servant by everyone but her cousin Edmund. As she grows up, she falls in love with him. Then one day some newcomers arrive...

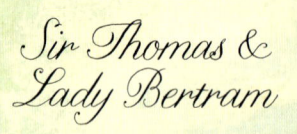

Sir Thomas & Lady Bertram
Fanny's very wealthy, stern uncle and placid aunt.

Mrs. Norris
Lady Bertram's overbearing sister who dislikes Fanny.

Fanny Price
Timid and gentle, Fanny is brought up to think she is a nobody. Will she ever be able to express her true feelings for her cousin Edmund?

Edmund Bertram
Younger son of Sir Thomas and Lady Bertram, destined to become a clergyman. He falls in love with Mary Crawford.

Tom Bertram
Extravagant and thoughtless elder son of Sir Thomas and Lady Bertram.

Julia Bertram
The younger Bertram sister. She is beautiful, but vain and selfish. She competes with her sister for Henry's attention.

Maria Bertram
The elder Bertram daughter. She is also beautiful and accomplished, but as vain and selfish as her sister.

Dr. & Mrs. Grant

The vicar of Mansfield village and his wife. Mrs. Grant is the half-sister of Henry and Mary Crawford.

Mary Crawford

A lively, intelligent young woman who comes to stay with Mrs. Grant. She falls for Edmund, but worries about his lack of wealth and prospects.

Henry Crawford

Charismatic, flirtatious and wealthy brother of Mary. He meddles with ladies' hearts and causes trouble.

Mr. Yates

A wealthy but shallow friend of Tom Bertram.

Mr. Rushworth

Wealthy but rather foolish young man who becomes engaged to Maria.

William Price

Fanny's beloved elder brother. When she leaves home, he joins the navy.

245

*S*OME TIME AGO, MISS MARIA WARD HAD THE GOOD LUCK to marry the very wealthy Sir Thomas Bertram who owned Mansfield Park, a magnificent country house in Northamptonshire. Everyone thought that since Maria's two sisters were just as pretty as she was, they would also marry well. But alas, there are not as many wealthy men in the world as there are pretty young ladies so, six years later, Maria's middle sister had to make do with Reverend Norris. The Reverend had very little money, but Sir Thomas gave him a position as vicar in Mansfield village, which came with a modest salary.

The third sister, Frances, fared even worse, as far as her family was concerned. She married Lieutenant Price, a penniless naval officer in Portsmouth. Frances's sisters disapproved, and argued bitterly with her. For the next eleven years they had no communication with her – although Mrs. Norris always seemed to find out whenever Frances had another child. And at the end of those eleven years, Frances had many children.

By now, Frances's husband was no longer working, and there was little money coming in. So, swallowing her pride, Frances wrote to Lady Bertram to tell her of her difficulties and say how very sorry she was for their disagreement. Her eldest was a boy of ten, and she wondered if Sir Thomas might find a position for him, perhaps at one of his offices in the West Indies. No situation would be beneath him…

The letter re-established peace. Sir Thomas sent advice on

professions, Lady Bertram sent money and baby clothes, and Mrs. Norris wrote the letters. Then Mrs. Norris had an idea: why not take on the eldest Price daughter? They could educate her and bring her up. A girl of nine would not be much trouble or cost.

"Yes, why ever not?" said Lady Bertram.

Sir Thomas hesitated. It would be a serious undertaking. Removing the child from her family could be more cruel than kind unless they made sure they provided for her properly.

"I know just what you are thinking," Mrs. Norris interrupted his thoughts. "But think of the advantages being brought up here would give her. It would be such a kindness. I am a poor woman, but have a kind heart. I would rather go without some of the necessary things in life than see her neglected."

Sir Thomas agreed. "So, shall she stay with you first, or with us?" he asked Mrs. Norris.

"Oh, she cannot possibly live with *me*!" Mrs. Norris replied, and came up with a number of reasons why not. She was perfectly happy doing good with Sir Thomas's money, but she had no intention of making a contribution that might cost her anything.

"Very well, her home shall be with us," Sir Thomas said. "It is important, however, that my daughters remain aware of who they are – without their looking down on their cousin, of course. The child must not forget that she is *not* a Miss Bertram. I would like the girls to be good friends, but they cannot be equals. Their rights and expectations will always be different. I hope I can rely on *you* to help us achieve this delicate balance, Mrs. Norris."

Mrs. Norris assured him that she would do her best.

Some months later, Fanny Price arrived at Mansfield Park. Now ten years old, she was small for her age, awkward, and very timid and shy. But she was pretty, and had a sweet voice. Although Sir Thomas tried to welcome her kindly, she found him terrifying.

Mansfield Park

There was a marked contrast between Fanny and her cousins. The Bertrams were tall and grown-up-looking, attractive and full of self-confidence. Tom and Edmund, at sixteen and seventeen, seemed like adults to little Fanny. Julia and Maria, at twelve and fourteen, did not know what to make of her – they were shocked that she only owned two sashes and spoke no French, and were offended when she did not seem to enjoy the piano duet they played for her – but they soon realized that she was no threat.

On that first day, Fanny was as unhappy as possible. She longed to go home, and could scarcely speak without crying. Mrs. Norris had told her repeatedly how lucky she was, and how grateful and well behaved she must be. This increased poor Fanny's misery, as she thought she must be wicked for feeling this way.

Over the following week, matters did not improve. Sir Thomas's stern looks, Julia and Maria's comments on her smallness and shyness, Mrs. Norris constantly telling her off… all these things just made her feel worse. The house was too large for her to feel at home, and she crept around it, terrified of breaking something. But no one would have known, had Edmund not come across her sitting on the stairs that led up to her tiny attic bedroom, weeping.

"My dear little cousin," he said gently, "what is the matter?" She would not tell him at first, but he persevered and eventually gathered that she was homesick, and missed her elder brother, William, especially. William had promised to write as soon as she did, but she could not write, as she had no paper.

Edmund took her by the hand, and led her downstairs, where he gave her some writing paper and a pen. Then, when she had finished, he slipped a coin inside the letter for her brother. Fanny was so grateful she could barely speak.

After this, she felt more comfortable at Mansfield Park. She became less fearful and, gradually, began to lose her awkwardness.

"My dear little cousin," Edmund said
gently, *"what is the matter?"*

Mansfield Park

Her uncle and aunts decided that, although she was not very clever, she would be no trouble.

In fact, Fanny *was* clever; she had simply not had much education. Perhaps she did not know all the kings and queens of England in order, but this did not make her any less intelligent than Julia and Maria – whatever they might think.

Mrs. Norris did everything to encourage her nieces' belief that Fanny was inferior to them: "Fanny has no *need* to be as accomplished as you are. In fact, it is better that she is not."

Gradually, however, Fanny began to think of Mansfield Park as her home. She was not *un*happy there. Julia and Maria's treatment of her was often humiliating, and Tom scarcely noticed her, but at least she had Edmund's friendship. No one ever thought to ask whether she would like to see her own family. Her brother William joined the navy, and she did see him once before he went to sea. But apart from that, Fanny was to see none of the Prices for some time.

Over the next eight years, life at Mansfield Park rarely varied. Lady Bertram spent her days lounging on the sofa, Sir Thomas divided his time between London and Mansfield, and Julia and Maria practised piano duets and tested their memories of the kings and queens of England. The two girls became even more beautiful, and Tom Bertram grew careless and extravagant, causing his father some concern. Edmund, meanwhile, became an upright, sensible young man, and planned to become a vicar.

In fact, in those eight years, only two events worth mentioning occurred. The first was the death of Reverend Norris, which forced Mrs. Norris to move out of the vicarage, and Dr. Grant, the new vicar, moved into it with his wife. The second was Sir Thomas's departure to Antigua. Some of his business interests in the West Indies were going badly, and he decided he must go there to sort them out. He expected to be away for a year.

Mansfield Park

Julia and Maria were pleased he was going. He was a strict father, and they looked forward to being able to do as they liked while he was away, knowing that neither their mother nor their Aunt Norris would stop them. Fanny was not pleased, but she was relieved. She was rather afraid of her stern uncle. Mrs. Norris saw his absence as an opportunity to 'help out' more at Mansfield Park. She was soon in her element organizing – or interfering in – her sister's affairs.

A year came and went, and Sir Thomas was forced to extend his stay in Antigua. Maria and Julia were now old enough to marry, and with their father away, Mrs. Norris took it upon herself to find suitable husbands. The beautiful Bertram sisters were widely admired in the local area. For years, Mrs. Norris had been showering them with praise – they could do no wrong in her eyes. As a result, they were supremely self-confident and very, very vain.

The best places to meet young men were parties and balls – accompanied by a parent, or in this case an aunt. While Julia and Maria were out enjoying themselves, Fanny kept Lady Bertram company at home. Although she was now eighteen, and old enough to go too, she was never invited. She never questioned this, as she did not think herself important enough to be included.

It did not take long for Mrs. Norris to find someone for Maria. Mr. Rushworth owned a fine house not far away. He was not, perhaps, terribly bright, but neither was he unpleasant. Maria knew him to be even richer than her father, so was happy to go along with the idea. Mr. Rushworth, struck by Maria's beauty, soon thought himself in love. After dancing at the appropriate number of balls, the two came to an understanding. Mrs. Norris was triumphant, Lady Bertram approved and Sir Thomas granted his permission – although the wedding would have to wait until his return. Only

Mansfield Park

Edmund had misgivings. He was dismayed that his sister thought money so important, and could not help thinking, "If this man were not so very rich, everyone would be more ready to think him very stupid."

In July, two visitors arrived at the vicarage. Mary and Henry Crawford were the wealthy half-sister and half-brother of Mrs. Grant, the vicar's wife. Mary was a lively and remarkably pretty young woman. Henry, although not handsome, was equally lively and had an attractive personality.

Within hours of their arrival, Mrs. Grant was already matchmaking for them. Tom Bertram was perfect for Mary, and Julia for Henry – seeing as Maria was already engaged.

Although Mary laughed off her sister's suggestion, in reality, marriage was her aim, provided she could marry well, and Tom Bertram sounded like a suitable match. Henry, on the other hand, enjoyed flirting too much to give up his life as a single man.

The Crawfords and Bertrams took to one another instantly. The Bertram ladies had no reason *not* to like Mary – they thought she was a sweet, pretty girl, and no threat. After the first meeting, Maria and Julia pronounced Henry to be very plain, but agreeable. After the second meeting, they thought him agreeable enough that one could almost forget that he was plain. And after the third, he was the most agreeable man they had ever met, and the word 'plain' was not used at all. Since her sister was already engaged, Julia regarded Henry as her rightful property, and by the end of the first week she was quite willing to fall in love with him.

Henry found the Bertram sisters attractive and saw nothing wrong in flirting with both of them, even if one *was* engaged. Mary, meanwhile, was impressed by both brothers, but slightly preferred Tom. The fact that he would one day inherit Mansfield Park, and become *Sir* Tom, did him no harm. When he went away soon after, she thought his brother Edmund would be dull company in comparison.

And what did Fanny think? Well no one asked her, of course, but she thought Mary pretty, and Henry plain – even after the third, fourth and fifth meetings.

Edmund, meanwhile, was increasingly unsure what to make of Mary. She was certainly pretty, but some of her views disturbed him. "What do you think of her, Fanny?" he asked his cousin.

"I like her very much," Fanny replied.

"But do you not think there is something not quite right about the way she talks?" Edmund persisted.

"Oh yes!" Fanny replied. "She ought not to have been rude about the admiralty, the other night at dinner, considering her uncle is an admiral, and how generous he has been to her. But perhaps that reflects her upbringing, rather than a flaw in her character?"

Edmund agreed. He and Fanny agreed with one another more often than not. But on the subject of Mary Crawford, their opinions would soon be in danger of differing in the extreme.

Over the next week, Edmund became more and more interested in Mary. He visited her every day to hear her play her harp. A young pretty woman, playing a harp as elegant as herself in a romantic setting, was enough to capture any man's heart, and Edmund was no exception. Without realizing what was happening, by the end of the week, he was in love.

In spite of herself, Mary had begun to like him too. She could not understand it. He was not pleasant by her usual standards: he did not flatter or make small talk, and his opinions were unbending. But there was a charm in his sincerity, his honesty…

Fanny had no idea what Edmund was feeling, but she found it natural that he should spend so much time with Mary. She would have loved to go and hear Mary play the harp herself. She did, however, think it odd that he no longer seemed to notice when Mary said things that were "not quite right". Fanny, on the other hand, was noticing more and more that was amiss in Mary's conversation, and was beginning to have doubts about her.

About a week later, Mr. Rushworth invited them all to visit his house, Sotherton. Fanny had longed to see it since she had first heard of it, but as usual, no one thought of including her, until Edmund asked, "What about Fanny?"

"She cannot come," Mrs. Norris was quick to reply. "She has to stay to keep her Aunt Bertram company. Anyway, there is no room for her in the carriage."

"Unless Henry takes his carriage," Edmund said. "If someone sits next to Henry as he drives, there will be room for Fanny."

Mrs. Norris was not pleased, but the rest were happy enough with the plan, especially Maria and Julia, who each imagined themselves to be the one sitting next to Henry.

The day of the trip was a fine one – fine enough for someone to sit next to Henry without fear of getting wet. But *who* was to sit next to him? It was Julia! Oh happy Julia! Fanny sat inside with Mary, Mrs. Norris and a very sulky Maria, while Edmund followed on his horse.

When they arrived at the house, Mr. Rushworth's mother took them on a guided tour. Fanny was enthralled, and hung on Mrs. Rushworth's every word as she told them its history. Eventually they reached the chapel.

"This chapel used to be in constant use both morning and evening," Mrs. Rushworth intoned. "Prayers were read here by a vicar, although the late Mr. Rushworth ended this custom."

"Every generation has its improvements," Mary whispered to Edmund.

Mansfield Park

"What a pity," Fanny said. "A whole family coming together regularly to pray is such a fine thing!"

"A very fine thing indeed," Miss Crawford laughed, "to force all the poor servants to drop everything twice a day to come and pray, while their employers are busy inventing excuses not to come."

"That is hardly what Fanny had in mind," Edmund said gravely.

"Perhaps," Mary replied, "but surely it is better to let people decide for themselves when and where they pray. All those poor young ladies, all the Miss Bridgets and Miss Eleanors, forced to get out of bed early to come here, their minds on other things... especially if the vicar were not handsome. I imagine vicars were even less good-looking in those days than they are now."

There was a stony silence.

Suddenly, Julia, who was on the other side of the room, said very loudly, "Oh, do look at Mr. Rushworth and Maria, standing side by side, as if they were about to get married!"

Henry moved closer to Maria and, in a voice that only she could hear said, "I do not like to see *you* so near the altar, Miss Bertram." Maria jumped and instinctively moved away from Mr. Rushworth.

"What a pity the ceremony cannot take place now, while we are all here together," Julia continued. "If only Edmund were already a vicar, he could marry them right this minute!"

Mary looked so aghast, it was almost comical.

"What!" she said, turning to Edmund. "You are to going to become a vicar?"

"Yes. At Christmas."

"If I had known that before, I would have talked about the clergy with more respect," Mary replied, and quickly changed the subject.

After the tour was over, the party wandered outside, and drifted into separate groups. Mary, Edmund and Fanny headed for a small

Mansfield Park

wood to seek some shade. They had been walking for a while when Mary turned to Edmund and said, "So you are to become a vicar. You *do* surprise me!"

"Well, I must have some profession, and I am sure you can see I am not cut out to be a lawyer – or a soldier or a sailor."

"True, but a *vicar* never occurred to me. Why a vicar? No one with any ambition chooses to be a vicar."

"There are many things a vicar cannot do, but it is still one of the most important jobs there are."

"Really? I think you are fit for something far better, Edmund. Now do change your mind and become a lawyer."

Edmund had nothing to say to that, and there was a short silence, before Fanny mentioned that she felt tired. The three went to sit down on a bench, but before long, Mary grew restless. Sitting still tired her, she claimed. So she and Edmund set off again, promising to return soon.

Fifteen minutes passed, then twenty, and still they did not return. Then suddenly Fanny heard voices. But they did not belong to Edmund and Mary. It was Maria, Mr. Rushworth and Henry. "Miss Price! All alone!" "My dear Fanny, how come?" "You should have stayed with us," they fussed. They then sat down, and continued their conversation as if she were not there.

After a few minutes, Maria was on her feet again. She had noticed a locked gate, and simply had to go through it, so Mr. Rushworth was sent off to fetch the key.

"So what do you think of Sotherton?" Maria asked Henry when Rushworth was gone.

"Very grand." Then he continued in a lower voice, "But I do not think I shall ever think it as beautiful as I do now. Next year will not improve it for me." Maria would, of course, be married to its owner by then.

There was an embarrassed silence.

"You seemed to enjoy your journey this morning," Maria pouted. "You and Julia were laughing all the way."

"Were we? I did not notice. Your sister does love to laugh."

"You think her more light-hearted than I am?"

"Perhaps, although you have much to be light-hearted about. This…" he indicated the house and land before them, which would all be hers when she married Rushworth.

"But right now, I feel restrained. I cannot get out." Maria indicated the locked gate. "Mr. Rushworth is taking so very long."

"I am sure it would be possible to squeeze around the edge of the gate, as long you do not think it is forbidden."

"Forbidden! Certainly not!" And to Fanny's horror, Maria began to do just that, aided, then followed, by Henry, and Fanny suddenly found herself alone again. She was mortified. Mortified by the way they had been flirting with one another, and mortified because she would be the one who had to explain where they had gone to Mr. Rushworth when he got back.

Before long, she heard footsteps again. This time it was Julia. She did not stay long either. Hearing what had happened, she too squeezed around the gate in search of Maria and Henry.

When Rushworth finally returned, he was unhappy to hear that the others had gone without him. "They might have waited for me," he said sulkily. Then, after a pause, he asked, "Miss Price, do *you* admire Mr. Crawford as everyone else seems to? Personally, *I* cannot see anything in him."

"I do not find him handsome," Fanny said carefully.

"Handsome! *Nobody* can call such an undersized man *handsome*. He is less than five foot nine! I think he is quite ugly. We were far better off before these Crawfords arrived."

Fanny sighed. She did not really feel she could disagree with him, so instead she encouraged him to follow them, and soon found herself alone again. In the end, tired of waiting, she went to look for Edmund and Mary.

When she found them, it was clear that they had enjoyed themselves. But what had they been talking about all this time? Fanny could not help but feel a little hurt that they had left her for so long. She was beginning to like Mary Crawford less and less.

When it was time to go home, Julia sat next to Henry again. But this time Maria did not sulk – now she knew *she* was the one Henry really preferred.

"Well, Fanny, what a fine day you have had," Mrs. Norris said in the carriage on the way back. "Nothing but pleasure from beginning to end! I hope you are grateful to your aunt and me for arranging it for you."

A few days later, a letter arrived to say that Sir Thomas would be coming home in November. Maria was dismayed. When her father returned, she was to marry Mr. Rushworth. It was a gloomy prospect. But it was still only August, and much could happen in thirteen weeks…

Mary took an interest in the news when she came to dinner that night. She knew that Edmund planned to be ordained when Sir Thomas returned. "It reminds me of those heroes from Greek legends," she laughed, "who, after performing great exploits in a foreign land, offered sacrifices to the gods on their safe return."

Edmund smiled. "I assure you it is no sacrifice on my part."

"It is fortunate that what you want also suits your father, I suppose. And I gather there is a parish waiting for you. That must be a comfort, at least," Mary said.

"I suppose you think that is my reason for doing it. It has, perhaps, influenced me, but I see nothing wrong in that. Do you think I should take orders without a parish?"

"No parish or salary? That would be madness! But I still fail to see the appeal. A vicar cannot be a hero or experience excitement or danger... I suspect men are tempted to become vicars because they are lazy. A vicar need do nothing all day but read the newspaper, watch the weather, and quarrel with his wife."

"I suspect these are not *really* your views, but your uncle's. He is an admiral, and so bound to think an exciting life preferable."

"Not at all!" Mary smiled mischievously. "These are entirely my own observations."

Edmund smiled too. He thought everything about Mary was marvellous, right down to the graceful way she walked. It was a pity that her views seemed so influenced by others...

With his father returning soon, Tom thought it best to come home as well. He was joined by his new friend, John Yates. Yates was the fashionable, extravagant son of a lord. He was *not* the sort of person Sir Thomas would approve of. He had been staying with some other friends, and they had been putting on a play. In fact, they had been within two days of performing it, when an elderly relative had died, bringing their fun to a premature end.

Yates could talk of nothing but acting, and before long the others had been swept up by his enthusiasm. Tom suggested they put on a play at Mansfield. Why not put on the very play Yates had been acting in – *Lovers' Vows*? They would need some bits and pieces, of course. A curtain – a few yards of green fabric would do. Oh, and a stage, some doors – they would need a carpenter. Some painted scenes that could be lifted up and down – they would have to get a painter in... They could do it in Sir Thomas's study! They would only need to move a couple of bookshelves...

Edmund listened in alarm as the plans grew grander and grander. "You are not serious about this, Tom," he said.

"Not serious! I most certainly am. I have never been more so! I fail to see why you do not approve."

"The subject matter is hardly appropriate," Edmund said, "especially not for Maria, given that she is engaged. And you know that Father would not approve."

"Oh, you are such a killjoy, Edmund. It will be a good distraction for Mother. She must be terribly worried, waiting for Father's ship to return safely."

They both looked over at their mother, who was sunk back on the sofa, falling into a gentle doze. Edmund shook his head, and Tom threw himself into a chair and laughed.

Maria and Julia turned out to be just as determined to act in the play, and Mrs. Norris had already ordered curtain fabric. All they had to do now was decide who would play who. They decided to offer the female role of 'Amelia' to Mary, which left only one other main female role, 'Agatha'. Maria and Julia both wanted to play Agatha – not least because Henry had been chosen to play 'Frederick', who had many scenes alone with Agatha. In the end, everyone agreed on Maria.

Julia did not take the news well. "If I am not to be Agatha, I shall do nothing else!" she declared, and stormed out of the room, leaving everyone feeling embarrassed. But the embarrassment did not last long. The play was *far* too exciting for anyone to care.

The next day, Mary readily accepted the part of Amelia. Yates was to play the 'Baron', and Rushworth the 'Count'. This left just two roles untaken: 'Anhalt', a vicar who was in love with Amelia, and the minor role of 'Cottager's Wife'.

"If *any* part could tempt *you* to act," Mary said quietly to Edmund, "I suppose it would be Anhalt. He is a vicar…"

"Not at all," Edmund replied. "I would be sorry to make such a character seem ridiculous by my bad acting."

Mary was offended, and moved her chair away from him.

"Fanny!" Tom suddenly said loudly. "We need you to play the

cottager's wife."

"Me!" Fanny looked terrified. "No! I cannot act. I – I mean, I could not. Really. Not if you offered me the world."

"If you are afraid of half a dozen speeches," Rushworth snorted, "what would you do with *my* part? I have forty-two to learn."

"No, it is not that." Fanny was shocked suddenly to find that she was the only one in the room speaking, and that everyone was looking at her. "I really cannot act."

"Oh, *that* does not matter! We are not asking for perfection. We can tell you what to do. You only have two scenes anyway and, as I shall be 'Cottager', I can push you about the stage so you do not even need to know where to go. All you need is the right costume, and if you will draw on a few wrinkles, you will make a very good little old woman!" Tom went on.

"Really, I cannot." Fanny was now bright red and very upset. She looked at Edmund, but he just gave her an encouraging smile, and suddenly everyone was urging her to agree.

"What a lot of fuss about nothing," Mrs. Norris said. "I am ashamed of you, Fanny, making such a fuss about helping your cousins, when they are so kind to you! Really, what an ungrateful girl you are – especially considering who and what you are."

Edmund was too angry to speak.

Mary looked in shock at Mrs. Norris, then at Fanny, whose eyes were now glistening with tears. "Never mind them, Fanny," Mary said to her. "Everyone is cross this evening. Pay no attention."

While Fanny did not love Mary Crawford, at that moment she was extremely grateful for her kindness. She went to bed very upset that night. Tom's attack, as she saw it, had shaken her to the core.

In the morning, Fanny left her attic bedroom and went to the East Room to think. The East Room had once been the schoolroom, but was now unofficially Fanny's room. She went there often, even though Mrs. Norris insisted that no fire be lit there just for her. It was somewhere to escape to, to be on her own, especially when something unpleasant happened. There was much to comfort her in there: her books, her plants, her writing desk, a picture of Edmund. But the room gave her little reassurance today. Was she *really* being selfish refusing to act?

Suddenly, she heard a knock at the door. It was Edmund.

"Fanny, may I speak to you? I need your opinion."

"My opinion?" Fanny shrank from the compliment, although it pleased her that he should ask.

"Yes. I do not know what to do. This acting scheme is getting worse and worse. Now they are talking about asking one of Yates's friends to play Anhalt. That would mean poor Miss Crawford would have to play love scenes with a complete stranger! So, I was thinking. If it *must* happen, would it not be better if *I* took the role of Anhalt? It is not that I want to. But I can see no alternative. Can you?"

"No, but…"

"But what? Think it over a little, Fanny. Put yourself in Miss Crawford's shoes. Do you not think her feelings should be respected? Fanny? Why are you hesitating?"

"I am sorry for her, yes, but more sorry to see you drawn in to doing something you had decided not to."

"But do you not see it will be for the greater good? I would have thought *you* would have been on Miss Crawford's side, after she was so kind to you last night."

"She was…" Fanny tried to sound warm, and failed. However, Edmund did not notice, and he left the room thinking he had her approval to do what he intended to do anyway.

Fanny could not believe it. After all Edmund's objections, he was going to act! How could he be so inconsistent? It was all Mary's doing!

Mansfield Park

Meanwhile Mary had persuaded her sister, Mrs. Grant, to play the cottager's wife, so Fanny was now safe. Safe, and relieved, but not at peace. She still could not forgive Edmund for deciding to act, and the fact that he seemed so *happy* about it made it even worse.

As the business of acting got underway, everyone around Fanny seemed happy and busy and important. She, on the other hand, was sad and insignificant. She was not part of it. No one noticed her when she was there, and she felt no one would miss her if she was not. Despite herself, Fanny became envious. She even began to wonder whether acting would be better than feeling this way.

Fanny was not the only one to suffer. Julia was miserable too. She was in love with Henry. She knew that he preferred Maria, and she was hurt and angry. Maria made no attempt to hide her triumph, and the sisters, who had been best friends, were now enemies. While Henry and Maria flirted shamelessly, Julia sulked and hoped that it would come to an unpleasant end.

As rehearsals progressed, people's tempers began to fray, and it was to Fanny that they each came to complain. Mr. Yates said the others could not act. Edmund had not yet learned his part. Mr. Rushworth did not seem *able* to learn his part, in spite of Fanny's attempts to help him. No one wanted to rehearse with him. Everyone thought that Mr. Yates shouted his lines, and no one was happy with their role. In short, no one was enjoying themselves any more. As well as listening to their complaints, Fanny became useful, helping people with their lines and making their costumes. She began to enjoy watching them rehearse, and had to admit to herself that Henry was the best actor.

Eventually, the day for the final dress rehearsal arrived, but there was some bad news: Dr. Grant was ill, so Mrs. Grant could not come. At once, all eyes turned to Fanny. Fanny must know all the words by now. She must do it! Even Edmund urged her.

As rehearsals progressed, Fanny became useful, helping people with their lines and making their costumes.

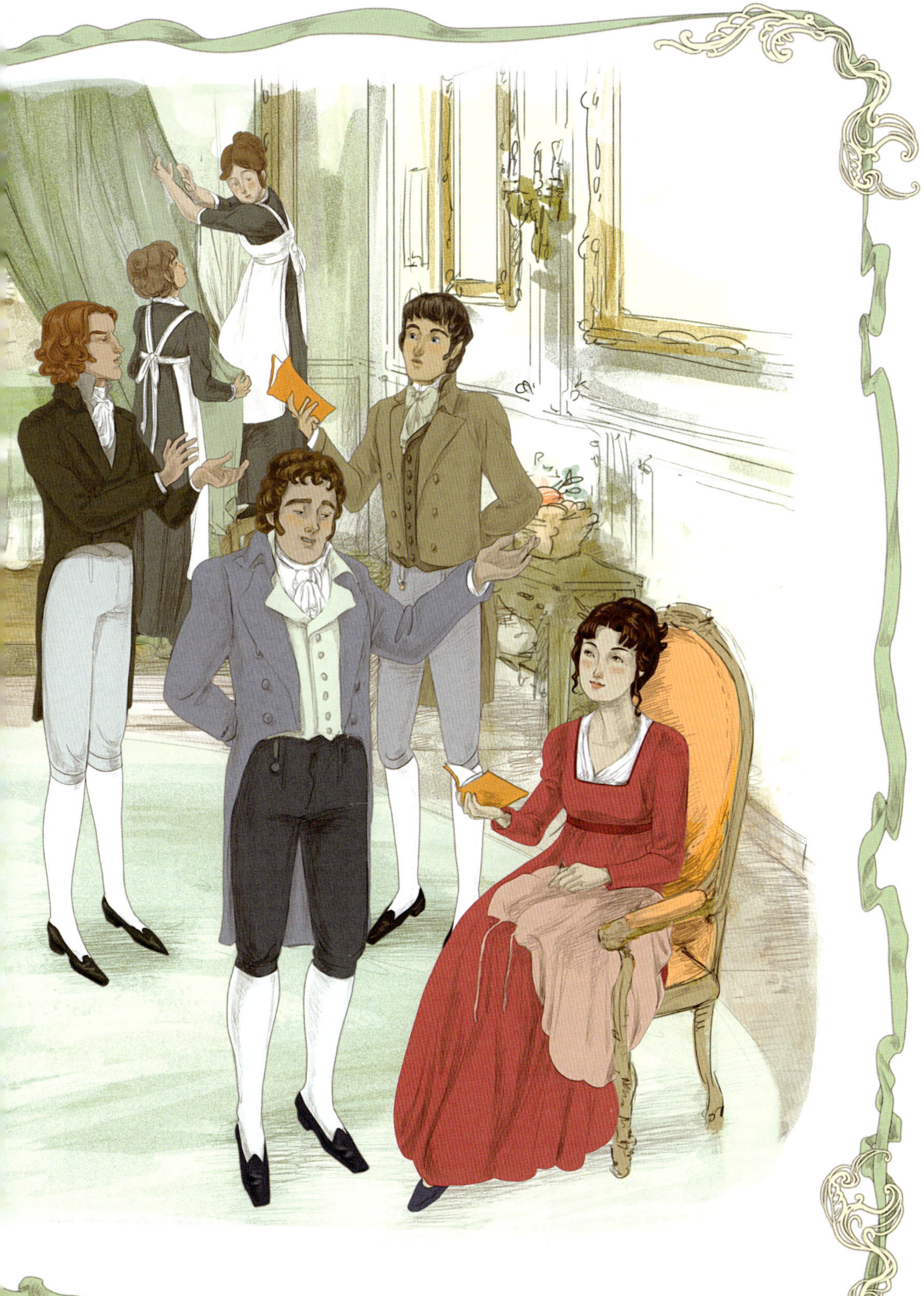

Mansfield Park

Poor Fanny. It was unbearable. But how could she refuse Edmund? Trembling and with her heart beating fast, she agreed.

They had just begun, when the doors into the room were thrown open. "Father has come!" Julia announced.

For a good half a minute, no one said anything. What a terrible, ill-timed, appalling stroke of bad luck! But while Yates and the Crawfords were annoyed, the Bertrams were positively alarmed. They knew their father would not approve of the play. Even Julia, who was not doing anything wrong, was so frightened she forgot to be jealous for a moment. That is, until she noticed Henry, who had been rehearsing with Maria, and was still holding her hand. Her resentment flooded back, and she swept out of the room, saying, "Well, at least *I* do not have anything to be afraid of!"

Julia's departure roused the others. Tom, Edmund and Maria left to greet their father, ignoring Mr. Rushworth's plaintive cries of, "Had I not better go too?" They did not think to ask Fanny to come, and nor did she really want to. Her childhood terror of Sir Thomas had returned. She dreaded to think how her uncle was going to react when he discovered what had been going on. Eventually, Fanny steeled herself and went to pay her respects to him in the drawing room. As she reached the door, her uncle was asking, "But where is little Fanny?" Timidly, Fanny went in, and to her surprise, Sir Thomas came over, smiling kindly, and gave her a kiss. He then asked her about herself and her family, and even complimented her on her appearance! He looked thin and tired, she noticed, and he had not even heard about the play yet...

Sir Thomas spent the next few hours telling his family all about Antigua. By the time he decided to take a look around the house, the Crawfords had gone home, leaving Mr. Yates rehearsing on his own. Sir Thomas was more than a little surprised to find a stage in his study, with a stranger there, talking to himself. Mr. Yates was introduced, and Sir Thomas was polite, but it was clear that he was not happy. It took him only five minutes to decide that Yates was not someone he approved of. And the stage and all its trimmings? Well, it was to be taken down at once. Mr. Yates left the next day.

Henry, meanwhile, had left almost as soon as Sir Thomas had arrived. He left the house, the vicarage and the area, without saying goodbye to anyone but Mary and the Grants.

Sir Thomas was disappointed by the whole business of the play, but was prepared to forgive his children. He felt rather less forgiving towards Mrs. Norris who, he felt, should have known better. For once in her life, Mrs. Norris was reduced to silence. She had not seen anything wrong in the play, but did not want to admit it. The only alternative was to admit that she had no influence over the young people. Instead, she changed the subject as quickly as she could, telling him how much she had helped his family while he had been away, and all the sacrifices she had made for them.

Life at Mansfield Park changed now Sir Thomas was back. He was reluctant to receive visitors, other than Mr. Rushworth, and everyone was in a subdued mood. Edmund missed Mary's company, although he did not say so. Only Fanny seemed to enjoy the evenings spent by the fire listening to Sir Thomas talk about Antigua. She found him less formidable than she had before, and even dared ask questions from time to time.

As Sir Thomas got to know Mr. Rushworth, he realized that, in spite of good first impressions, he was not the son-in-law he had hoped for. He was clearly as ignorant about business as he was about books, and seemed entirely unaware of his failings. Worse still, Maria did not even really seem to like him. Even though the marriage would be advantageous, Sir Thomas did not want Maria to marry Rushworth if it would make her unhappy.

He asked her if she would like to break off the engagement.

Mansfield Park

Maria, after only a moment's struggle, assured him that she thought very highly of Mr. Rushworth and had no doubt that she would be happy with him. Sir Thomas did not argue. Rushworth might improve, he reasoned. And to break off the engagement would be embarrassing…

In fact, Maria did not think highly of her fiancé. Rather, he filled her with contempt. But Henry had gone. He had left her to her fate without a care, and she was determined for him not to know that he had destroyed her happiness. Marrying Rushworth would prove to Henry that she did not care for him. It would also free her from the constraints of her father.

The marriage took place in early November. Everything was as it should have been: the bride looked prettier than anyone else; the father gave her away; the mother was moved to tears; the aunt tried to cry. After the service, the bride and groom went off in a carriage. It was done and they were gone. And soon, so was Julia, who joined the couple in Brighton a few days later.

After Maria and Julia had departed, Fanny became a more important member of the household. "Where is Fanny?" was now a frequent question, and not just because someone needed her to do something for them. Mary regularly invited her to the vicarage, and she and Fanny began to become friends, although Fanny still had reservations about her mischievous and sometimes disrespectful way of talking about people.

Their friendship pleased Edmund immensely, although some of Mary's views still bothered him, too. She placed far too much importance on money, and seemed to think that happiness depended on it. If money was so important to her happiness, how could she ever be happy with him? As a vicar, he would never earn much or live in a grand house. He certainly could not afford a house in London, as she desired. And he very much wanted her

Mansfield Park

to be happy with him, for Edmund had decided that he wanted to marry Mary. The question was, would *she* want to marry *him*?

A few weeks after Maria and Mr. Rushworth's wedding, Mrs. Grant invited Fanny to dinner, along with Edmund. Lady Bertram could not quite understand it. "Fanny *never* dines there. I am sure she does not want to go." But Fanny *did* want to go. Simple as such a thing might seem to others, to her it was of great importance. She had hardly ever dined out before.

Mrs. Norris, when she heard, seemed intent on taking Fanny's happiness away. "Upon my word, Fanny, you are very lucky! You ought to be very grateful to Mrs. Grant. I hope you are aware that there is no real reason for your being invited, or ever dining out at all. Do not expect to be invited again. And do not think of it as a compliment. Mrs. Grant is just being polite. If your cousin Julia had been at home, you would not have been asked at all."

Mrs. Norris caught her breath, and then continued, "And make sure you do not put yourself forward, Fanny, or talk, or give your opinion as if you were one of your cousins. And you are to stay just as long as Edmund chooses, and if it rains, which I think very likely, do not expect to go by carriage."

"What time would you like the carriage, Fanny?" Sir Thomas asked a short time later, on entering the room. "Will twenty past four suit you?" He looked at Mrs. Norris's red face and added, "I cannot have a niece of mine *walking* to a dinner engagement at this time of year."

"You are far too kind to her," she spluttered. "But, I suppose it is really for Edmund."

But Fanny knew that the carriage was not really for Edmund at all. It was for her.

It was a short drive to the vicarage. When they got there, they noticed another carriage already in front of the house. It was

Mansfield Park

Henry Crawford's.

"What a surprise!" Edmund exclaimed. "I shall be glad to see him." Fanny did not feel the same way, but said nothing. She was anxious enough as it was and the thought of another guest only made it worse. On the other hand, the more people there were, the easier it might be for her to stay silent and remain unnoticed.

It turned out that the conversation flowed perfectly well without her joining in. When she was spoken to, she kept her answers as short as politeness would allow, particularly when Henry spoke to her, which he did with alarming frequency.

The conversation turned to the play. "Poor Rushworth and his forty-two speeches!" Henry laughed. "Nobody can ever forget them. Ah, I see him now – all hard work and despair. Well, I would be surprised if his lovely Maria will ever want him to make forty-two speeches to her." Then, more seriously: "She is much too good for him." And then changing his tone yet again he turned to Fanny. "*You* were Mr. Rushworth's best friend. Your kindness and endless patience can never be forgotten, trying to help him learn his part – trying to give him the brain which nature did not. He might not have sense enough himself to value your kindness, but I may venture to say that everyone else noticed it."

Fanny blushed, but said nothing.

"I shall always look back on our acting days with pleasure," Henry continued. "Oh, how alive we all were! I was never happier."

"Never happier than when you were flirting with an engaged woman!" Fanny thought indignantly.

"Such a pity," Henry continued quietly, so only Fanny could hear, "that your uncle returned and brought an end to it."

"As far as I am concerned, sir, I would not have delayed Sir Thomas's return one moment more. In my opinion, everything had gone quite far enough." Fanny had never spoken so much at once to him before, and never so angrily to *anyone*, and when she had finished, she trembled and blushed at her own daring.

He was surprised, but after a few moments' silent consideration, replied in a graver tone, "I believe you are right. It was more fun than sensible. We were becoming too noisy." And then, changing the subject, he tried to engage her on a different topic, but she was so shy and reluctant, he got nowhere.

He turned to his sister instead. "I hear Edmund is to be ordained as a vicar in a few weeks. He will have not less than seven hundred pounds a year," he smiled. "I am sure he can live on that."

"I would like to see *you* try to live on that little," was Mary's retort. She tried to laugh it off, but the idea of Edmund being ordained so soon came as a blow. She had secretly hoped it would not happen, or at least not for a long while. Her feelings soon changed to annoyance. She had thought her influence over Edmund was greater – that she would be able to make him change his mind. He *must know* that she would never stoop to marrying a vicar. Clearly he had no true feelings for her if he intended to become one anyway. And she had begun to feel so fond of him, too. From now on, she decided, she would regard his attentions to her as nothing more than an amusing distraction.

The next day, Henry had an announcement to make to Mary: "I plan to make Fanny Price fall in love with me."

"Oh, really, Henry!" Mary snorted. "Were her two cousins not enough for you?"

"No. I cannot be satisfied without making a small hole in Fanny Price's heart. Clearly you have not noticed how she has blossomed in the last few weeks. She is really quite pretty now. And she must have grown at least two inches since October."

"Phoo! She has not changed at all! You only see these things because there is no one to compare her to, now her cousins are gone. She has a sweet smile, yes, but you will never convince me that you are interested in her because you find her attractive."

Henry smiled. "I do not know what to make of Miss Price," he said. "I have never spent so long in a girl's company without her warming to me. It is as if she is determined not to like me."

"Ah, now I understand. You only want her because she is not interested in you!" Mary laughed. Then, looking more serious, "Henry, please do not make her *too* unhappy. A little in love perhaps, but no more. She is a good creature and feels deeply."

"I am only staying for a fortnight. How much harm can I do in that time? I only want her to look kindly at me, to give me smiles as well as blushes, to keep a chair for me next to her and liven up when I talk to her. All I want is for her to be interested in everything about me, to try to keep me longer at Mansfield, and to feel, when I go away, that she will never be happy again. Nothing more."

"Such modest ambitions!" said Mary smiling, and without making any further objections, she left Fanny to her fate. A fate which, had not Fanny's heart been protected in a way Mary did not suspect, would have been harder than she deserved. For although there are, no doubt, young ladies of eighteen who cannot be persuaded to fall in love against their better judgement, there was no reason to suppose that Fanny was one of them. Nor was there any reason to think Fanny might have survived Henry's 'courtship' with her heart entirely undamaged, were it not for one thing: Fanny Price was already in love – with Edmund.

Nonetheless, after just a few days of Henry's campaign, Fanny had already begun to dislike him less. He was clever, as well as persistent, and adapted his approach to her gentle personality. She had by no means forgotten the past. She still disapproved of him, but… he was entertaining, and so very polite that it was impossible not to be polite back.

Mansfield Park

Henry's cause was helped a little by some news that made Fanny happy with everyone. Her brother William was on leave from the navy, and Sir Thomas had invited him to stay.

Just ten days after the invitation was sent, he arrived. It was years since Fanny had seen her brother, and it took a little while to get used to the new William. But he was so warm, open and affectionate, that they were soon spending every morning walking and chatting. Fanny had never known such happiness and freedom as she did in these conversations with her brother. He opened his heart to her and told her all his hopes and fears and plans.

Henry saw how happy and full of life Fanny was with William, and it made her even more attractive to him. It was clear that her love for William was deep and strong. It would be something to be loved by such a girl. Now she interested him all the more. A fortnight was not long enough! Henry decided to stay indefinitely.

With William staying, and Henry back at the vicarage, the atmosphere at Mansfield Park seemed almost as it had been before Maria and Julia had left. Even Sir Thomas seemed to become more sociable, and accepted an invitation for dinner at the vicarage. It was on this visit that he noticed Henry's interest in Fanny. In fact, that evening, it was impossible *not* to notice how much Henry seemed to admire her. Fanny had clearly grown up a lot since Sir Thomas had been away. It really was time Fanny was introduced to society… William had said how much he would like to see her dance, so why not hold a ball at Mansfield?

"Ah yes, a ball," Mrs. Norris said when he mentioned it. "If only Maria and Julia were here. *Then* we could have one."

"I am sure my daughters are having plenty of fun in Brighton," Sir Thomas replied seriously. "This ball will be for Fanny."

Mrs. Norris was so shocked, she was silent for a few minutes. A ball without Julia and Maria! Still there would be plenty for her to organize. But, as it turned out, there was not. Sir Thomas had already thought it all through, right down to who would be invited, and the date it would be held. It was to be on the day before William left. Invitations were sent out, and many a young lady went to bed that night in a happy flutter of excitement.

Fanny was happy too, but also worried. What would she wear? And which necklace? She had no chain for the cross that William had bought her. She could not very well wear it on a ribbon, as she had in the past – not to an event as grand as a ball.

While Fanny worried about the ball, Edmund had two very different matters on his mind – his ordination as a vicar, and marriage. He was to leave the day after the ball to be ordained a month later. That would decide half of his future, but what about the other half? He knew his own mind about marriage, but was less sure of Mary's. They did not always agree, but he thought that their disagreements could be overcome by love. There were times when he was sure she loved him, but then other times… She seemed to dislike the idea of a quiet life in the country, preferring a busy London life, which, given his plans to become a country vicar, made him think she would either reject him outright, or accept him, but expect him to change his plans.

It boiled down to two questions: firstly, did Mary love him enough to give up what she thought essential – wealth, London society and so on? And secondly, did she love him enough to stop thinking she really needed these things? It was the second question, in particular, which he kept asking himself over and over. More often than not, the answer was 'yes', but sometimes it was 'no'. With this going around and around in his head, Edmund took little interest in the ball except that he hoped to have the first two dances with Mary.

The day before the ball, Fanny still could not decide what to wear, and decided to ask Mary for advice. After settling the matter of the dress, conversation turned to the question of the necklace. "So will you wear your brother's cross?" Mary asked, when Fanny told her about William's gift.

"I am not sure. I have no chain for it…"

Mary nodded and smiled, then held out a small box containing several gold chains. "You see how many I have. More than I ever wear or think of. They are not new," she quickly added, seeing Fanny's look of horror. "Please do take one."

"I – I cannot. They are too valuable."

"Nonsense. Not at all. Please take one. To please me?"

Mary could be very persuasive, and in the end Fanny gave in. Mary seemed to point to one more than the others, so Fanny chose that one, hoping it was the one Mary least wanted to keep. Mary seemed very pleased with her choice.

"I shall always think of how kind you are when I wear it," Fanny said, as Mary fastened it around her neck.

"And you must think of another too," Mary smiled, "Henry gave me this one."

Fanny immediately took the chain off and gave it back to Mary. "If it was a gift, I cannot possibly take it."

Mary laughed, "My dear child, why ever not? Do you think Henry and I are in league? That we have plotted together to trick you into taking his chain? That perhaps it was his idea?"

Fanny blushed. No such thing had occurred to her, but now she felt obliged to accept the chain to prove that it had not. She still felt very uncomfortable about it. It was impossible not to have seen the change in Henry towards her. The way he had been behaving was uncomfortably like the way he had behaved towards her cousins. He seemed to be trying to steal her peace of mind as he had theirs. And Mary, she sensed, was more loyal to her brother than to her friends.

When Fanny got home, she went straight up to the East Room,

where, to her surprise, she found Edmund writing a note. "Fanny," he said, "I have a small gift for you." He held out a chain. "It is for William's cross."

Fanny thanked him from her heart, but felt pained. Now she had a chain she wanted to wear, and one that she did not, but felt obliged to wear. "I need your advice," she confessed, and told him about the chain Mary had given her. She hoped Edmund would advise her to return it, but he would hear nothing of it.

"You must certainly not, Fanny. It might offend Mary, and I would not want you two to fall out, when you are the two dearest objects I have on earth."

Fanny's heart sank. She tried to be glad that she was one of the dearest objects in the world to him, but when the *other* was Mary… This was as close to a declaration of love that Edmund had come. Although in her heart of hearts, Fanny already knew he loved Mary, this was still a stab. It might have been more bearable if she thought Mary deserved him. But Edmund had surely been taken in. He gave Mary virtues she did not have, and he no longer saw her faults. It was clear. Edmund loved Mary and he would marry her.

After Edmund left, Fanny could not help herself. She burst into tears. She told herself to stop being so selfish. Edmund's happiness was more important than hers. Besides, even if he did not love Mary, he could never love *her*, except as a sister or friend.

So Fanny made a heroic resolution to be rational, and not to let her feelings have the upper hand. But those feelings were very powerful, so she still folded up the scrap of paper on which Edmund had been writing to her, and put it in her box of treasures along with the chain. It was the closest thing to a letter she had ever had from him, and she might never receive another. After locking them away, she was able to go downstairs and get on with her usual tasks without appearing in the least bit heartbroken.

The day of the ball came, and with it a note from Henry Crawford. He had to go to London the following day, and he wondered if William would accompany him, as he was due to leave then too. William was happy to agree. It would be a more pleasant journey with company and, indeed, a more comfortable one in Henry's carriage. Henry also invited him to have dinner with his uncle, the Admiral, in London.

Fanny's nerves about the ball increased as the day went on. It was just as well she did not realize that, as this was her first official appearance at such an event, she was regarded by the guests as the queen of the evening. Her hopes were modest: to have partners to dance with and to dance without being noticed too much, and without getting too tired. She hoped to dance a little with Edmund and not much with Henry, to see her brother enjoy himself and to keep away from Mrs. Norris.

Unfortunately, she could not avoid Mrs. Norris, and Mrs. Norris was in a bad mood. By the time Fanny went upstairs to get ready, she felt tired and miserable. But an encounter with Edmund on the stairs lightened her mood. He had been to the vicarage to ask if Mary would have the first two dances with him. She had said yes, and that this would be the last time. "She said she has never danced with a clergyman, and never will!" Edmund said. "I cannot understand her Fanny. I know she is as naturally sweet and faultless as you are, but sometimes she says such dreadful things. I know it is playfulness, but it still upsets me. I begin to think that she and I do not have a future together."

Fanny suddenly felt happier than she had been for some time. Now full of energy, she dressed with the happy flutter one might expect a young lady to have before her first ball. Better still, Mary's chain turned out to be too big to go through William's cross, so she put the cross on Edmund's chain, but wore Mary's chain too, so as not to offend her or upset Edmund. In no time at all, Fanny was ready, and went downstairs to join her aunts and uncle.

When he saw her, Sir Thomas only commented on her dress, but as soon as she left the room, he praised her beauty and elegance.
"Well, she should look presentable, with all the advantages of being brought up in this family," Mrs. Norris said. "What would she be without us taking her in?"
Sir Thomas said no more.
Fanny was happy, and happier still when Edmund asked her to keep two dances for him. Her happiness only faltered when she heard the sound of carriages outside and realized that she would soon be surrounded by strangers. Then, as the guests came in, there was the terror of being spoken to, and having to reply and curtsey. But luckily, familiar faces – the Grants and Crawfords – soon appeared and she was able to relax a little… although Mary looked all loveliness, and where might *that* end when Edmund saw her?
Henry asked her for the first two dances, which was a mixed blessing. On the one hand, it was a relief to have a dancing partner – she believed she was the last person anyone would want to dance with. On the other hand, she did not like the pointed way he asked, and she saw him glancing at the chain Mary had given her with a smile which made her blush and feel wretched.
As they moved into the ballroom, it became clear that she was to lead the first dance, and there was no getting out of it. She could hardly believe it. That *she* was being placed above all the other elegant women in the room. It was treating her as an equal to her cousins! What would Maria and Julia think if they could see her now? Especially when the first dance was with Henry Crawford!
And the dancing began.
There were few there who did not admire Fanny. She was

Mansfield Park

beautiful, she was modest, she was Sir Thomas's niece, *and* she was said to be admired by Mr. Crawford. Sir Thomas was proud of her.

Mary, seeing how happy Fanny looked, thought it must be something to do with Henry. But Henry had nothing to do with it. Indeed, he was making her feel very uncomfortable. She was happy to see William dance, though, and looking forward to dancing with Edmund. In the meantime, since dancing with Henry, she had been asked to dance by one young man after another.

Edmund, however, was less happy.

"I have been talking incessantly all night, but had nothing to say," he complained, as he took Fanny's hand to dance. "But with you, Fanny, there will at last be peace. *You* will not need to be talked to. Let us have the luxury of silence." Mary was the cause of his low mood. She had been in high spirits, mocking his chosen profession again. They had not exactly argued, but they had parted feeling annoyed with one another. Fanny had noticed from afar, and although it was terrible to witness Edmund's suffering, she could not help feeling glad about the reason for it.

Once her two dances with Edmund were over, Fanny was too tired to dance any more. Sir Thomas noticed, and insisted that she go to bed. Fanny took one last look at the scene, then went upstairs thinking that a ball was indeed a delightful thing.

The next morning, after an early breakfast, William left for London with Henry. Edmund left a few hours later, and nothing remained of the ball but memories, and no one to share them with. The week passed quietly, but peacefully, at Mansfield Park.

At the vicarage, Mary was anything but peaceful. She missed Edmund and she hated the reason he had gone – to prepare for ordination. Even though she was angry with him, she began to regret some of the things she had said at the ball. To make things worse, at the end of the week, instead of returning to Mansfield as planned, he extended his stay with a friend. A friend with sisters. And Mary began to feel an unpleasant emotion that she had never felt before: jealousy.

Henry also stayed longer than expected in London. And when he returned, he left again almost immediately to go to Mansfield Park. It was over an hour before he was back. "I could not get away sooner," he told his sister later. "Fanny looked so lovely. My mind is made up. Will it astonish you? No! You must already know! Mary, I am quite determined to marry Fanny Price."

Mary was astonished. It had never occurred to her that he might do any such thing, and he had to repeat himself before she believed him. "Lucky, lucky girl!" she said, when she could speak again. "I approve. You will have a sweet little wife. She will be so grateful, and devoted to you, I am sure. Exactly what you deserve, and what an amazing match for her! Tell me all about it! When did you start to have real feelings for her?"

Henry found it hard to answer that question, but he was more than happy to talk about it – and Fanny. Indeed, Henry could not stop talking about Fanny – her sweetness, her beauty, her gentleness, her modesty, her intelligence, her manners, her sense of what was right... Henry went on and on, but Mary was almost as happy to listen as he was to talk.

"What are your plans?" Mary asked eventually. "Does Fanny know any of this yet?"

"She does not."

"Then what are you waiting for? Even if she does not yet love you – and I am sure she does – you have nothing to fear. I do not think she would marry unless she were in love – she is not an ambitious girl – but if you ask her to love you, she cannot refuse. You know, the more I think about her, the more I see how right this is. I would never have chosen her for you, but I can now see that she will make you happy. Your wicked scheme to make her love you has come to some good in the end."

"Yes, that was wrong of me," Henry admitted, "but I did not know her then as I do now. I shall make her happy – happier than she has ever been. And I shall rent a house for us near here, too."

"Yes, settle here in Northamptonshire. We will all be together!" The words had no sooner fallen from her lips than Mary wished they had not. To her relief, Henry only supposed her to mean that she would still be staying at the vicarage, not that she hoped she would be married to Edmund.

"If only you saw her earlier, Mary," Henry continued, "helping her stupid aunt with such sweetness and patience, her hair arranged neatly, but one little curl falling forward as she leaned over – had you seen her, Mary, you would understand how much I love her."

"My dearest Henry," Mary smiled, "how glad I am to see you so much in love! But what will Maria and Julia say?"

"What do I care? But they will now see their cousin treated as she ought to be, and I hope they will feel ashamed of the dreadful way *they* have treated her. They will be angry," he added, after a moment's silence, "but they will get over it quickly enough."

Henry was at Mansfield Park again early the next day. It was a while before he was able to speak to Fanny alone, but when he did, he had some news for her. The dinner at which he had introduced William to his uncle, the Admiral, had gone well: "It is my great pleasure to tell you that your brother is now a lieutenant."

Fanny could not speak, but she had no need to. To see all her emotions – doubt, confusion, then utter delight – chase each other across her face was enough for Henry.

"I received a letter from my uncle this morning, and came here as soon as I knew," he added.

"This is all your doing? How very, very kind. But how?"

Mansfield Park

Henry explained. This had, of course, been what his trip to London had been about. He had asked his uncle, the Admiral, to put in a word on behalf of William to the friend of a friend. Fanny could hardly take it in. "You are so kind. I must go and tell my uncle!" and Fanny jumped up, but Henry stopped her.

"Please stay. Please just give me five more minutes." Henry took her hand and led her back to her seat.

In the minutes that followed, Henry told her how much he loved her, and loved her as he had loved no woman before, and that everything he had done for William was because he loved her. Fanny was distressed, confused, astonished, even horrified, and for some moments she was unable to speak. It must all be a joke, a trick. How could he treat her this way? What had she done to deserve this? But after what he had done for William... What could she say? In the end, she stood up, and merely said, "Please, Mr. Crawford, I beg you. Stop. I cannot bear it."

But he continued to talk, describing his love, asking for her love in return, and, finally, in words so plain as to bear but one meaning, even to her, he offered himself, his fortune, his everything, to her.

"Fanny, will you marry me?" There. He had said it.

"No, no, no!" Fanny cried, hiding her face. "This is all nonsense. Please stop it. Your kindness to William makes me more obliged to you than words can express, but I do not want... I cannot bear... I must not listen... I know you do not mean it."

Suddenly, they both heard Sir Thomas's voice outside, and Fanny fled the room before her uncle had the chance to enter it. She ran straight up to the East Room, where she paced up and down, her mind in turmoil. She was upset, happy, miserable, grateful and very, very angry. It was all beyond belief! Inexcusable! He clearly could not do anything good without mixing it with something evil. One moment, he had made her the happiest person on earth, the next, he... he had done this! He could not be serious.

But at least he would never propose to her again after the way she had reacted.

Fanny stayed upstairs until she thought Henry must have gone. When she went back down, she managed to talk calmly to her uncle about William's promotion and was beginning to feel like herself again, when Sir Thomas told her that he had invited Henry to dine with them that evening.

Henry sat near to her at dinner. He had brought her a note from Mary:

> *My dear Fanny,*
>
> *I could not resist sending a note to congratulate you and tell you that I heartily approve! There can be no reason for you to refuse him, and I trust you will send him back to me this evening very happy.*
>
> *Yours affectionately,*
>
> *M.C.*

It was clear what Mary meant, but was she sincere? It was all too confusing and upsetting. Fanny could barely eat. Thoughts whirled around in her head. What on earth were Henry and Mary up to? Everything pointed to it being a cruel joke. Everything, that is, apart from Henry's words and the way he had behaved. He had *seemed* sincere, but how could she possibly have made a man like him – a man who had flirted with so many women, all far superior to Fanny – fall in love with *her*? And how could she believe that Mary, with all her ideas about marriage and money, could approve of Henry marrying her, when she had nothing?

Mansfield Park

Soon, Fanny had almost convinced herself that Henry could not possibly really be in love with her. Yet… when he looked at her, the *way* he looked at her, it was very hard to believe that he was not.

The evening seemed to go on forever, but at long last it drew to an end, and Henry said he must go. Fanny inwardly breathed a sigh of relief, but at the last moment Henry turned to her and asked her if she had a reply for Mary's note. Fanny was flustered, embarrassed and desperate to get away. Hastily, she wrote a note and gave it to him:

> I am very much obliged to you, my dear Miss Crawford, for your kind congratulations, as far as they relate to my dear William. The rest of your note I know really means nothing, and I hope you will excuse my begging you to forget the matter. I have seen too much of Mr. Crawford not to understand his ways. If he understood me as well, he would, I am sure, behave differently. I would be very grateful if you would never mention the subject again.
>
> With many thanks for your note,
> Yours,
>   Fanny Price

The next day, Fanny was in the East Room when she heard a familiar, heavy step on the stairs. It was her uncle. He stopped short as he entered the room. "Why have you no fire?"

"I am not cold, sir. I do not sit in here too long, though, at this time of the year."

"You do not generally have a fire?"

"No, sir."

"How can this be? I understood you used this room. I know you cannot have a fire in your bedroom, but in here… The room should be kept warm. Your aunt cannot be aware of this."

"Aunt Norris…" Fanny faltered.

"I understand. Your Aunt Norris has always been an advocate of young people not being overindulged, but I think in this case a little more lenience might have been given."

However, Sir Thomas had not come to discuss Mrs. Norris. The reason for his visit was Henry. Henry had come to ask Sir Thomas for permission to marry Fanny, and he now wanted her to come downstairs where Henry was waiting. Fanny was shocked, but not as shocked as Sir Thomas was at her response.

"Oh no! I cannot be with him. He should never have… I told him yesterday. I told him plainly that I do not like him, and I cannot possibly ever return his feelings."

"I do not catch your meaning," Sir Thomas sat down, astounded. "What is all this? I know he spoke to you and, or so I am led to understand, you gave as much encouragement as a young lady could properly give under the circumstances. But now he has asked openly… what difficulties can you still have?"

"I – I do not know why Mr. Crawford thinks I encouraged him. I cannot remember my exact words, but I told him that I could not marry him and asked him not to mention it again. In fact, I begged him not to. I am sure I said that and more. Perhaps I should have said more still."

"Am I to understand," said Sir Thomas after a few minutes, "that you intend to refuse Mr. Crawford?"

"Yes, sir."

"*Refuse* him?"

"Yes, sir."

"But why?"

Mansfield Park

"I… I cannot like him well enough to marry him."

"How very strange," Sir Thomas said, sounding displeased. "It is entirely beyond me, in fact."

For how could Fanny possibly reject such an agreeable young man, the brother of her close friend, the person who had helped William get promoted? As he proceeded to point these things out, Fanny was filled with shame.

"You cannot have formed an attachment to someone else…?"

Fanny's lips formed a "No," but no sound came out and her face turned scarlet. She would rather die than admit the truth. Luckily, Sir Thomas interpreted her blush as modesty.

Sir Thomas continued to question her for some time, but in the end concluded that he was getting nowhere. His parting words to Fanny were severe. He had formed a high opinion of her since he had returned from Antigua. He had thought her incapable of being stubborn or wilful. But now she had proved him wrong. She was also selfish, not thinking about how her brothers and sisters might benefit from such a marriage. And she was ungrateful… It was a long speech and long before it was over, Fanny was crying bitterly.

"I wish I could do otherwise," she sobbed, "but I am convinced I could never make him happy and I would be miserable myself."

Sir Thomas sighed. "Yes, well, dry up your tears. I suggest you go for a walk. The air will do you good."

Fanny did as he suggested, and when she got back, the fire in the East Room had been lit, and, as she soon discovered, Sir Thomas had ordered that it now be lit every day.

Fanny knew she would have to speak to Henry again, but after that, it would all be over, and everything would return to normal. Henry would not be upset by her refusal for long. He would be off to London soon and would quickly find someone else to attach himself to. In fact, Fanny had almost stopped worrying about it when Sir Thomas sent for her, and she soon found herself alone again with Henry Crawford.

But the meeting was neither as short nor as final as Fanny had hoped. Henry, it seemed, was not going to give up easily.

At first, Henry told her, he had thought that she must love him without knowing it. Now, he realized that she did not love him, but he believed he could make her. He was in love. Very much in love. Of course, Henry had no idea that Fanny loved someone else. As far as he was concerned, she simply did not understand how much he loved her, but when he had *made* her understand, she would love him back. He fully believed that if he kept on trying, he would not, *could* not, fail to make her love him.

Fanny could not understand *any* of this. How could Henry keep trying when she had made her feelings so clear?

Almost two weeks later, Edmund came back to Mansfield Park. His uncomfortable conversation with Mary at the ball had led him to stay away an extra fortnight to avoid her, believing that she would be in London by the time he got back. He was surprised – and happy – to see her in the village, and his feelings for her were instantly rekindled.

He was, of course, also surprised to hear about Henry's proposal… and Fanny's refusal. Urged on by his father, he did everything he could to persuade her to give Henry a chance, and to convince her that Henry would make her happy, and she him. Like everyone else, he seemed unable to understand why she could have turned Henry down. But nothing he said seemed to change Fanny's mind. As a last attempt, he dragged Mary into his arguments. "Mary is angry with you, Fanny," he told her. "I am sure she will come to see you before she leaves for London, and will forgive you, as she is such a kind-hearted person. But neither she nor Mrs. Grant can understand why you have refused Henry."

Fanny had quietly endured all Edmund's attempts to persuade her to marry Henry, but this last statement prompted her to speak.

"I would have thought that any woman could understand that even the most attractive man will occasionally come across a woman who does not love him," she said. "But, that aside, Mr. Crawford took me by surprise. How was I suddenly to love him the instant he declared his love for me? And even if I had suspected his feelings, surely it would have been improper of me to assume that he really was interested in me. Do we not think badly of women who can turn their feelings on and off so quickly and easily?"

"Ah, *now* I have the truth of the matter," Edmund smiled. It was just a matter of time, he thought. Fanny just needed to get used to the idea. But, of course, Edmund only had some of the truth. He had no idea that Fanny was in love with him.

After the conversation with Edmund, Fanny lived in dread of a visit from Mary. She tried to stay by Lady Bertram's side as much as possible, and avoided solitary walks in the garden to escape sudden attack. And she succeeded! She was safe in the breakfast room with her aunt the morning Mary arrived. But Mary was a determined woman and told Fanny she had to see her alone. So they went up to the East Room.

"Oh, Fanny," Mary began, "when I realize this is the last time I shall see you – I fear it is – I realize how much I love you."

Well this was not what Fanny had been expecting, and she could not help herself. She burst into tears.

"I hate to leave you," Mary continued, "but I still believe we will be sisters. How I wish I could take you with me to London so you could see how much Henry is admired there. No one will be able to believe that you have refused him! *Everyone* wants to marry him. Only you, Fanny, could be so indifferent to him. Do you really care for him as little as you claim? No, I see you do not. I shall not tease you, but I will say that you cannot have been so very surprised at his proposal after the way he behaved at the ball, and after all, you did accept his necklace just as we planned."

"You mean your brother *knew* about the necklace?"

"Knew about it? It was all his doing."

"I half suspected it, but if I had known for sure, nothing would have made me accept it," Fanny cried. "And as for the ball, yes, I was aware that he was paying me attention, but I never thought he was serious. Especially after the way he flirted with my cousins last year. I was quiet, Mary, but I was not blind."

"I cannot deny it and I cannot defend him. But I really believe that he has never felt for anyone the way he feels for you. He loves you with all his heart and will love you for as near to forever as any man can. He was never happier than when he succeeded in getting your brother's promotion. He must have gone to a lot of trouble."

Mary had hit upon the most difficult part of the situation. How could Fanny have rejected Henry after all he had done for William?

When the two went back downstairs and said their goodbyes, Mary made Fanny promise to write to her. Fanny would have preferred not to, but felt she could not say no. But at least the meeting had not been as painful as she feared, and her secret love for Edmund had not been revealed.

Fanny said goodbye to Henry that night too, hoping that if she ever saw him again, he would be married to another woman. And the next day, the Crawfords were gone.

But Fanny could not stop thinking about Mary and Edmund. Since he had got back, Edmund had not stopped talking about Mary. He was clearly head over heels in love with her, and Fanny was now sure that he would propose to her at the next opportunity. And that opportunity might well come sooner rather than later. Edmund intended to go to London, and Mary had said she had hoped she would see him there. And if he did propose, would Mary say yes? Something told Fanny that she would.

Soon afterwards, William was on leave again, but he was unable to be away from Portsmouth for long. To Fanny's astonishment, Sir Thomas suggested that she go to see him, and stay with her family for a while. Little did she know, Sir Thomas's motives were not as generous as they seemed. He hoped that seeing her family might make Fanny regret her decision about Henry. Her family had so little to offer her, he thought, that being with them would surely make her realize how much she would gain from marrying a wealthy man. So, it was arranged. Fanny would go to Portsmouth and spend two months with the family she had now been separated from for half her life.
Fanny was delighted. She believed that going home would heal every pain that the separation from her family had caused her.
William came to collect her, and as they travelled, she thought about how she would soon be in a circle of people who loved her – how she would feel love without restraint or fear, and how she would feel equal to those around her. She would also be safe from mention of the Crawfords.

It took two days to reach Portsmouth. As the carriage rattled down a narrow street and stopped in front of the small house where the Price family lived, Fanny's heart was beating fast. They were met at the door by a scruffy-looking housemaid who stared at her, then told William that his ship had come into port. Eventually, Fanny was ushered into the house and down a narrow passageway and into the arms of her mother. Her two sisters, Susan and little Betsey, were there too, full of curiosity about their big sister. Her mother, who looked like a faded version of Lady Bertram, bustled back down the hall to welcome William and to tell him about his ship, before coming back in to kiss Fanny and comment on how she had grown.

"Dear me, what a sad fire we have," she commented, when they finally sat down. "I cannot think what Rebecca has been doing. Susan, you should have brought some coals."

"I was upstairs moving my things to make room for Fanny," Susan replied in a fearless, self-defensive tone that Fanny found shocking. If Mrs. Price had intended to respond, she was interrupted by her young son, Sam, entering the room arguing loudly with Rebecca, the maid. And then Mr. Price arrived, kicking Fanny's bags as he strode down the hall swearing. When he entered the room, he either did not notice, or was not interested in Fanny. But he was interested in William's ship, which he talked about at length, his sentences punctuated with swearing, until William drew his attention to Fanny. Mr. Price then gave his daughter a hug, observed that she had grown into a woman, and then seemed to forget about her again.

William went upstairs to change into his uniform. If his ship was in, he would have to leave soon. As he went up, two rosy-faced, dirty little boys, of around eight and nine years old, rushed into the room. Tom and Charles were eager to see their sister, but even more eager to talk about William's ship. They endured Fanny's kisses but, unable to stay still, were soon running about and slamming doors enough to make Fanny's head ache. Perhaps it was as well her other two brothers no longer lived there.

Fanny had now seen all the members of her family that she would see, but she had not yet heard all the noise they could make. The smallness of the house and the constant running about and shouting was unbearable. Fanny was at home, but it was not the home she had expected, and nor had she had the welcome she had long imagined.

Fanny was at home, but it was not the home she had expected, nor the welcome she had imagined.

Mansfield Park

Some time later, the maid had still not brought the tea. Susan had to go and fetch it. As she carried it into the room, she looked torn between triumphantly showing her sister how useful she could be, and being ashamed of having to do something she thought beneath her.

William came downstairs in his new lieutenant's uniform, with the happiest smile on his face. Fanny stood up in speechless admiration. She flung her arms around his neck and sobbed, knowing that he would soon have to leave.

The chaos continued after William had gone and Fanny was grateful when her mother suggested that she must be tired from her journey and might wish to go to bed early.

The next morning the house was quieter, and Fanny felt more optimistic. But by the end of the week, had Sir Thomas known how she was feeling, he might have been sure that Fanny would now accept Henry. William was gone, and Fanny was left in a home where nothing was done as it should be, everyone was noisy, and nobody listened to anybody when they spoke. And she had thought that this home would put Mansfield out of her head! She could think of little else. Although Mansfield might sometimes be a source of pain, Portsmouth could give no pleasure.

And as for her parents… She had not had high hopes for her father, but he was far worse than she had feared – he was rude, he swore, he drank a lot and was dirty and smelly. Her mother was kind enough, but clearly felt little for Fanny. But at least Fanny was beginning to get to know Susan better, and Susan had begun to look up to her, eager for her advice and guidance.

Over the next few weeks, Fanny heard nothing from Mary. At first this was a relief, but as she became more and more homesick, she began to long for a letter. But when one finally arrived, it was rather a disappointment. It was full of trivia: what Maria and Julia were getting up to, the fact that Mr. Yates seemed to be pursuing Julia… None of it was very interesting apart from one thing. It was evident that Mary had not seen Edmund, so at least they could not yet be engaged.

One morning, about a week later, there was a knock at the door, and Fanny heard a voice. A voice that made her turn pale.
It was Henry Crawford.
Thankfully, Mrs. Price's manners were at their best on this occasion and, thankfully, Mr. Price was out. They talked about William, a topic of which Mrs. Price never tired. Then Henry suggested a short walk. Mrs. Price declined, but was happy to let Fanny and Susan go. Just ten minutes later, Fanny found herself unhappily walking down the High Street with Henry and Susan. Matters got worse when they bumped into Mr. Price, and Fanny had to introduce him to Henry. Surely Henry would be so embarrassed by him that he would, at last, now give her up… Of course, this was what Fanny wanted, but not for this reason. At any rate, Mr. Price seemed a different man in Henry's company. He came over as quite sensible, and he did not swear once!
As they walked down to the dockyard together, Henry chatting amiably, Fanny found herself thinking that, while Henry was and always would be completely unsuited to her, he might have more good qualities than she had previously thought. He seemed more likeable than when she had last seen him – gentle and attentive.
The next day, Henry called again, and the whole family set off for a walk by the sea. It was a lovely day – it was still March, but felt like April. It was mild, there was a gentle wind, and the sun shone brightly. It all looked so beautiful that Fanny could not help but feel happy, in spite of everything.
Even though it was a relief when the day was over and Henry had gone, Fanny felt strangely low. But he was a friend of sorts, she

supposed, and her one connection to Mansfield, so perhaps this was not so very odd.

A couple of days later, Fanny received another letter from Mary. She opened it fearfully, but it contained little news. It said that she had seen Edmund three times, but said nothing more about him. So Edmund had still not proposed to her. The only other information the letter conveyed was that Mary was planning to arrange a meeting between Henry and Maria. There was to be a house party, and they were both to be invited.

Fanny had been in Portsmouth for seven weeks when she received a letter from Edmund. It was a very long letter, and she prepared herself for a detailed account of how happy he felt, and how wonderful his fiancée was. But it turned out that he had not written before because he felt he had so little to say.

Edmund had seen Mary often in London, he said, and she had changed. In fact, she had changed so much that after their first meeting, he had almost left London straight away. She was surrounded by people who were a bad influence, the woman she was staying with in particular. "But I cannot give Mary up, Fanny," he wrote. "She is the only woman in the world whom I could ever think of as a wife."

Well, sadly, Fanny could believe it. Even if Mary refused him, he would still be wedded to her forever. So he had not yet asked her to marry him, but he intended to. The only questions were, when and how? All Fanny wanted now was for him to end the suspense, and propose to Mary.

There was some bad news in the letter too. Although her Aunt Bertram missed her, she would not be fetched home until after Easter. How could she possibly bear to stay in Portsmouth that much longer?

Mansfield Park

A few days later, another letter arrived, this time from Lady Bertram to tell her that Tom had been taken ill, and was in grave danger. He had developed a fever while staying at a friend's and Edmund had gone to fetch him. A week later Edmund wrote that his condition was even worse. It was very worrying indeed.

Easter came and went, with no mention of Fanny going home. It was now nearly three months since Fanny had left Mansfield and how she longed to return. Before coming to Portsmouth, she had loved referring to it as home, but now… Well, Portsmouth was Portsmouth, but Mansfield Park was home, and Fanny missed it terribly.

It had been a long time since Fanny had heard from Mary, when another letter from her finally arrived:

> Forgive me, my dear Fanny, for my long silence. I hear poor Tom has only a slim chance of recovery from his illness. Is it true? I beg you to let me know. I really am quite upset. But Fanny, I see you smile and look cunning. Of course I do not want him to die, but if he were to, well, I would not be afraid to say that wealth and the title of 'Sir' could not fall into hands more deserving of them than Edmund's.
>
> Write to me, Fanny. And do not feel guilty for thinking the same way as I do about Tom.
>
> Yours ever,
>
> Mary
>
> P.S. Henry just came in - he saw Maria this morning in Richmond. Rest assured, he cares for nobody but you.

Mansfield Park

Fanny was disgusted by the letter, disgusted with Mary's cold-hearted ambition. A week later, she received another letter from Mary. Its contents were startling:

A scandalous story has reached me, and I write to warn you not to believe it, should it reach you. I am sure there is some mistake, and that a day or two will clear it up. At any rate, Henry is blameless, and in spite of a brief, careless slip, he thinks of nobody but you. I am sure it will be all hushed up, and nothing proved but Rushworth's foolishness. If they are gone, I bet it is only to Mansfield Park, and Julia with them.

Yours,

Mary

Fanny was aghast. What could it mean? It suggested that something had happened at the Rushworths' house – something which Mary thought would make Fanny jealous – something Henry had done. Well, Mary need not have worried on her account, but it was still strange. Before this, Fanny had begun to believe that Henry really did love her.

She wondered when she would find out more. No letter arrived the following morning, but later that day, Fanny was sitting with her father, when he suddenly looked up from his newspaper and said, "What was the name of that grand cousin of yours in town, Fan?"

Fanny jumped. "Rushworth, sir."

"And do they live at Wimpole Street?"

"Yes, sir."

He held out the newspaper. "Well then, look here. Much good may such fine relations do you…"

Mansfield Park

Fanny took the paper and read: "It is with infinite concern that we announce a matrimonial disturbance in the family of Mr. R. of Wimpole Street. The beautiful Mrs. R., who had promised to become such a brilliant leader in fashionable society, has left her husband's home in the company of the well-known and captivating Mr. C., close friend of Mr. R., and it is not known even to the editor of this newspaper where they have gone."

"It must be a mistake, sir," Fanny said instantly. "It cannot be true. It must be about someone else." But everything in Mary's letter suggested it was true. Fanny had never felt so shocked in her life. Maria had not been married six months, and Henry was supposed to be in love with *her*... It was just too awful!

After another two days, a letter with a London postmark arrived. It was from Edmund:

Dear Fanny,

You know our present awful situation. We have been in London two days, but there is nothing to be done. They cannot be traced. You may not have heard the latest news. Julia has run off with Yates and they are married. I write to ask that you come home for my mother's sake. I shall be in Portsmouth the morning after you receive this, and hope to find you ready to leave. My father wishes you to invite Susan to come and stay with you at Mansfield for a few months. Arrange it as you like. I will see you in the morning.

Yours,

Edmund

Mansfield Park

Leave Portsmouth tomorrow! Fanny felt in sudden danger of being exquisitely happy in the midst of so much misery. She could barely help herself, and for a while she had to tell herself to be upset. Her parents granted their permission for Susan to go with her, and Susan was ecstatic. To her it was like a dream come true.

Edmund arrived at eight the next morning. "My Fanny, my only sister, my only comfort now!" he whispered as he embraced her. His voice trembled and he did not look well. They set off soon after, and passed the first day of the journey in silence.

It was just before dinner time the next day when they arrived at Mansfield Park. Fanny was dreading meeting her aunts and uncle in the circumstances, but was excited to see her home again. Susan was anxious because soon all the good manners she had recently learned from Fanny would be put to the test. Edmund, meanwhile, was leaning back in the carriage, sunk into a gloom, his eyes closed.

As they stepped into the house, Lady Bertram, who had never before felt such impatience, hurried to Fanny and flung her arms around her neck, saying, "Dear Fanny! Now I shall feel better."

They were a miserable group of people that evening, each believing themselves to be suffering more than the rest. Mrs. Norris, touched by the disaster that had befallen her beloved Maria, was a different person – for once, she made no effort to control everyone around her. She was angry with Fanny. If Fanny had accepted Mr. Crawford, she thought, none of this would have happened.

It was through Lady Bertram's rather disjointed account that Fanny eventually pieced together everything that had happened. Maria had gone to stay with friends in Richmond while her husband was visiting his mother. While she was there, Henry had started visiting her. Sir Thomas received a letter from a friend warning him that something was amiss, but before Sir Thomas was able to get to London to put a stop to it, Maria had run off with Henry. Then it was discovered that Julia had run away too, with Yates.

It was three days before Edmund finally spoke to Fanny on the subject. It was clearly very painful to him. Fanny found his first words alarming: he said that he had seen Miss Crawford.

Mary had invited Edmund to come and see her, and he had gone, assuming it would be their last meeting. He had thought he would find her racked with shame and misery, and had felt full of love for her. She met him looking very serious, he told Fanny, but then she had said, "I heard you were in town. I wanted to see you. Let us talk over this sad business. How foolish our two siblings have been!" Edmund had not replied, trusting that his expression said it all. She had then continued by saying she did not mean to defend Henry at his sister's expense. But then…

"How she went on, Fanny. It was hardly fit to be repeated to you," Edmund told her. "She said that she was angry Henry had been so foolish as to be drawn in by a woman he had never cared for, at the cost of losing the woman he adored. She was even more angry with poor Maria, for sacrificing her situation because of a foolish, false belief that she was loved by a man who had long ago made his indifference clear. Can you believe it? She did not think it was so terrible at all, what he had done! She thought they had only been foolish, and that it was only bad because they had been caught! She then went on to talk about you, Fanny, and what a loss you were to him – how you might have made him better, would have made him happy. She spoke of you affectionately, but even then… she almost *blamed* you, Fanny! She said that, if you had accepted him, he would never have done this! The charm is broken, Fanny. My eyes are opened. Perhaps it is for the best… But I would far rather have had the pain of her saying 'no' to me than that of discovering her true nature."

But this had not been the end of it. Mary had also said that Henry must be made to marry Maria, and the best way to ensure this was to encourage Maria to keep on living with him. If she left him, a marriage would be less likely to happen.

Edmund had been scandalized. How could she suggest that they not only accept, but support Maria and Henry's current situation? "Mary is not the woman I thought she was, and I told her that it was for the best that we parted ways. She was astonished, Fanny. More than astonished. She turned bright red, then she gave a sort of laugh, and tried to look as if she did not care. I told her from my heart that I wished her well, and made for the door. I had gone a few steps, when I heard her say, 'Mr. Bertram.' I looked back. 'Mr. Bertram,' she said, with a smile, a flirtatious, playful smile, which invited me to come back, but I walked on. Such was the end of our friendship. And what a friendship it has been! How I have been deceived!"

Edmund fell silent.

But five minutes later, they started discussing Mary again, and at last, Fanny felt free to speak her mind. She told him about the letter Mary had sent her, in which she seemed to hope that Tom would die so that Edmund would become heir to Mansfield Park. It was all very painful for Edmund. Time, he knew, would lessen his pain, but for now he was sure that he could never meet another woman whom he could love. In the meantime, thank goodness he had Fanny's friendship to cling to.

In the time after this, Fanny was happy – happy in spite her sympathy for the unhappiness of those around her. She was back at Mansfield; she was loved and needed; she had escaped Henry Crawford; Sir Thomas was no longer angry with her for refusing

Mansfield Park

Henry – in fact, quite the contrary – and Edmund was no longer Mary Crawford's fool.

Sir Thomas blamed himself for his daughters' actions. He had not known them well enough, and had allowed them to grow up to be selfish. But after a while, things seemed less bleak. Julia's marriage turned out to be not quite as disastrous as he had thought. She had eloped with Mr. Yates partly because she feared a backlash from her father after Maria's actions – that her freedom would be severely restricted if she went home again. But she was now humble and wished to be forgiven, and Mr. Yates, eager to be accepted by the family, looked up to Sir Thomas and was willing to be guided by him. He was a weak character, but there was some hope for him as a son-in-law.

Tom recovered, and lost his thoughtlessness and extravagance. He had suffered, and he had learned to think: two advantages he had never had before. At twenty-six, he became what he ought to be: useful to his father rather than merely living for himself. Edmund grew happier, and after sitting beneath the trees on a warm summer evening with Fanny, was almost cheerful.

Maria refused to leave Henry at first… until she realized that he would never marry her. Then, her love turned to hatred. Henry, meanwhile, came to resent her for causing him to lose Fanny. So when Maria left him, she did not even have the satisfaction of knowing that doing so would hurt him – it did not. She had to make do with knowing that at least he would never be able to marry Fanny, after what they had done.

Mrs. Norris wanted Maria to return to Mansfield, but Sir Thomas refused to allow it. In the end, Mrs. Norris left Mansfield Park to devote herself to Maria. A house was found for them in the countryside, where they were shut up together with little other company. With no affection on Maria's side and no intelligence on Mrs. Norris's, they became each other's punishment.

Mansfield Park

Mrs. Norris's departure from Mansfield Park was a huge relief to Sir Thomas. His opinion of her had been sinking since the day he had returned from Antigua. He had begun to feel her an hourly evil, which was made worse by the fact that he could see no end to it other than one of them dying. She was missed by no one at Mansfield. She had never been able to win the affection of anyone – not even those whom she loved.

Henry Crawford, it could be argued, had been ruined by early independence. Perhaps, if he could have been satisfied with winning the love of one woman, he might have been happy. He had made some progress with Fanny. His love for her had changed the way she felt about him. Had he persevered, perhaps he would eventually have deserved and won her hand in marriage. If his sister had not pressed him to go to that fateful party at which he met Maria again, perhaps things might have turned out differently. But curiosity, vanity and the temptation of immediate pleasure got the better of him. He was not in the habit of sacrificing these things for what was right.

What had happened at that party was that Maria had rebuffed him. He had found this intolerable. Determined to defeat her display of resentment, he set about re-igniting the old feelings from the days of the play by flattering and flirting with her. The problem was that she really did love him, and once he became involved with her, it was hard to escape. In the end, he ran away with Maria simply because he could not help himself, even though he regretted the loss of Fanny as he did so, and all the more once the excitement of the affair had died down.

As a man he suffered less from the disgrace of his actions than Maria did, but he was still punished by the loss of a woman he loved passionately with both his heart and his head.

After all of this, the Grants – the connection between the Bertram family and the Crawfords – moved to London. Mary moved with them, and when Dr. Grant died, stayed with her sister. Mary, though perfectly resolved against ever attaching herself to a younger brother again, had many eligible suitors. There were plenty of dashing young men, some of them heirs to great fortunes, who were attracted by her beauty… and her £20,000. But none seemed to satisfy the high standards she had acquired at Mansfield. None seemed to promise any hope of the domestic happiness she had learned to value there. And none could put Edmund Bertram sufficiently out of her head.

Edmund, meanwhile, had scarcely finished telling Fanny that he could never again find a woman he could love, when it began to strike him that perhaps a very different sort of woman might suit him just as well, or, in fact, a good deal better. He began to realize that Fanny might be growing even dearer to him in all her smiles and ways, and that she might be persuaded to swap her sisterly love for something else. Edmund stopped caring about Mary Crawford and began to be as anxious to marry Fanny as Fanny herself might wish him to be.

And what could be more natural than this change? He had been loving, guiding and protecting her since she was ten years old. She had been so greatly influenced by his care, as she grew up, and she had been important to him all along. What was there now to add, other than that he should learn to prefer soft, light eyes to sparkling, dark ones? And since he spent almost all his time with her, telling her his thoughts and feelings, and she gave him all of her attention, it could not take long for those soft, light eyes to win him over.

Having once set out on what he thought must be a road to happiness, there was nothing to delay him. No doubts about her nature, or about differing opinions and tastes. No fears of deception, no reliance on future improvement. He was already aware of Fanny's intellectual superiority. She was, of course, too good for him, but as nobody minds having what is too good for them, this did not put him off. Fanny, timid, anxious, doubting as she was, soon gave him the gentle encouragement he wanted. It was some time, however, before she told him the whole delightful and astonishing truth about her love for him. His happiness in discovering that he had been loved by her for so long must have been immense.

Their parents did not object. In fact, Sir Thomas was very happy. Fanny was the daughter he wanted, and he and Fanny became very close. Once she and Edmund had moved into the vicarage, he made a point of visiting her there most days, if she did not come to Mansfield. Lady Bertram was not so happy to have to part with "dear Fanny," but at least she now had Susan. Susan happily slipped into the role that Fanny had once had, and she was as well suited to it by a desire to be useful as Fanny had been by her sweetness of temper. Very soon, Susan became even more beloved by Lady Bertram than Fanny had been.

And Fanny and Edmund? They were as happy together as is possible in this life, and their house was filled with love.

Persuasion

Persuaded to give up an engagement when she was young, Anne Elliot is unhappy and overlooked by her family. Can a change in circumstances throw her in the way of a better fate? Will her true value be understood at last by those who matter to her...?

Sir Walter Elliot
Anne's vain father, a baronet, has fallen into debt and has to give up Kellynch Hall.

Lady Russell
A friend and advisor of the Elliot family, particularly Anne.

Elizabeth Elliot
The eldest of Sir Walter's daughters. Proud and snobbish like her father.

Anne Elliot
Sir Walter's middle daughter. Disappointed in love, she has lost her bloom. Ignored by her father and sisters. Will anyone see her true value?

Mrs. Clay
Elizabeth's fortune-seeking friend.

Mrs. Smith
Anne's poor but charitable friend in Bath.

Admiral & Mrs. Croft
Captain Wentworth's sister and her wealthy navy husband, who rent Kellynch Hall from Sir Walter.

Mr. & Mrs. Musgrove

Charles Musgrove's parents, who live in the Great House (Uppercross) nearby and see Charles and Mary every day.

Mary & Charles Musgrove

The attention-seeking, peevish youngest sister of Anne and Elizabeth and her tolerant, friendly husband, who have two little sons.

Captain Wentworth

Engaged to Anne years ago, until she broke it off. He has returned to the area, determined not to forgive Anne, but looking for someone to marry.

Louisa Musgrove

Charles's sister. Merry, determined and full of life, she sees Captain Wentworth as a catch.

Henrietta Musgrove

Charles's sister, who neglects her beloved Charles Hayter when she meets Captain Wentworth.

Captain & Mrs. Harville

Captain Wentworth's friends in Lyme.

Captain Benwick

A melancholy, poetic friend of Captain Harville's.

William Elliot Esquire

The estranged heir of the Kellynch Estate. Will his reappearance on the scene change everyone's fate?

Sir Walter Elliot, of Kellynch Hall in Somerset, never read any book for his own amusement except one: *The Baronetage*, which listed the upper classes of England. He always leafed directly to the page on which he himself was listed, "Walter Elliot of Kellynch Hall", with the date of his marriage, and the birthdates of his children, Elizabeth, Anne and Mary. Sir Walter had added the details of Mary's marriage, and the date on which he had lost his wife.

Sir Walter Elliot was vain through and through: about his looks and his position in society. To him, being handsome was almost as important as being a baronet. He, Sir Walter Elliot, was both.

Lady Elliot had been a better wife than he had truly deserved. She had softened and concealed her husband's faults for seventeen years. When she died, her young daughters had been left to the guidance of their vain, silly father. Thankfully, Lady Russell, a family friend, provided them with kind and thoughtful advice.

After his wife's death, Sir Walter had remained single for his dear eldest daughter's sake. The two others did not concern him. The youngest, Mary, had married into an old country family he thought insignificant, and was now Mrs. Musgrove. And Anne, whose elegant mind and sweet character would have made anyone of real understanding value her, was nobody to either her father or her elder sister. Her word carried no weight; she was only Anne.

To Lady Russell, however, she was a very dear, highly valued god-daughter and friend. She loved them all, but Anne, who took after her mother, had a special place in her heart.

A few years before, Anne Elliot had been a very pretty girl, but her bloom had vanished early. Her father had never thought much of Anne – her delicate face and mild, dark eyes were so different from his own; now he thought nothing of her at all. He had no hope of reading her name elsewhere in his beloved book. Mary had gained no title through her marriage, so everything now rested on Elizabeth. Elizabeth still had her looks; Elizabeth would, he told himself, one day marry suitably.

Elizabeth was not quite as contented as her father. She did not doubt her own good looks, but she was aware of the danger of already being twenty-nine, and would have been glad of a marriage proposal from a baronet within the next year or so. Then she might enjoy looking at her father's book. Now, she did not.

It reminded her of a particular disappointment from the heir to the Kellynch estate, a distant cousin, William Elliot. As a young girl, knowing that he would become the future baronet (as she had no brother to inherit the title), she had meant to marry him, and her father had approved. After her mother's death, they had tried to get to know him. One spring in London, they had met.

He was at the time a very young man, and Elizabeth had liked him very much. He was invited eagerly to Kellynch Hall, but he never came. The next thing they heard was that he was married. Instead of accepting the fortune marked out for him as the heir of the house of Elliot, he had bought independence by marrying a rich woman of a lower status.

Mr. Elliot offered no apology and showed no interest in the family. All contact with him ceased. In addition to his terrible marriage choice, they had heard through friends that he had spoken disrespectfully of them, and that they could not forgive. Years later, Elizabeth was still angry about it. There was not another baronet in the country she considered her equal. But even now, when they had heard his wife had passed away, she could not reconsider him.

Something else had been bothering Elizabeth lately: her father was running out of money. While Lady Elliot was alive, she had kept him within his income. Since she had died, he had exceeded it with a lavish lifestyle. He was dreadfully in debt.

Neither Elizabeth nor her father could see how to lessen their expenses whilst keeping their dignity and the comforts they could not bear to do without. Dividing the estate was unthinkable. Kellynch must be passed on whole, as Sir Walter had received it. Their two confidential friends, Lady Russell and Mr. Shepherd, were called upon to advise them.

Mr. Shepherd, a cautious and polite lawyer, was reluctant to suggest anything disagreeable to Sir Walter, and so recommended they follow Lady Russell's excellent judgement on the matter.

Lady Russell gave the subject much serious thought. She found it difficult to come to a decision because of two conflicting principles: she wanted to save Sir Walter's feelings as much as the family's money. He was a baronet, after all, and some compassion had to be felt for his present difficulties.

She thought of ways to cut back with the least possible pain to Sir Walter and Elizabeth. And she did what no one else had thought of doing: she consulted Anne. "If I can persuade your father to accept these measures," Lady Russell said, showing Anne her calculations, "in seven years he will be clear of debt."

Anne suggested more severe cutbacks, believing they should get out of debt rather than save face. However, Sir Walter said he would sooner leave Kellynch Hall than cut back on anything at all.

"Kellynch Hall demands a certain standard of living… elsewhere, you could choose for yourself how to live," Mr.

Shepherd volunteered.

So it was decided: they would leave Kellynch Hall. But where should they go? Mr. Shepherd felt Sir Walter could not be trusted to live modestly enough in London. Bath would be safer: he could be important there at comparatively little expense.

Anne suffered her usual fate, and was ignored. She disliked Bath, yet it was Bath that was to be her home.

Lady Russell approved of the plan but, knowing Anne's feelings about Bath, invited Anne to spend some time at her house, Kellynch Lodge, before moving there. All in all, however, she thought the change might do Anne some good.

Another reason for Lady Russell to approve the plan to move to Bath was this. Elizabeth had lately been forming an unsuitable friendship with a Mrs. Clay, the widowed daughter of Mr. Shepherd. Lady Russell was not sure of Mrs. Clay's character. She was clever, and knew how to please people... Caution was needed, and any move which would leave Mrs. Clay behind was good news.

As for Kellynch Hall, it was to be let out. This, however, was to be a secret. Sir Walter could not bear it to be widely known that he was letting his house. It was Mr. Shepherd's job to find a suitably wealthy tenant discreetly.

"The present political situation is in our favour, Sir Walter," observed Mr. Shepherd one morning at Kellynch Hall, laying down his newspaper. "Peace will bring our rich naval officers ashore..."

"A naval gentleman would be lucky to find himself in a house like this," said Sir Walter.

"They would bless their good fortune!" said Mrs. Clay. "Sailors would be sure to look after it, and keep the gardens in order."

Sir Walter sniffed. "I have not made up my mind whether to include the gardens. I might not grant a sailor the privilege."

Here Anne spoke: "The navy has done so much for us. They

deserve at least the same privileges as anyone else."

"The profession has its uses, but it offends me on two points," said Sir Walter. "First, it raises men from low families to undeserved distinction. Second, the sea air ages a man dreadfully. Sailors are so horribly sea-battered and wrinkled."

In fact, the very first applicant turned out to be a naval officer, an Admiral Croft.

"I suppose his face is orange?" Sir Walter said suspiciously.

"He is only a little weather-beaten," Mr. Shepherd assured him. He pointed out the advantages of having him as a tenant: he was married without children. "His wife is the sister of a gentleman who lived in this area once. I forget. What was his name?"

After a long moment, when nobody else came to his aid, Anne answered, very quietly, "You mean Mr. Wentworth, I suppose."

"Yes! He was the vicar of Monkford," cried Mr. Shepherd.

A vicar did not impress Sir Walter, but nonetheless, he was eventually won over, and a day was fixed for the house to be seen.

Anne, meanwhile, who had listened quietly to everything, left the room with flushed cheeks. Outside, in the cool air of the garden, she said to herself with a gentle sigh, "A few months more, and *he*, perhaps, may be walking here."

He was not Mr. Wentworth, the vicar of Monkford, but his brother, Captain Frederick Wentworth, who had come to Somerset eight years ago, after being made a commander but having no ship immediately available. He was a fine young man – intelligent, brilliant and lively; and Anne was an extremely pretty girl – gentle, modest, and full of feeling. They had fallen rapidly and deeply in love and, for a short time, were intensely happy.

But troubles soon arose. When asked for Anne's hand in marriage, Sir Walter had met the request with coldness and silence. He thought the marriage beneath her.

Persuasion

Even Lady Russell had thought it an unfortunate match. She found it unbearable that Anne Elliot, with all her beauty and high birth, should throw herself away at nineteen in an engagement to a young man who had nothing but himself to recommend him. If, by friendly persuasion, she could prevent it, she would.

Wentworth had no fortune, but was confident that he would soon be successful in his profession. That was enough for Anne. But Lady Russell saw his easy confidence as dangerous. He was brilliant but headstrong, and, Lady Russell feared, unwise.

Such opposition was more than young, gentle Anne could fight. She thought Lady Russell, whom she loved and relied upon, could not be advising her in vain. Wentworth did not take the news well. He was angry and heartbroken, and left the area as a result.

Their relationship had begun and ended within a few months; but Anne's suffering did not end so quickly. Her sorrow clouded her youth. She lost her bloom and the effect was lasting.

Eight years had passed since then. But she had not met anyone else who could compare to Frederick Wentworth. Once, when she was twenty-two, she had been asked to marry someone, but she had declined, and that man had found a more willing partner in her younger sister, Mary. Lady Russell had been sorry about Anne's refusal, and was now worried that she would never be tempted to marry anyone at all.

They did not know one another's opinion, for they never spoke about it, but Anne, at twenty-seven, thought very differently from the way she had been persuaded to think at nineteen. She did not blame Lady Russell, nor did she blame herself for being guided by her; but she felt that if anyone in similar circumstances ever asked her advice, she would never lead them to such wretchedness.

Wentworth's confidence, as it happened, had been justified. Soon after their engagement had ended, he had been given a ship and everything he had said would happen, did. Anne knew from reading the navy lists in newspapers. He had gained rank and made a fortune. She presumed he was also, by now, married.

How persuasive Anne Elliot could have been on the side of young love and confidence against caution! She had been forced to be wise in her youth; she learned to be romantic as she grew older.

With all these memories, she could not think of Captain Wentworth's older sister living at Kellynch Hall without some pain, and it took many sighs and strolls in the garden to get used to the idea. Fortunately, only three people knew her secret: Lady Russell, her father and Elizabeth, and they all seemed to have forgotten about it, or were pretending to. And so she hoped that meeting the Crofts would not be too awkward.

On the morning that Admiral and Mrs. Croft came to see Kellynch Hall, Anne took her daily walk to Lady Russell's and kept out of the way till it was over.

The meeting went well and it was decided at once. The Crofts were to move in on the 29th September. As Sir Walter planned to move to Bath in August, he and Elizabeth decided to go to Bath right away to choose a house to live in.

Mary had been a little unwell recently. When she heard they might all be going to Bath, she demanded that Anne come to help her. "I cannot possibly do without Anne," she said.

"Then Anne had better stay," was Elizabeth's reply, "for nobody will want her in Bath."

Anne was glad to be of use and certainly not sorry to remain in the countryside. Lady Russell was going away to visit friends, but invited her to stay when she returned. So it was settled that Anne would divide her time between Mary and Lady Russell, until after Christmas, when Lady Russell would accompany her to Bath.

To Lady Russell's dismay, Sir Walter and Elizabeth were taking

Persuasion

Mrs. Clay with them to Bath. Lady Russell was offended on Anne's behalf that she was considered of no use while Mrs. Clay was declared indispensable.

Anne was hardened to such insults, but was worried about Mrs. Clay's intentions. Although she did not think it had occurred to her father yet, Mrs. Clay was young, and clever enough to know what she was doing… If she married their father, Elizabeth would suffer most, so Anne tried to warn her before they left.

"Mrs. Clay," Elizabeth retorted hotly, "never forgets her station. She hates inequality in marriage. As for our father, he has kept himself single for our sakes so need not be suspected now. If Mrs. Clay were beautiful, there would be some danger, but she has a tooth that sticks out and those freckles! At any rate, it is unnecessary for you to advise *me* about anything!"

Sir Walter, Elizabeth and Mrs. Clay set off merrily in a carriage to Bath. At the same time, Anne walked up, in a sort of desolate tranquillity, to the Lodge to see Lady Russell, who was no happier than herself. Shortly after, Lady Russell started off on her trip, and dropped Anne off at Mary's house, Uppercross Cottage.

Mary was lying on the sofa. She greeted Anne with: "Here you are at last! I began to think I would never see you! I am so ill I can hardly speak. I have seen no one all morning."

"I am sorry you are unwell," said Anne. She asked after Charles, and Mary replied that he had gone out shooting. "And have you had your little boys with you?" Anne asked.

"As long as I could bear the noise," Mary said. "Little Charles pays no attention to a word I say, and Walter is growing as bad."

"You will soon be better," Anne said cheerfully. "How are all the other Musgroves at the Great House?"

"I only saw them through the window today. I told them I was ill, and they did not come in. Oh, Anne. I am so unwell. It was unkind of you not to come on Thursday."

"Mary, you wrote that there was no need to hurry, remember? Besides there was so much to do in leaving Kellynch Hall."

"What could you possibly have had to do?"

"A great deal. I made catalogues of all Father's books and pictures, and had to pack my own things. It all took time."

Little by little, with patience and forced cheerfulness on Anne's side, Mary seemed to be cured. In a while, she could sit up, and soon, forgetting herself, she was at the other end of the room, arranging flowers and wondering if they should go for a walk.

They decided to call at the Great House, where Charles's parents lived, and so they went, and sat for half an hour chatting to them. Mr. and Mrs. Musgrove were good people – not so highly educated or elegant, but friendly and welcoming. They had numerous children, but the only grown-up ones apart from Charles were Henrietta and Louisa, who were nineteen and twenty. They had finished school, and now lived to be merry. They were pretty, fashionably dressed and had pleasant manners. As a result, they were popular everywhere they went. Anne thought they were the happiest creatures she knew, but envied them nothing but their sisterly affection, of which she herself had known so little.

Coming as Anne did, with a full heart at leaving Kellynch Hall, she had expected a little curiosity or sympathy from the Musgroves. But all she received was a brief remark, "So, your father and sister are gone. Where in Bath do you think they will live?" which was followed, without waiting for a reply, with the Miss Musgroves exclaiming, "I hope we can visit Bath this winter, Papa!"

The Musgroves had their own concerns, and it was right that it should be so. And Anne was looking forward to fitting into their little circle for the next two months. Mary, for all her complaints, was not as cold and unsisterly as Elizabeth, and Anne was always on friendly terms with her brother-in-law. The children, who loved her dearly, kept her busy and amused.

Charles Musgrove was very good-tempered, and his past proposal to Anne did not cause any awkwardness. He bore his wife's unreasonableness with very good humour, much to Anne's admiration. All in all, they seemed a happy enough couple.

Her visit began well. She was cheered by the change of place. Mary's ailments lessened by having her company, and they saw the other Musgroves every day. Their cheerful faces and their singing, laughing daughters certainly did a lot to keep a happy mood.

The Musgroves had lots of dinner parties and visitors. They were very popular. The girls were wild for dancing, and often the evening ended in a little impromptu ball. Anne, preferring the job of musician to dancer, played the piano for them hour by hour.

The first three weeks flew by, and September arrived, when the Crofts were to move into Kellynch Hall. Anne's heart lurched as she imagined her beloved home being home to other people.

The Crofts moved in with naval precision on the 29th, and a plan was made to visit them. Mary persuaded Charles to drive her over one day. Fortunately for Anne, there was no room for her in the carriage. She was glad to be in, however, when the Crofts returned the visit. Charles was not at home, and Anne ended up talking to Mrs. Croft, while the Admiral sat by Mary and played with her little boys.

Mrs. Croft had a vigorous uprightness to her figure which made her seem important. She had bright, dark eyes, and a pleasant face, though her weather-beaten complexion (from being at sea almost as much as her husband) made her seem older than her thirty-eight years. She was open and easy, confident and good-humoured. She seemed considerate of Anne's feelings about Kellynch Hall, which was much appreciated. Anne was feeling very calm, in fact, until a moment electrified by Mrs. Croft suddenly saying, "It was you, not your sister, that my brother knew when he lived in this area?"

Anne hoped she had outlived the age of blushing; but the age of emotion she certainly had not.

"Have you heard that he is now married?" Mrs. Croft went on. She explained that she meant Edward, rather than Frederick, and Anne felt able to offer her congratulations.

The rest of the visit passed smoothly, until, as they were leaving, Anne heard the Admiral say to Mary, "We are expecting Mrs. Croft's brother soon; I dare say you know him—" but then he was attacked by the two little boys, who clung to him and declared that he was not allowed to leave.

Anne persuaded herself, as best she could, that he must mean Edward, rather than Frederick, but she could not be entirely sure.

The Musgroves were due to spend the evening with Mary, Charles and Anne, and they were just listening out for the carriage when Louisa walked in. She had come on foot, she said, to leave room for the harp in the carriage. "The Crofts called this morning," she said, "and told us that Mrs. Croft's brother, Captain Wentworth, has just returned to England, and is coming to see them. Mama thinks he was poor Richard's captain before he died. So she is all melancholy and we must cheer her up with the harp!"

The Musgroves had had a troublesome son, Richard, who had gone to sea before he was twenty. In truth, the family had found him completely unmanageable on shore and had not cared to talk about him, nor had they heard from him much, until news of his death had reached Uppercross, two years ago. He had served for six months under Captain Wentworth, under whose influence he had written the only two letters home in which he had not asked for money. Mrs. Musgrove had reread these letters, in which he spoke well of his captain, and was now full of renewed grief for her son.

Persuasion

When they arrived at the cottage, there was a lot of discussion about Captain Wentworth, which Anne found a trial to her nerves. She told herself that she must learn to be less sensitive to such remarks, especially since he was soon to be in the area. The Musgroves seemed determined to meet him as soon as possible.

A few days more, and Captain Wentworth had arrived. Mr. Musgrove had called on him at Kellynch, and returned full of praise, having invited him to dinner the following week. A week, thought Anne. Another week and she would have to see him.

But he repaid Mr. Musgrove's visit quicker than that. In fact, he must have been at the Great House at the very time Anne and Mary were on their way to call there. But they were prevented by Mary's elder son, Charles, being brought home after a bad fall. The poor little boy had dislocated his collarbone and hurt his back in an alarming way. It was a distressing afternoon, and Anne was kept busy: she had to send for the doctor, and for someone to tell his father, prevent his mother from having hysterics, keep the younger child out of the way and soothe the poor suffering one. The doctor arrived, and put the collarbone back in place. He looked solemn, but said they could hope for a full recovery in time.

The Musgroves came, and Louisa and Henrietta said that Captain Wentworth was the most handsome and agreeable man they had ever met, and he was coming to dinner tomorrow! Mr. Musgrove said he was sorry that Charles and Mary would miss it, as they would not want to leave their little boy.

At first, Mary and Charles agreed. But the following day, after the doctor's second visit, they felt the boy was out of danger, and began to waver. "I would like to meet Captain Wentworth," Charles said, "and there is nothing to be done here. So I think I will go over for dinner at the Great House."

When he had left the room, Mary said to Anne, "How

unfeeling! Off he goes to enjoy himself, and I am left behind to cope with a sick child. I am sure I am not even the best person to deal with him. As his mother, my feelings are so affected by it all."

"But, with a mother's feelings, could you be happy leaving him for a whole evening?" Anne asked.

"Yes!" said Mary. "His father is, so why should I not be? I was worried yesterday, but today is different. His nurse can send a message if anything changes."

"Well, then why not go to dinner too? I can stay and look after little Charles," Anne suggested.

Mary's eyes brightened. "Are you serious?" she said. "What an excellent idea, Anne! I shall go and get ready immediately."

Anne saw them both off in the carriage. She hoped they would be happy, however odd it seemed, and she was glad she herself did not need to go. She could care for her poor little nephew. What was it to her that Captain Wentworth was only half a mile away!

She would have liked to know what he felt about them meeting. He must either be indifferent or unwilling. Had he ever wished to see her again, he could have found her at any time before this.

Her sister and brother-in-law returned later, delighted with the evening, and with him. There had been music, singing, talking, laughing, and Captain Wentworth had been charming and friendly. He had agreed to come shooting with Charles the very next day.

The following morning, Mary and Anne were having breakfast, when Charles popped in to collect his dogs. He said his sisters were coming to see Mary and little Charles, and Captain Wentworth was also going to call in, too, if not inconvenient. Captain Wentworth had asked him to go ahead to let them know.

Mary was delighted, while a thousand feelings rushed through Anne, the most consoling of which was that it would soon be over. And it was. In two minutes, they were in the drawing room.

Her eyes half met Captain Wentworth's; a bow, a curtsey; he said something to the others; and in two minutes they had gone.

"It is over. It is over," she repeated to herself. She had seen him. They had met. They had been in the same room again! She tried to reason with herself. Eight years had gone by since they had given up what they had. Alas, to her feelings, eight years seemed nothing.

Later, Mary told her: "Henrietta asked Captain Wentworth if he remembered you, after they left, and he said you had changed so much he would not have recognized you."

Mary was not thinking of Anne's feelings as she said this, and did not realize how deeply wounding these words would be.

Anne was mortified. "Changed beyond recognition," she thought to herself. It was probably true. But she could take no revenge: the years seemed to have improved his looks. To her, he was the same Frederick Wentworth as ever.

Captain Wentworth had not realized his words would reach Anne's ears. Yet he had thought her wretchedly changed. He had not forgiven Anne Elliot. She had deserted and disappointed him; and worse, she had given him up to please others. She had allowed herself to be over-persuaded. He saw that as unbearable weakness.

He had been so in love with her. He had never met a woman since whom he thought her equal; but, apart from curiosity, he had no desire to see her again. Her power with him was gone for ever.

His plan now was to marry. He was rich, and had come ashore intending to marry anyone who could tempt him. He was ready to fall in love with as much speed as a clear head could allow. He had a heart for either of the Miss Musgroves, or any pleasing young woman who came along. Anyone except Anne Elliot.

"A little beauty, a few smiles, compliments to the navy, and I am a lost man," he said to his sister carelessly. "That will be enough for a sailor, will it not?"

But his bright, proud eyes spoke volumes of how particular he really was. And Anne Elliot was not out of his thoughts when he, more seriously, described the woman he hoped to meet. "A strong mind, with sweetness of manner," was all he wanted. "And if that makes me a fool," he added, "then so be it, for I have thought about the subject more than most men."

From this time, Captain Wentworth and Anne were in the same circle. As soon as the little boy's health could no longer be used as an excuse, they dined together at Mr. Musgrove's.

It was a good test of whether old feelings would be revived. Whenever something came up that had happened in the year of their engagement, he referred to it as "the year before I went to sea". Although his voice did not falter, nor did his eye stray toward her, Anne found it impossible to imagine that he did not remember.

They did not talk to one another, beyond a few polite words. There had been a time, when they would have found it difficult to stop talking to one another! Now they were strangers; worse than strangers, for they could never get to know one another again.

When he talked, she heard the same voice and the same mind that she had known. As the Miss Musgroves asked him all about life on board a ship, he gently teased them for showing surprise at his answers. It reminded Anne of the days she had asked the same questions, and been pleasantly teased in the same way.

Mrs. Musgrove got out the navy list, to find the ships Captain Wentworth had commanded. "Your first was the *Asp*, I remember," she said.

"You will not find it listed there," said Captain Wentworth. "I was the last to command her. She was hardly fit for service – but I was sent to the West Indies!" He smiled, "The admiralty amuses itself sometimes by sending men to sea in a ship fit to sink."

"What nonsense!" the Admiral guffawed. "The *Asp* was a good ship! He was lucky to get a ship at all so early in his career!"

"I did feel lucky, I assure you," Captain Wentworth replied seriously. "At that time in particular, I needed to be kept busy."

"But to be given such an old ship!" Louisa cried.

"Ah, the dear old *Asp*," he said, smiling again. "I knew we would either go to the bottom of the sea together, or she would be the making of me. I never had two days of bad weather all the time I was at sea in her. In fact, I brought her into Plymouth only six hours before a gale came on which would have sunk us."

The Miss Musgroves exclaimed in horror, and Anne shuddered. The girls hunted for the listing for his next ship, the *Laconia*, and Captain Wentworth took the book and fondly read the description aloud. "Those were pleasant days," he sighed.

"I am sure it was a lucky day for us, when you were captain of that ship," Mrs. Musgrove said, her voice low with feeling.

Captain Wentworth looked up expectantly.

"Mama is thinking of poor Richard, our brother," whispered one of the girls.

"Poor dear!" continued Mrs. Musgrove. "It would be a happy thing if he were still with you!"

A flicker of an expression crossed the Captain's face at this, a mere glance of his bright eye, a slight curl of his lip, which convinced Anne that he felt rather differently about poor Richard, but it was too quick to have been seen by anyone who knew him less well than she did. The next moment it was gone. He moved to the sofa to sit next to Mrs. Musgrove, and talked to her about her son with kindness and sympathy.

They were actually on the same sofa, separated only by Mrs. Musgrove. It was no insignificant barrier, as Mrs. Musgrove was a comfortable size, and Anne's slender form and pensive face were almost completely hidden from Captain Wentworth while he attended to Mrs. Musgrove's sighs.

Persuasion

The conversation moved on. Mrs. Croft said she had often been at sea in her fifteen years of marriage. "The happiest days of my life have been on board a ship. It was when my husband was at sea without me that I suffered. As long as we were together, there was nothing to fear!"

The evening ended with dancing, and Anne was only too glad to offer her services on the piano. Though her eyes sometimes filled with tears as she sat there playing, she wanted nothing more than to be unobserved.

It was a merry party, and no one seemed in higher spirits than Captain Wentworth. How could he be otherwise – with the admiration of everyone, particularly the Miss Musgroves, whose friendship with one another was the only thing keeping them from being rivals for him.

Anne thought about this while her fingers faultlessly played. Once she felt he was looking at her, perhaps trying to remember the face that had once charmed him; and once he asked if Miss Elliot ever danced? The answer was, "Oh no, she has given up dancing. She would much rather play." Once too, he spoke to her. She had left the piano, and he had sat down, trying to play something to the Miss Musgroves. She had returned and he had risen immediately and said coldly, "I beg your pardon. This is your seat." That cold politeness, to Anne, felt worse than anything.

Captain Wentworth was at Uppercross almost every day after that, welcomed by the Musgroves, and admired by all. But this changed a little when Charles Hayter returned to their circle.

Charles, a friendly young gentleman, was a cousin of the Musgroves. He was a curate and lived at his father's house, within walking distance of Uppercross. He and Henrietta had grown fond of each other. But his short absence had left her unguarded at a critical period, and when he returned, her behaviour had changed.

He was mortified. Before he left, she had been very interested in the idea of his obtaining a curacy in Uppercross. But alas! When he told her now that he had been promised the curacy, Henrietta was hardly listening. Louisa was watching out of the window for Captain Wentworth, and Henrietta said half-heartedly, "I am glad. It is no surprise though, is it?... Is he coming, Louisa?"

Mr. and Mrs. Musgrove had noticed Charles's attention to Henrietta without disapproval. Mrs. Musgrove and Mrs. Hayter were sisters. Both families had money, but Mr. Hayter's property and standing in society was nothing compared to the Musgroves'. However, there was no envy or pride on either side, and the Musgroves had nothing against the match. "If Henrietta likes him…" they had said. And Henrietta *had* thought she liked him, until Captain Wentworth had come along.

Mary and Charles talked about it constantly. Charles thought Captain Wentworth preferred Louisa, Mary thought Henrietta. She preferred the idea of Henrietta marrying him, as it would put an end to Charles Hayter's intentions. She looked down on the Hayters, and did not want to be connected to them by marriage.

"Nonsense," said her husband. "Charles is the eldest son, and will inherit some of the best land in the country from his father. He would not be a bad match for Henrietta at all."

Which of the two sisters Captain Wentworth preferred was not yet clear, as far as Anne could tell. She thought it more important that he choose soon to avoid endangering the happiness of either.

One morning, Captain Wentworth walked into the drawing room of the cottage to find Anne alone with little injured Charles, who was lying on the sofa. The surprise of finding himself almost alone with Anne Elliot ruffled him. He could only say, "I thought the Musgroves were here – Mrs. Musgrove said so," before he went to the window to gather his wits and work out how to behave.

"They are upstairs with my sister. They will be down in a few moments," Anne answered naturally enough. But it was only little Charles's request that she do something for him that prevented her from fleeing the room herself.

Captain Wentworth stayed by the window. "I hope the little boy is better," he said, and then was silent.

She knelt down by the sofa to deal with little Charles, and busied herself for a few minutes when, to her relief, she heard someone else come in. Unfortunately it was Charles Hayter, who was probably no more pleased at the sight of Captain Wentworth than he had been at the sight of Anne. "Would you like to sit down?" Anne said. "The others will be here soon."

Captain Wentworth came from his corner, apparently intending to make conversation, but Charles Hayter prevented him by sitting down and picking up a newspaper, so he returned to his window.

Another minute brought someone else. It was Walter, the younger brother of two years old, who went straight to the sofa to see what was going on. He wanted to play, and fastened himself onto his aunt's back in such a way that she could not get him off.

She spoke to him, ordered him, begged him, but all in vain. Walter did not let go.

In another moment, Anne felt someone lifting him off her back to free her, and he was carried away, before she knew Captain Wentworth had done it.

She was speechless at the discovery. She could not even thank him. She could only bend over little Charles in confusion. It had been so kind – but the fact Captain Wentworth was making a lot of noise with little Walter at that moment seemed to prove that the last thing he wanted was for them to speak to one another.

At last, Mary and the Miss Musgroves came in, and she could leave the room. It might have been a chance to observe the four all together, but she could not wonder about others' feelings while her

*In another moment, Anne felt someone
lifting him off her back to free her...*

own were so disturbed. She hurried away, ashamed to have been overcome by such a trifle. It took a while for her to recover.

Soon, Anne had been with the four often enough to have an opinion. She could not agree with Charles or Mary for, while she considered Louisa to be preferred, she could not help but think that Captain Wentworth was not really in love with either. They were more in love with him; yet even that was not really love. There was a kind of fever of admiration, which could end in love.
Charles Hayter seemed to feel slighted, and Henrietta sometimes seemed divided between them. Anne did not think any of them were being sly or manipulative, however. And she was pleased that Captain Wentworth seemed unaware of any pain he might be causing. He probably never knew of any claim Charles Hayter may have had on Henrietta. His only fault was in accepting the flattering attentions of two women at once.
After a short struggle, Charles Hayter seemed to give up. He stopped coming to Uppercross, and refused an invitation to dinner.

One morning, Charles Musgrove and Captain Wentworth had gone shooting together, when the Miss Musgroves came to the cottage to see Anne and Mary. It was a fine November day, and they were on their way for a long walk, but assumed that Mary would not like to come. "Oh yes I would," said Mary. "I am very fond of long walks!"
Anne was sure by the looks of the girls that they did not really want Mary to go. So, when they rather more cordially invited her as well, she accepted, thinking perhaps that she could persuade Mary to turn back at some point. They were just setting off, when the gentlemen arrived. Their sport had been spoiled by a young, disobedient dog they had with them, so they were just in the mood to join a walk. Soon everyone had decided to go together.

Persuasion

Anne tried her best not to be in the way, keeping with her sister and brother-in-law. She found pleasure in the views of the last tawny leaves on trees, and concentrated on remembering verses and poetic descriptions of autumn as they went along. But whenever she was in earshot of Captain Wentworth's conversations, it was impossible not to listen. One particular conversation he had with Louisa struck her.

"My sister and the Admiral are taking a drive today," Captain Wentworth was saying. "I wonder where he overturns the carriage today! It happens so often, but my sister does not seem to care."

"I would be the same!" Louisa cried. "If I loved a man as she loves the Admiral, nothing would separate us – I would rather be overturned in a carriage by him than driven safely by anyone else!"

"Would you?" he said warmly. "Then I think very highly of you!" And there was a silence between them for a little while.

The sweet scenes of autumn went right out of Anne's mind for a while. After half a mile of gradual descent through farmland, they saw Winthrop, the Hayters' property, stretched out before them. "Bless me, it is Winthrop!" Mary cried. "I had no idea! We had better turn back now; I am tired."

Henrietta was ashamed and, seeing no Charles Hayter walking along any path, was ready to do as Mary wished. But Charles Musgrove and Louisa protested. Charles declared to call on his aunt, Mrs. Hayter. Mary refused to. After a short debate, it was decided that Charles and Henrietta would go down for a few minutes, while the rest of them waited at the top of the hill. Louisa went down with them a little way, talking to Henrietta, and Mary took the opportunity to say scornfully to Captain Wentworth, "It is so unpleasant to be connected to such people!"

She received no answer other than an artificial smile, and a contemptuous glance as he turned away. Anne knew the meaning of that glance perfectly.

Persuasion

The brow of the hill was a cheerful spot. Louisa returned and drew Captain Wentworth away to look for some nuts in the hedgerow behind. Mary, sure that Louisa must have found a better spot, followed but could not see them. Anne found a nice seat for her on a sunny bank near the hedgerow but Mary wandered off. So Anne sat down herself, glad of the rest.

Soon, she heard Louisa and Captain Wentworth talking on the other side of the hedgerow. Louisa was in the middle of some eager speech. "…so I made Henrietta go! Would I be turned back from doing something I wanted to do? No, – I would never be so easily persuaded. When I have made up my mind, that is it."

"Your sister is amiable, but *you* are the one with the firm character, I see. A character that is too giving cannot be depended upon. Those who want to be happy should be firm," he said. He picked a nut, and playfully went on, "Here is a good example – a glossy nut, that has outlived all the storms. Not a weak spot anywhere." Then he continued earnestly, "Anyone I am interested in must be firm. If Louisa Musgrove wants to be beautiful and happy in her life, she will value her power of mind…"

There came no answer. It would have surprised Anne if Louisa had been able to answer such a speech – spoken with such warmth. She could imagine what Louisa was feeling. As for herself, she did not dare move, for fear of being seen. A low, rambling holly bush protected her from view just then, and soon they moved on. Before they were out of hearing, however, Louisa said, "Mary's pride annoys me sometimes. We so wish Charles had married Anne instead – I suppose you know he wanted to marry Anne?"

After a pause, Captain Wentworth said, "So she refused him?"

"Oh yes."

"When did that happen?"

"About a year before he married Mary. Mama and Papa thought Lady Russell persuaded Anne to refuse him."

Persuasion

Their footsteps faded away, and Anne heard no more. Her own emotions rooted her to the spot. It was clear to her how Captain Wentworth saw her character; and he had shown just enough curiosity about her to make her extremely bothered about it.

As soon as she could, she went back to find Mary. They were rejoined by the others, and Charles and Henrietta returned with Charles Hayter. Anne did not understand what had happened, but Charles and Henrietta seemed very happy together, devoted to each other, in fact, as they all set off back to Uppercross.

Everything now marked out Louisa for Captain Wentworth; nothing could be plainer. Anne walked with Charles and Mary, tired enough to be very glad of Charles's arm.

Their path crossed over a lane, and there they met a carriage, with the Admiral and Mrs. Croft in it. They were on their way home, and offered anyone a seat who was tired of walking. Everyone refused the offer, and Anne said nothing. But Captain Wentworth said something to his sister, who said to Anne, "Miss Elliot, I believe you are tired. Do give us the pleasure of taking you home!" Then Captain Wentworth offered his arm, and she found herself in the carriage, riding home, lost in thought.

He had noticed her tiredness. He had perhaps not forgiven her, but he could not see her suffer, without coming to her aid. It was a thought that gave her such pleasure and such pain that she did not know which was stronger.

For the first part of the journey, she barely noticed the Crofts, but when she began to listen, she found they were talking about Frederick. "He certainly means to marry one of those girls," the Admiral was saying. "He has been running after them so long he cannot make up his mind. In times of war, we could not afford to have long courtships. How long was it my dear, between when we met and when I asked you to marry me?"

"If Miss Elliot knew how short a time it was," Mrs. Croft smiled, "she would never believe we could be happy."

"Ah, well, I hope Frederick marries one of them. They are both so pleasant, I cannot tell one from the other," the Admiral said.

"They are very unspoiled, lovely girls," Mrs. Croft said, in a tone which made Anne wonder whether she thought them not entirely worthy of her brother. "Watch that post!"

Mrs. Croft took the reins herself, and drove them safely out of danger. Amused at their style of driving, which she thought was probably a good representation of their marriage, Anne was deposited safely at the cottage.

It was nearly time for Lady Russell's return, and Anne was looking forward to joining her when she arrived. But the end of her stay at Uppercross was more eventful than she had imagined.

Captain Wentworth, having received a letter from an old friend, had been to visit him and his family in Lyme for two days. His friend, Captain Harville, had been badly injured two years before, and had not been in good health since. Captain Wentworth spoke so warmly of him, and of Lyme, that everyone decided that they – Charles, Mary, Anne, Henrietta, Louisa and Captain Wentworth – would go and visit. They would spend the night at an inn, and return the following day.

They set off the very next morning, and by noon were driving down the long hill into Lyme. After booking into an inn, and ordering dinner there for later, they walked down to the sea. They wanted to take a walk around the Cobb, the breakwater wall around the bay, from which there is a charming view of the line of cliffs stretching east from the town.

Captain Wentworth brought Admiral Harville and his wife to meet the others at the Cobb, along with a Captain Benwick who was staying with them. He was a fine young man, Captain

Wentworth had told them, a captain in the navy. Sadly, he was mourning the death of his fiancée, Captain Harville's sister. Poor Fanny Harville had died last summer while Captain Benwick was at sea. Captain Wentworth said no man could have been more in love, or more affected by grief. Benwick now lived with the Harvilles, who had taken a house by the sea partly for his benefit.

They all met, and were introduced. Captain Harville had a kind face, and was a little lame in one leg from his injury. Captain Benwick was younger, and looked pleasant but quiet and sad.

Captain Harville and his wife welcomed the whole party as friends. They seemed very fond of Captain Wentworth, and their warmth was so genuine rather than dutiful that Anne felt a pang of sadness. "These would have been my friends," she thought.

They went back to the inn for dinner, and Captain Harville visited them in the evening, bringing along Benwick. Captain Wentworth and Harville led a merry conversation about their good old days on one side of the room. Captain Benwick and Anne were left together on the other. Gently, she began a conversation with him, and soon they were talking about poetry, which he loved reading. They compared poems, and he mentioned, tremulously, one he liked which was about a broken heart.

Anne ventured to say that she hoped he did not only read poetry, for although those with deep feelings understood it best, they were also the ones who should read it sparingly.

He did not look pained, but pleased, that she had mentioned his feelings, so she felt bold enough to go on. She recommended books for him to read. He wrote down the titles, and promised to read them.

Anne and Henrietta were the first up the next morning, and went for a stroll on the shore before breakfast. Before long, Louisa and Captain Wentworth joined them. As they went back up the steps, a gentleman at the top drew back to let them pass, and Anne could not help but notice him looking intently at her. In fact, she was looking very well, her face once again blooming and fresh from the fine sea air. It was clear that the gentleman admired her. Captain Wentworth noticed, and looked around at her too, his momentary bright glance seeming to say, "That man finds you striking and even I, just now, see something of Anne Elliot again."

When they returned to the inn, Anne ran into the gentleman on the way from her room to the dining room. He was staying at the same inn! It was clear from his gaze that he thought her lovely, and Anne felt that she should like to know who he was.

They had nearly finished breakfast, when a carriage drew up outside the window, and the same man got into it. "It is the man we passed," said Captain Wentworth, with half a glance at Anne. When the servant came in, he asked, "Could you tell us the name of the gentleman who just drove away?"

"Yes, sir, it is Mr. Elliot – a gentleman of large fortune. He is on his way to Bath and London," replied the man.

"Bless me," said Mary, "that must be our cousin Mr. Elliot! He is my father's heir! I wish I had looked closer. You must mention this to our father, Anne, when you go to Bath."

Anne stayed silent. She felt that after Mr. Elliot had caused their father such offence, it might be wiser not to mention him.

Breakfast was not long over, when they were joined by Captain and Mrs. Harville and Captain Benwick, for their last walk before they set off for home. Captain Benwick walked with Anne, and they talked about poetry. As they walked on, she found Captain Harville by her instead, and he said quietly, "You have done a good deed, getting that poor fellow to talk. I wish he had more company – it is bad for him to be alone with us so much."

"Yet his bad news is still fresh," said Anne.

"Yes, he only heard of Fanny's death last August," said Captain Harville. "It was Captain Wentworth, that good man, who broke the news to him. He travelled night and day to Portsmouth, and rowed out to the ship to tell him. He did not leave his side for a week. He is very dear to us for that."

They decided to walk along the Cobb one last time, but Captain Harville could not manage any more, so they left him and Mrs. Harville at their door.

There was too much wind to walk along the high part of the breakwater wall, and so they went down the steps to the lower part. Louisa insisted on being jumped down from the steps by Captain Wentworth. On their country walk, he had had to jump her down from all the stiles, as she enjoyed it so much. He was less willing here, as the pavement was hard, but he did it to oblige her. No sooner was she safely down, than she ran up the steps to be jumped down again. He advised against it. "I am determined I will," cried Louisa, and she jumped… He put out his hands, but too late, and she fell onto the pavement, and lay there, still!

She looked lifeless. There was no wound, no blood, no visible bruise; but her eyes were closed, she did not appear to be breathing and her face looked like death. Everyone stood around, horrified.

Captain Wentworth kneeled and took her in his arms, and looked at her with a face as pale as her own.

"She is dead!" screamed Mary.

Henrietta fainted, and was caught by Anne and Captain Benwick together.

"Will nobody help me?" were the first words which burst from Captain Wentworth, in a tone of despair.

"Go to him!" Anne cried to Captain Benwick. "I can hold Henrietta. Rub her hands and temples, to see if it revives her!"

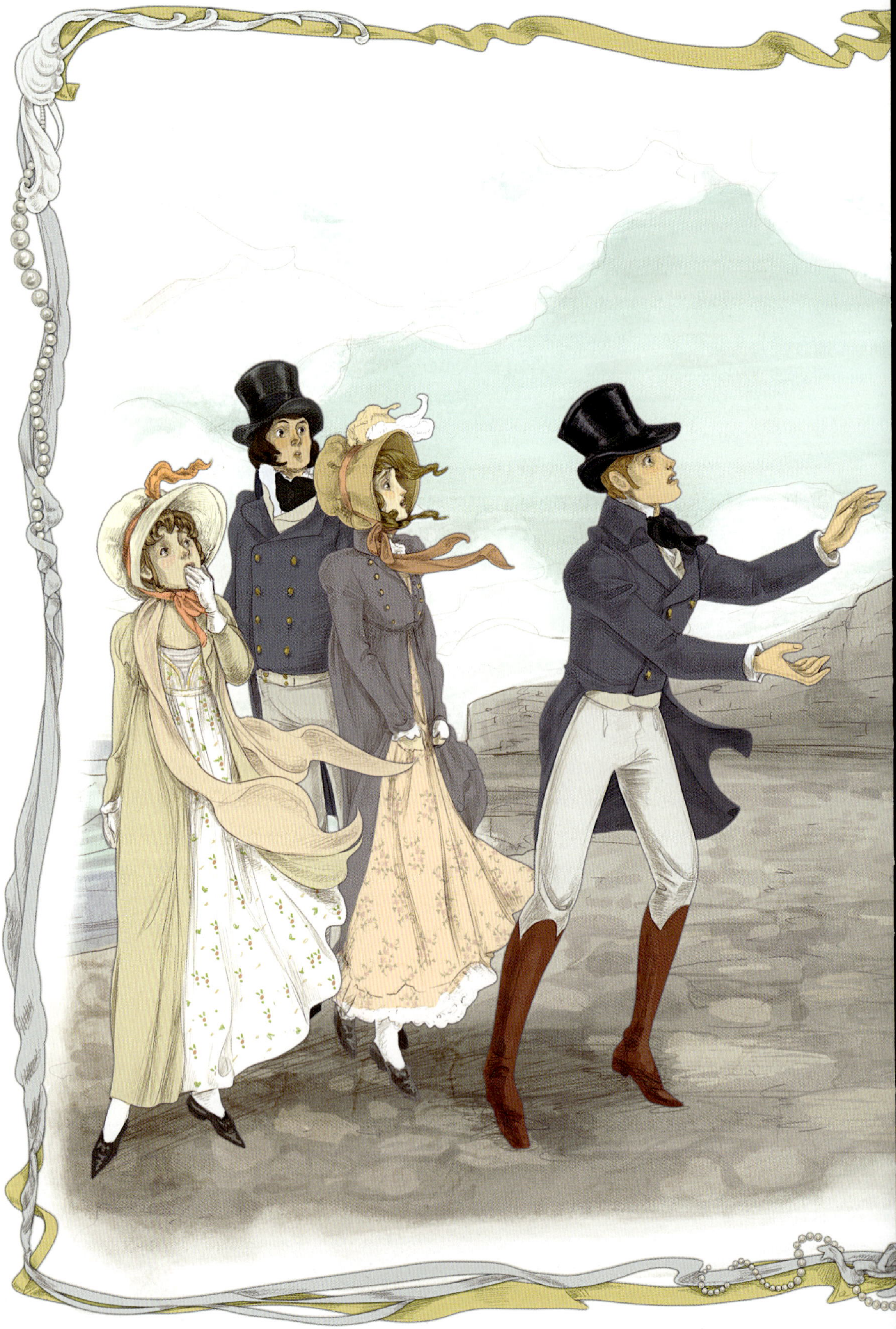

"I am determined I will,"
cried Louisa, and she jumped...

Captan Benwick and Charles rushed forward to help. They raised Louisa up and did what Anne prompted, in vain; while Captain Wentworth staggered against the wall, exclaiming, "Oh God! Her father and mother!"

"A doctor!" Anne cried.

The word seemed to rouse him, and he was about to dart away, when Anne suggested, "Captain Benwick might know where to find one." In a moment, Captain Benwick had rushed off.

It was hard to tell which of them was more distraught – but Anne pulled herself together. She tried to rouse Henrietta; she comforted the others; quietened Mary; encouraged sobbing Charles; and soothed Captain Wentworth's anguish. Both the men seemed to look to her for direction.

"Anne," cried Charles, "what shall we do next?"

"Carry her gently to the inn," Anne decided.

Captain Wentworth picked her up, and strangers rushed to help.

Supporting Henrietta, who had awoken, the group set off along the Cobb. The Harvilles rushed out, having seen Captain Benwick flying past, and told them to come to their house – it was closer than the inn. They put Louisa to bed in Mrs. Harville's room, and waited, sick with horror, for the doctor to come.

When the doctor had examined her, he reported that she had a severe concussion to the head. He had seen worse, he said, fairly cheerfully, and he thought that she would recover, given time.

"Thank God!" Captain Wentworth cried.

The group now had to decide what to do. Without doubt Louisa had to remain where she was. The Harvilles silenced all worries about that matter. Mrs. Harville was an experienced nurse and well able to look after her, with help from their nursery maid.

There was some debate as to who should stay, and who should go and break the news to Louisa's parents at Uppercross. Charles could not bear to leave. As Anne was quietly coming down the stairs from seeing Louisa, she heard Captain Wentworth say, "Then it is decided: you stay here and I shall escort Henrietta home. As for who should stay to help, it must be Anne. There is no one so proper, so capable as Anne!"

The others heartily agreed.

When Anne reappeared, Captain Wentworth turned to her, as warm as he had ever been, and said, "You will stay and nurse her?"

She flushed, and he gathered himself and moved away.

She said that she was more than happy to stay. But then Mary rejoined them, learned of the plan, and complained bitterly that it was unfair for Anne to stay rather than her. She was Louisa's sister-in-law, and Anne was nothing to Louisa. She went on and on until Charles gave way, and so no one else felt they could argue.

Anne had never submitted so reluctantly to Mary's jealousy, and Captain Wentworth was very dismayed. As he helped her into the carriage, she wondered whether he only valued her as far as she was useful to Louisa. He sat between her and Henrietta, but turned towards Henrietta and focussed all his attention on her. He seemed to be trying to keep her from becoming upset again. Only once, when she said she wished they had not taken that last walk, did he burst out, "Do not talk about it! If only I had not given way to her! But she was so determined and eager – dear, sweet Louisa!"

Anne wondered whether it might strike him now that firmness of mind should have its limits, and that a persuadable character might sometimes bring just as much happiness.

It was dusk when they finally arrived at Uppercross, and they had been silent for some time. Henrietta was leaning back in the corner, having cried herself to sleep. Suddenly Anne found Captain Wentworth turning to her and saying quietly, "I have been wondering what we had best do. Henrietta must not go in first.

Persuasion

I thought perhaps you should stay in the carriage with her while I go and break the news. Do you think that is a good plan?"

She did; he was satisfied, and said no more. But she felt pleased that he had asked her – it was some proof of their friendship, and deference to her judgement.

After the news had been broken, Henrietta and Anne had gone in, and everyone was as calm as they could be, he announced his intention to return to Lyme at once, and was off.

Early the next morning, Charles brought news from Lyme before dashing back there. He said there would be no speedy cure, but everything was going as well as could be expected. Louisa was becoming conscious for longer spells of time. He also said Mrs. Harville was such a good nurse that there was nothing left for anyone else to do. Mary had become hysterical, so had been sent for a walk with Captain Benwick. He wished she had been persuaded to come home instead of Anne... He said Captain Wentworth had not moved from Lyme.

Anne was due to move to Lady Russell's house in two days' time. She spent the last of her time at Uppercross helping poor Mr. and Mrs. Musgrove. They all dreaded her departure – what would they do without her? Anne persuaded them to go to Lyme, and find a place at an inn. At least they could help by entertaining Mrs. Harville's children while she cared for Louisa. They liked the idea so much, they went the following morning.

Anne's last few hours in the house were spent alone. What a difference a few days had made! But if Louisa made a full recovery, all would soon be well. In Anne's mind there was no doubt what would follow her recovery...

A few hours' contemplation on a dark November day, with thick rain blotting out the view from the windows, was enough to make the sound of Lady Russell's carriage very welcome. Though Anne was sad to leave the cottage – much had passed there which made it precious to her.

Lady Russell greeted Anne joyfully, and with some anxiety. She knew Captain Wentworth had been at Uppercross, and worried about the effect on Anne. However, Anne's looks seemed to have improved – she was rosier and looked more like she used to.

When they came to talk, Anne became aware of a change within herself, too. The subjects that had weighed heavily on her heart on leaving Kellynch did not seem so important any more. She had forgotten all about her sister and her father in Bath, and the worry about Mrs. Clay. Her mind was still full of her friends in Lyme.

She felt awkward while telling Lady Russell about the accident in Lyme. She found she could not quite look her friend in the eye until she had told her about the attachment between Captain Wentworth and Louisa. After she had, she found she could mention his name more easily.

Lady Russell listened with composure, saying she wished them happiness, but internally her heart revelled in contempt, that a man who at twenty-three saw the value in Anne Elliot could, eight years later, be charmed by a Louisa Musgrove.

After a few quiet days, Lady Russell said, "I must call on Mrs. Croft. Anne, do you have the courage to come with me, and pay a visit to the house? It will be a trial to us both…"

But Anne did not mind. "I have become quite used to the idea," she said. She could have said more – in fact she had so high an opinion of the Crofts that, however sorry she was for having to leave Kellynch Hall, she felt it could not have been in better hands.

Mrs. Croft met her with kindness, as always. They talked about the accident at Lyme, comparing their latest accounts of Louisa's progress. Anne learned that Captain Wentworth had asked after her, saying he hoped she was no worse for her exertions. As to the catastrophe itself, both sensible women judged it to be the result of rash behaviour. The Admiral wound it all up by exclaiming, "It is a strange new way to declare love to a lady, for a fellow to break her head, is it not Miss Elliot?"

The tone may not have pleased Lady Russell, but Anne found his good heart and simple character irresistible.

"This must be awful for you," he suddenly observed, "to find us here. Do look around the house, if you would like."

Anne declined politely.

"We have only made a few alterations," the Admiral said. "I had some of the huge looking-glasses in the dressing room put away. Your father must be very fashion-conscious for a man of his age. There was no getting away from yourself!"

Anne, amused despite herself, was searching for a suitable answer, when the Admiral, fearing he had not been very polite, went on to say, "When you next write to your father, do say that we are settled in very well, and there is no house we like better."

When Lady Russell invited the Crofts to return the visit, Mrs. Croft said that they were going away shortly, and might not return before Lady Russell had left for Bath.

So ended all danger to Anne of meeting Captain Wentworth at Kellynch Hall, or of seeing him in the company of Lady Russell. She smiled over the anxious feelings she had wasted on the subject.

Charles and Mary were the first to return from Lyme, and came straight away to visit Lady Russell. They brought the news that Louisa was now able to sit up, though she was still very weak.

Mrs. Musgrove had taken Mrs. Harville's children out as much as possible. Mrs. Harville had insisted they come to dinner every day, and both sides had been extremely helpful to one another. Mary was cheerful – she had enjoyed her stay – she had bathed, visited the library, had many walks, and had felt so very *useful*.

When Anne asked after Captain Benwick, Mary pulled a face. "He is very odd. We asked him to Uppercross. At first he seemed delighted, but a few days later he said he would not be coming."

Charles laughed. "It was all your doing," he said to Anne. "He thought you would be there. When he found out you would not, he did not want to come. He talks of you in such high terms."

"He hardly mentions her," said Mary peevishly.

"He is reading every book you recommended," Charles continued, "and wants to talk to you about them. I overheard him describing you to Henrietta… 'Elegance, sweetness, beauty!'"

Anne admitted that she was flattered. But Mary said, "Even if he did, there is little credit in it, is there, Lady Russell? Miss Harville only died last June!"

"I must meet this Captain Benwick, before I decide," said Lady Russell, smiling. Then she tactfully changed the subject.

Mary began talking of Mr. Elliot, but Lady Russell's disapproval checked her enthusiasm. "He is a man I have no wish to see. His treatment of the Elliot family has left a bad impression."

So then Mary spoke of Captain Wentworth, who seemed happier as Louisa improved, but who had not actually spoken to her since the accident. He seemed worried about doing so. On the contrary, he was planning to go away for a week or so to Plymouth.

Soon, Mr. and Mrs. Musgrove came back, leaving Henrietta with Louisa, but bringing with them the Harvilles' children. Uppercross once again became busy and bursting with life. Anne and Lady Russell visited to find chattering little girls cutting up gold paper, and riotous boys feasting on pies by a roaring Christmas fire. Mr. Musgrove tried to talk with Lady Russell but could barely be heard above the noise of the children on his knees. All in all, it was a fine family scene.

"Remind me never to visit again in the Christmas holidays," Lady Russell remarked to Anne afterwards.

Everyone has their own level of tolerance for different types of noise. A short time later, as Lady Russell and Anne were entering Bath on their way to Sir Walter's lodgings at Camden Place, Lady Russell did not complain about the clattering of carriages and bawling of newsmen. Anne, on the other hand, did not share her cheer at this point. She disliked Bath, and looked back, with fond regret, to the bustle of Uppercross and the quiet of Kellynch.

Elizabeth's last letter had mentioned that Mr. Elliot had called in on them in Bath, many times, and had seemed keen to renew their connection. Lady Russell was curious, and wanted to see him. Anne felt she would rather see him than not, which was more than she could say for anyone else in Bath. Lady Russell left her in Camden Place, and drove on to her own lodgings.

Elizabeth and Sir Walter gave Anne a much warmer welcome than she had expected, even if it was only to boast about their house. As usual, they had no inclination to listen to her. They talked mostly about themselves. They liked Bath; their house was the best in Camden Place; everybody wanted to know them; everyone wanted to visit them.

They were happy about Mr. Elliot too. Not only was he pardoned, they were delighted with him. He had apologized for his past behaviour, and explained it all away. He said it was all a misunderstanding – he had thought *they* had rejected *him*. And he indignantly denied ever having slighted the family name. Anyone who knew him would tell them how he boasted of being an Elliot.

Anne listened to all of this, without quite understanding it. There seemed to be something more behind Mr. Elliot's wishing to be on good terms with them after so long. He had nothing to gain by it materially – he was probably richer than Sir Walter, and he would inherit the estate whatever they thought of him. She could only think of one reason: Elizabeth. Perhaps he had liked her before, and it had been circumstances that had drawn him away. Elizabeth was certainly elegant and beautiful. Anne hoped closer knowledge of her character would not put him off. Elizabeth also seemed to think herself the reason for his attentions. A glance or two between her and Mrs. Clay said as much.

Anne mentioned she had seen him at Lyme, but nobody took any notice of her. They were more absorbed by their own descriptions of him – his gentlemanly appearance, his elegant, fashionable air. They talked on and on about him, when there came a knock at the door. It was ten o'clock – who could be calling so late? Mrs. Clay said it was Mr. Elliot's knock, and she was right. The next moment, the butler ushered him into the room.

Anne drew back a little, as the others greeted him and he apologized for calling so late. Then Sir Walter introduced her, and Anne, smiling and blushing, showed Mr. Elliot the pretty face which he had by no means forgotten. By his look of surprise, it was clear he had not known in Lyme who she was. He looked pleased. His eyes brightened, and he said that they had met. He was just as good-looking as he had been at Lyme.

He sat down with them and talked with Anne about Lyme, comparing opinions of the place, and saying what a coincidence they had found themselves at the same inn. The conversation soon led to Anne having to tell him about the accident. In contrast to her father and sister, Mr. Elliot seemed really to want to understand what had happened, and seemed concerned about what she must have suffered while witnessing it.

The clock on the mantelpiece struck eleven – he had been there an hour before anyone had realized. Anne could not have thought it possible that her first evening in Bath would go so well!

Anne would have been happy to know whether Mr. Elliot was in fact in love with Elizabeth, but more than that, she wanted to know whether her father was in love with Mrs. Clay. Mrs. Clay certainly seemed to meet his approval. As Anne came down for breakfast the next morning, she overheard Mrs. Clay whisper to Elizabeth, "Now Anne is here, I suppose I am no longer wanted."

Elizabeth replied, in less of a whisper, "She is nothing to me, compared with you."

"My dear, you cannot run away from us now," her father added. "There is much more here for your fine mind to enjoy."

Mrs. Clay stole a glance at Elizabeth and Anne at that, and promised to stay.

The same morning, Sir Walter complimented Anne on her complexion and asked her whether she had used something on it. When Anne said not, he exclaimed, "Mrs. Clay has been using a cream on my recommendation, and it has removed her freckles!"

Anne thought Mrs. Clay's freckles looked the same as ever. Perhaps it was her father's opinion of Mrs. Clay that had changed… If Elizabeth were to marry Mr. Elliot, at least it would lessen the evil of this possible marriage.

Lady Russell's manners were put on trial at the sight of Mrs. Clay so favoured and Anne so overlooked. But she seemed to mind less as she got to know Mr. Elliot. He so impressed her that she exclaimed to Anne, "Can this be the same Mr. Elliot?" To her, everything good was united in him: good understanding and a warm heart, together with a feeling of family honour, without pride or weakness. He seemed to value what he ought.

Anne knew that she and Lady Russell sometimes thought differently. It did not surprise her, therefore, that Lady Russell did not see anything suspicious in Mr. Elliot's desire to reconcile himself to his family. Lady Russell thought it was natural – that it had been an error of his youth that made him think otherwise. When Anne mentioned Elizabeth as a possible motivation, she looked thoughtful and said, "Time will tell."

Anne had to accept that. However it might end, he was still the pleasantest person she knew in Bath. She enjoyed talking to him about Lyme, which he seemed as eager to see again as she was. And they talked of their first meeting there. He recalled when he had first looked at her on the steps. And she remembered how another person had looked then too...

Mr. Elliot and Anne did not always think alike. He valued rank and connections more than she did. He shared her father and sister's excitement about a subject she thought unworthy of them: the arrival of the Dowager Viscountess Dalrymple and her daughter, which was announced in the newspaper one morning. The Dalrymples were cousins of the Elliots, and for a few days Sir Walter and Elizabeth talked of nothing but "our cousins the Dalrymples" all day long. Anne found herself in the usual position of wishing they had more pride.

Sir Walter wrote a fine, lengthy letter introducing himself to Lady Dalrymple, and received a card in return, saying she would be happy to see them. Sir Walter told everyone he met, and Anne was ashamed. Still more so, when they finally met Lady Dalrymple and found her no more than civil.

When Anne spoke to Mr. Elliot about it, he said the Dalrymples were good company to have. "My idea of good company," Anne smiled, "is the company of clever, well-informed people who have something to talk about."

"That is not just good company," he said gently, "that is the best. For good company, you only need high enough birth and good manners. Ah, but you are shaking your head. My dear cousin, you have a better right to be fussy than almost any other woman

I know. But will it make you happy? Would it not be better just to enjoy the connection to the Dalrymples as far as possible?"

Anne smiled at herself. "I suppose I have more pride than any of you, but it vexes me that we have taken so much trouble to make a connection with them, which they do not care about in the least… I am proud, too proud to enjoy a welcome which depends so entirely upon place in society."

"I love your indignation," he said. "I am proud too, when it comes to this family. In fact, we might have the same aim in the end." He lowered his voice, "Do you not agree that any new person in your father's circle might divert his thoughts from those who are beneath him…" he glanced over at a chair that Mrs. Clay had just vacated and Anne, although she did not agree that they had the same sort of pride, was glad he did not like Mrs. Clay.

While Sir Walter and Elizabeth were busy pursuing high connections, Anne had been seeing a friend of a different description – an old school friend whom she had heard was in Bath. Miss Hamilton, now Mrs. Smith, had been kind to Anne as a girl of fourteen when her mother had died, and Anne was fond of her.

Mrs. Smith was a widow, and poor. Her husband had left her in terrible debt when he had died two years before. In addition to this, she had been suffering from rheumatic fever, which had crippled her legs. She had come to Bath for its healing waters.

It had been twelve years since they had seen one another, but within ten minutes they were like old friends. Anne was astonished by the cheerful determination with which her friend faced her difficulties. Mrs. Smith told her that she had been so ill on first reaching Bath, that she had needed to hire a nurse. But the nurse had turned out to be a good woman, who had become a friend and taught her how to knit. Now Mrs. Smith spent her time knitting things to raise money for poor families in the area.

Persuasion

Anne had called on her friend several times before mentioning it to Sir Walter and Elizabeth. One morning, they told her Lady Dalrymple had invited them all that evening. Anne declined, saying she had promised to see Mrs. Smith.

Sir Walter was indignant, "You have the strangest taste in friends," he raged. "Who is Miss Anne Elliot to be visiting some poor widow with no connections? Put her off until tomorrow."

"I am afraid I cannot," Anne replied.

Anne kept her appointment; and the others kept theirs. Lady Russell and Mr. Elliot joined them. Lady Russell told Anne afterwards that when she had explained Anne's absence to Mr. Elliot, he had called her a model of female excellence.

Lady Russell had now decided what she thought of Mr. Elliot. She was convinced he meant, in time, to ask Anne to marry him, and she thought he deserved her. She hinted as much to Anne.

Anne smiled, blushed, and shook her head. "I think highly of Mr. Elliot in many respects," she said. "But we are not suited."

"I would be delighted to see you as Lady Elliot, mistress of Kellynch Hall, like your mother," Lady Russell said.

Anne had to walk away to try to subdue this bewitching image. The idea of returning to her home forever was almost irresistible. But she thought of Mr. Elliot, and the charm faded. She could never accept him. It was not only because her feelings were still averse to every man save one; it was her judgement too, which was against Mr. Elliot.

She had known him now for a month, but did not feel she knew his character, and she still could not explain his past conduct. Mr. Elliot was rational and polished, but he was not open. There was never any burst of feeling, any indignation or delight, at the evil or good of others. This, to Anne, was a definite flaw. She prized the frank, the open-hearted, the eager character beyond all others.

Persuasion

Warmth and enthusiasm captivated her. She felt she could depend more on the sincerity of those who sometimes looked or said a hasty, careless thing, than those whose presence of mind never varied, whose tongue never slipped.

Lady Russell, however, saw nothing to distrust. She thought Mr. Elliot was everything Anne deserved, and she hoped to see them married by the end of the year.

It was the beginning of February, and Anne was eager for news from Uppercross and Lyme. She was thinking intently about them all one evening when a thick letter from Mary was delivered to her – with a note saying the Crofts had brought it. "The Crofts must be in Bath," thought Anne with surprise, before reading the letter.

After the first few pages of peevish complaints, and a mention of the Crofts coming to Bath to cure the Admiral's gout, she reached a part which read, "Louisa is finally home, and guess what news I have? She is engaged to be married – to Captain Benwick! We are all so pleased. It is not as good as her marrying Captain Wentworth, but far better than Charles Hayter. Well this is an end to Captain Benwick being supposed to be an admirer of yours!"

Anne had never been more astonished. Captain Benwick and Louisa Musgrove! She slipped away to her room to try to understand it. How would Captain Wentworth feel? She could not bear it if his friend had betrayed him. Joyous, high-spirited Louisa Musgrove and thoughtful, bookish Captain Benwick – they were so dissimilar! What could have been the attraction? She could only think it was situation – they had been thrown together, both in a vulnerable state. She *had* felt that Captain Benwick had been drawn to her, but she was sure that any woman who had been sympathetic to him might have received the same compliments. He had an affectionate heart. He needed to love somebody.

She saw no reason for the pair to be unhappy – they would

become more like each other in time: he would gain Louisa's cheer and she might begin to read poetry. Anne smiled at the thought.

There was nothing to regret about the match. No, it was not regret making her heart thump, or her cheeks flush when she thought of Captain Wentworth unshackled and free. She had some feelings she was ashamed to investigate. They were too much like joy, senseless joy!

Anne longed to see the Crofts, to see if they knew how Captain Wentworth had taken the news, but her father would not associate with them now that the Dalrymples were in town. It was a few days before Anne, walking by herself, came across the Admiral looking at a painting of a ship in a shop window. "I am just wondering how anyone could venture to sea in an old cockleshell like this!" he said cheerfully when she stopped. "Well, now, can I be of any use?"

"No, thank you, unless you would like to walk with me a little way?" Anne replied.

As they strolled along the street together, the Admiral told her that Captain Wentworth had written to him with news of Benwick and Louisa's engagement. "That young lady he was courting week after week!" he exclaimed.

Anne saw her chance. "I hope Captain Wentworth does not feel ill-treated by his friend?" she asked.

"No, no, not at all. He wishes them the best. You would never guess that he had thought anything of this Miss – what is her name again? – at all. But poor Frederick. Now he must begin all over again with someone else. I think we must get him to Bath to find someone. Do you not think, Miss Elliot, that we had better try to get him to Bath?"

In fact, while the Admiral and Anne were talking about Captain Wentworth coming to Bath, he was already on his way there. And the very next time Anne went out, she saw him.

Persuasion

Mr. Elliot, Elizabeth, Anne and Mrs. Clay were out walking when it began to rain. They turned into the sweet shop to shelter from it, and Mr. Elliot went out to ask Lady Dalrymple, who was passing, to take them home in her carriage. There was only room for Elizabeth and Mrs. Clay, and so Anne had decided to walk home with Mr. Elliot. She was sitting by the window, when she saw Captain Wentworth walking down the street.

She lost sight of him, and suddenly thought she might go outside to see whether it had stopped raining. But she had just reached the doorway, when he came right into the shop with a group of people, and she had to beat a hasty retreat. The moment he saw her, he turned bright red. She felt something intense, too – something between delight and misery.

He said good day, and then turned away. He seemed embarrassed. But then he came and spoke again. Neither of them really knew what they were saying to each other. They had been calm enough in each other's company before, but something had changed. Now he could not even pretend to be comfortable.

Just then, Lady Dalrymple's carriage drew up, and Elizabeth and Mrs. Clay left to get in it. Captain Wentworth offered Anne his arm to help her into it too, but she said, "Oh no, I prefer to walk."

"Then please make use of my umbrella," he said, offering it.

She thanked him but said the rain would come to nothing. "I am just waiting for Mr. Elliot. He will be here in a moment."

She had hardly spoken the words, when Mr. Elliot came through the door – Captain Wentworth clearly recognized him as the man on the steps in Lyme who had admired Anne. Mr. Elliot apologized to Anne for keeping her waiting, and a moment later walked off with her arm in his.

As soon as they were out of sight, the ladies in Captain Wentworth's group started talking. "You can guess what will happen with those two. What a good-looking man!"

"Yes, and Anne Elliot is very pretty. Everyone thinks her sister is the beauty, but I admire her more. She is so delicate."

Anne would have appreciated it if Mr. Elliot could have walked all the way back without speaking. She could not pay attention to him, her mind was so full of Captain Wentworth. Was he disappointed about Louisa or not? Until she knew, she could not be herself. She hoped to be wise and reasonable in time, but, alas, she was not wise yet.

A day or two more passed without Anne seeing him. The Elliots spent their evenings in private parties, rather than the theatre or assembly rooms, where they might meet him. But then a concert was announced, which Lady Dalrymple was to attend, and the Elliots planned to go too. Captain Wentworth was fond of music. If only she could have a few minutes' conversation with him again… She excused herself from an evening with Mrs. Smith in order to join her family at the concert.

The following evening, Sir Walter, his two daughters and Mrs. Clay were standing by the fire waiting for Lady Dalrymple to arrive, when Captain Wentworth walked in. Anne spoke to him, so he stopped, and asked how she was. Then he said with a little flush, "I have hardly seen you since Lyme. What a frightful day!" But then he smiled, "However the outcome is far from frightful, with Benwick and Louisa engaged!"

"Yes, I hope it is a happy match."

"I do too, with all my soul. They have no opposition. The Musgroves are anxious only for their daughter's happiness. All this makes it easier for them, than perhaps—" He broke off suddenly and turned red. Then he cleared his throat and continued, "I must confess though, that I think there is some difference between them. Louisa is a sweet girl, but Fanny Harville, Benwick's fiancée who died, was more than that. And he loved her so. A man does not recover from such devotion! He ought not – he does not!"

He stopped there. The room buzzed around them, and Anne, intent on every word, began to breathe very quickly. She felt a hundred things in one moment. It was impossible for her to answer, but she had to say something. So she said, after a pause, "You stayed a good while in Lyme, I believe?"

"Yes, I was too deeply involved in the accident to be at peace otherwise. It was my doing – chiefly mine. She would not have been obstinate if I had not been weak…" he said. "I should think you would never like to go back to Lyme, after such horrors!"

"The last few hours were painful," Anne admitted, "but one does not love a place less for having suffered in it, unless it was nothing but suffering. When the pain is over, the memory often becomes a pleasure. My memory of Lyme is very agreeable."

The entrance doors opened, and Lady Dalrymple entered the room. Sir Walter went to greet her, bringing Anne, Elizabeth and Mrs. Clay with him, and so she was separated from Captain Wentworth. Their all-too-interesting conversation had to be stopped for now.

She took her place for the concert, brimming with happiness. Her eyes were bright, her cheeks glowed. Everything about their conversation – his view of Benwick and Louisa, his glance, his manner, it all led her to one idea: he must love her.

Mr. Elliot sat down next to her and the music began. In her high spirits, she felt she had never enjoyed anything more. When the interval came, she was explaining the words of an Italian song to Mr. Elliot, sharing the concert bill between them. "Such a perfect translation!" Mr. Elliot exclaimed.

"Oh no, I am a poor Italian scholar," Anne protested.

"Anne Elliot, you are too modest for someone with so many talents," said Mr. Elliot.

"This is too much flattery," Anne said, bending over the bill.

"Perhaps," whispered Mr. Elliot, "but I have known of you for longer than you think. Someone told me of you before we met."

Mr. Elliot was not disappointed – this remark raised Anne's curiosity. How could it not? But he would not say who he had spoken to. "Some other time, perhaps. The name of Anne Elliot has interested me for years," he said. "If I dared, I would breathe my wish that the name might never change, not even by marriage…"

But just then, Anne's attention was caught by Lady Dalrymple behind her, saying to her father, "Such a fine young man!"

"Good-looking," her father agreed. "I know his name: it is Captain Wentworth."

Anne looked around to see Captain Wentworth standing a little way away. As her eyes fell on him, he looked away. He did not look back, and the performance was restarting. When she next glanced over, he had gone.

The first act was over, and much of the audience went for tea, including Mr. Elliot, but Anne stayed in her seat. She waited and waited but Captain Wentworth did not reappear. It was only when the audience was coming back in that she saw him again. He looked as if something was the matter. Slowly, he came near enough to talk to her, and as she spoke to him of the performance, he began to smile a little. He even glanced down as if he might sit by her, but then she felt a tap on her shoulder. It was Mr. Elliot, asking if she could explain the Italian again. Reluctantly, Anne did so as quickly as she could. But when she turned back, Captain Wentworth was saying goodbye to her.

"Is this song not worth staying for?" Anne asked, suddenly feeling that he might need some encouragement.

"No!" he replied impressively. "There is nothing worth my staying for!" and he was gone.

Was he jealous? Of Mr. Elliot? That could be the only

explanation and yet she would not have believed it only three hours ago! For a moment, the pleasure was exquisite, but then she wondered how she could ever get the truth to him? It was misery to think that Mr. Elliot's attentions might have a terrible effect.

Anne went to visit Mrs. Smith the next day. Prettier thoughts of love and devotion could never before have passed along the streets of Bath. It was almost enough to spread perfume all the way.

She told Mrs. Smith all about the concert, and who had been there. "You do not need to tell me whether you had a pleasant evening," Mrs. Smith said. "I can see it in your eyes. Last night, you were in the company of one person who interests you more than anyone else in the world."

Anne blushed and could not say a word.

"So thank you for sparing the time to come and see me," Mrs. Smith said. "I expect that soon you will no longer have time for visits to me. Does Mr. Elliot even know I am in Bath?"

"Mr. Elliot?" Anne asked, surprised. "You know him?"

"It has been a long time since we saw one another."

"If I had known, I could have mentioned you," Anne said.

"I would like you to. He could do something for me, if you would not mind using your influence with him to ask," said Mrs. Smith.

"Of course, but I think you suspect me of having more influence over him than I do," Anne hesitated.

"Oh, I am sorry for speaking too soon. Do let me know when you announce your engagement officially," Mrs. Smith said.

"That will not ever happen!" Anne cried. "I am not going to marry Mr. Elliot. It is not who I was thinking of—" She stopped and blushed deeply. "Do tell me what made you think I was."

Mrs. Smith looked surprised. "You have spent so much time together," she explained. "It would be fitting for your family too…

and also my friend, Nurse Rooke, heard it from a Mrs. Wallis."

Anne laughed. "Well, there was no news to tell. Did you know Mr. Elliot a long time ago? I am curious to learn what he was like as a young man," she said.

"I knew him before he was married. But I have not seen him for three years," Mrs. Smith replied gravely. "I am not sure what to tell you. I do not want to speak badly of anyone, or make mischief…" She paused, deliberated, then burst out, "Oh dear, but I think you should know Mr. Elliot's real character. He has no feeling for others. He can lead people to ruin and then desert them without a thought. He is black at heart, hollow and black!"

Anne was astonished.

"I have startled you," Mrs. Smith said more calmly. "I was allowing my feelings to get in the way. I feel angry… wronged… But I will try to tell you the facts, so they can speak for themselves. He was my husband's friend, and seemed very pleasant. He was poorer than us at the time, and struggling to support himself. My husband helped him, and he had a home with us whenever he needed it. We were very close. He intended, then, to make his fortune by marrying someone rich. I know that he drew back from your family, as he thought that your father intended for him to marry your sister. It did not suit his ideas of wealth and independence. He told me the whole story – he talked about one Miss Elliot, and I thought fondly of the other…"

Anne suddenly had an idea, "Did you tell him about me?"

"Naturally. I used to boast of my Anne Elliot," said Mrs. Smith.

"Ah, that explains something he said last night," Anne said.

"Well, back then, he did not value Kellynch or your family name at all – they were as cheap as dirt to him. But do not take my word for it." Mrs. Smith sent Anne to fetch a little box, from which she took an old letter from Mr. Elliot to her husband.

As Anne read, her cheeks began to glow at what Mr. Elliot had written: "I have got rid of Walter and Miss. They have gone back to Kellynch, and almost made me swear to visit them this summer. But my first visit to Kellynch will be to see how much I can sell it for – unless the baronet marries again and produces a male heir. He is a fool. I am sick of the name of Elliot!"

She was so taken aback, she could not speak for a moment. After pausing to recover herself a little, she asked, "But how can you explain his interest in the family now?"

"He is different now. I have no letter as proof this time, but he confides in his friend Mr. Wallis, whose silly wife tells everything to Nurse Rooke. After he made his fortune with his first marriage, he had nothing left to want but a title. He cannot bear the thought of not becoming the baronet. He heard of Mrs. Clay's attention to your father, and worried that your father would marry her. Any boy child they might have would be heir instead of him, and he is desperate not to allow that to happen. Apparently he was delighted to find the woman he had admired in Lyme was actually Anne Elliot. I think he genuinely wants to marry you. Of course, there was no harm in pleasing your father too – he would be less inclined to remarry if *your* children would inherit Kellynch. When I believed Mr. Elliot loved you, I hoped, perhaps, that you might change him for the better…"

"I am very glad to know all of this," Anne said thoughtfully. "Mr. Elliot is evidently an artificial, manipulative man, who has only ever been guided by selfishness."

Mrs. Smith now came to the part that she felt bitter about. After his marriage, Mr. Elliot had still spent a lot of time with them. Now he was rich, he had persuaded Mr. Smith, who was fond of him and easily led, to live beyond what he could afford. In short, he had led him into dreadful debt. The Smiths had been ruined. Mr. Smith had died before learning the whole truth, leaving Mr. Elliot as the executor of his will. Mrs. Smith's husband had owned property which, if sold, could make Mrs. Smith comparatively rich. But Mr. Elliot refused to act for her. She showed Anne letters from him, answers to her pleas of help that were cold and indifferent to her suffering. It was in this matter that she had hoped to ask Anne to persuade Mr. Elliot.

Anne shuddered at the thought that she might have been persuaded by Lady Russell to marry Mr. Elliot. The misery that would have followed!

Anne went home to think about all she had heard. Mr. Elliot had called while she was out, and Elizabeth said he was coming again that evening. "He gave so many hints," Elizabeth smirked, "that I had to let him."

Mrs. Clay looked pleased, and Anne could not help but admire her acting. She must dread the arrival of the person who was getting in the way of her aim, if she wanted to marry Sir Walter.

When Mr. Elliot did appear, Anne could hardly bear the sight of him. She saw how insincere his behaviour was, compared to the letter he had written. She was very pleased to learn that he would be out of Bath for the next few days.

On Friday morning, there came a knock at the door, and, to everyone's surprise, Mary and Charles Musgrove were ushered in. Anne was really glad to see them, and the others were glad to have someone to boast of their fine house to.

As Mary was shown around, Charles told Anne that they had come to Bath with his mother, Henrietta and Captain Harville. The Captain was coming on business and they had decided to come along, to buy clothes for Henrietta's wedding. It was going to take place in a few months, along with Louisa's.

"I am so glad!" Anne cried. "Particularly that they should both be happily married at the same time. Is Louisa fully recovered?"

Charles hesitated. "Yes, but she has changed. There is no more dancing about. And Benwick reads verses to her all day long."

Anne laughed, "That cannot be much to your taste, I know," she said, "but I do believe him to be an excellent young man."

"I do not doubt it," Charles assured her.

Elizabeth proposed that they should all come to a card party the next evening, and be introduced to Lady Dalrymple. Mary was happy with that, and Anne accompanied them back to the White Hart, where they were staying with Mrs. Musgrove and Henrietta.

Anne went eagerly to see her friends. Henrietta and Mrs. Musgrove welcomed her, begging her to stay as long as possible, and to see them every day. It was a sincere warmth, and Anne soon found herself falling into her role of listening to their news and helping with every little thing, from arranging trinkets to recommending shops.

Charles went out and returned with Captain Harville and Captain Wentworth, which was a surprise. Anne feared from his sombre looks that whatever had been the matter at the concert was still there. He did not seem to want to talk to her. She tried to stay calm, and leave things to take their course. "Surely," she told herself, "if we truly love one another, our hearts must understand each other before long."

"Anne," Mary said, looking out of the window, "there is Mrs. Clay talking to Mr. Elliot. They are deep in conversation…"

"It cannot be him," Anne said quickly. "Mr. Elliot said he was leaving Bath for a few days. He does not return until tomorrow."

She felt Captain Wentworth look at her and, embarrassed, wished she had not said so much.

"Come and look for yourself," Mary insisted.

So Anne did, partly to hide her embarrassment. She was just in time to see that it was indeed Mr. Elliot, before he and Mrs. Clay parted and went different ways.

Charles said, "I have booked us a box at the theatre tomorrow. Captain Wentworth is coming, and will you come, Anne?"

"How could you have forgotten? We are going to the party tomorrow night to meet Lady Dalrymple!" exclaimed Mary.

"I think I would rather go to the play," Charles said.

"Charles! It would be unpardonable not to go. You need to meet the Dalrymples and Mr. Elliot! He is my father's heir. The future representative of the family!"

"If I will not go for your father, I certainly will not go for Mr. Elliot. What is he to me?" Charles scoffed.

Captain Wentworth was listening with all his soul, and Anne saw these words bring his questioning eyes from Charles to herself.

Mrs. Musgrove said, "We can change it to Tuesday. Anne will have to go to the party. If we go tonight, she will not be able to come, and we cannot go without Anne."

Anne was grateful, and it gave her the chance to say, "I would much rather go to the play with you than the party. But perhaps it would be better to change it." She trembled, conscious of Captain Wentworth listening to her words, but did not dare observe their effect on him.

Before long, Captain Wentworth made his way towards her. "You do not prefer an evening party to going out?" he asked her.

"Not usually... I am no card player."

"I remember you were not before. But time changes things..."

"I have not changed all that much!" Anne cried, and stopped, fearing how he would take it.

"Eight and a half years is such a long time!" he burst out.

Just then, the door was flung open and in walked Sir Walter and Elizabeth. To Anne's dismay, a cold hush descended on the room. But Elizabeth and her father only stayed long enough to invite everyone graciously to the party tomorrow night, giving them all an invitation card, including Captain Wentworth.

Anne's spirits sank as she saw him examine the card as though considering whether to accept.

"Captain Wentworth is so delighted to be included he cannot put the card down!" Mary whispered audibly.

Anne caught his eye, saw his cheeks glow, his mouth twist in disdain, and turned away, so she could see no more to pain her.

Soon, they went their separate ways, and Anne returned to her lodgings at Camden Place. Mrs. Clay and Elizabeth were there, busy discussing details of the party. Before going to her room, Anne told Mrs. Clay that she had seen her with Mr. Elliot, and watched her reaction carefully. It was gone in an instant, but a distinct look of guilt passed over Mrs. Clay's face, before she claimed, "I was so surprised to meet him still in Bath! He was prevented from going away as planned – but I forget how. He asked about tomorrow, so he is certainly coming."

The following morning, Anne returned to the White Hart as she had promised, hurrying there between bouts of rain. She arrived to find Henrietta and Mary had gone out, but Mrs. Musgove said they had asked her to stay until they returned. Captain Wentworth was there again, with Captain Harville, and Anne sat down quietly while Mrs. Musgrove chatted to Mrs. Croft.

"I will write that letter we were talking of now, Harville," Captain Wentworth said. He sat down at a separate table, with his back to them all, and began to write.

Captain Harville gestured to Anne to join him at the window near Captain Wentworth's table. So she went, and he showed her a little portrait of Captain Benwick he had in his hand. "It was made to send to my poor sister, but now it is being given to another." He looked at Captain Wentworth, writing away. "He is doing it for me." His lip quivered. "Poor Fanny," he said, "she would not have forgotten him so soon!"

"I can believe that," Anne said gently. "It would not be in the nature of any woman who truly loved."

Captain Harville smiled at that, and Anne said, "You smile but it is true. We do not forget you as soon as you forget us. Perhaps it is because we have no profession to take us back into the world and distract us."

"But that does not apply to Benwick. He has been living peacefully with us," Captain Harville countered.

"Perhaps it is nature that is responsible, then," said Anne.

"No, it is not in man's nature. I would say a man's feelings are like his body – strong and capable of bearing out rough weather."

"Man may be more robust than woman, but he does not live longer. Indeed it would be too hard on men, to deal with all the struggles of life, *and* have a woman's feelings…" her voice faltered.

There was a clatter – Captain Wentworth had dropped his pen. Anne was startled to realize he was closer than she had supposed.

"Have you finished?" Captain Harville asked.

"Just a few more lines," he replied.

Captain Harville turned back to Anne. "If only you could see how deeply a man feels when he sails away from his loved ones!"

"I do not think only women capable of true love!" Anne cried. "I only claim that women love longest, when all hope is gone."

She could not have said another word; her heart was too full.

"You are a good soul," Captain Harville said, patting her arm.

Captain Wentworth was folding up a letter in great haste, and he and Captain Harville left the room.

But then Captain Wentworth returned, saying he had forgotten his gloves. He crossed to the writing table, drew a letter from under the scattered paper, and placed it before Anne with eyes of glowing entreaty fixed on her. Then he collected his gloves and was gone. It all happened in an instant! The letter was the one he had been folding so hastily. While he was writing a letter for Captain

*He placed the letter before
Anne with eyes of glowing entreaty.*

Benwick, he had also been writing to her! She sank into the chair he had occupied, and her eyes devoured the following words:

> *I can listen no longer in silence. I must speak the only way I can. I am half in agony, half hope. Tell me I am not too late, that those feelings are not gone forever! I offer myself to you, with a heart even more yours than when you broke it eight and a half years ago. I have loved none but you. You alone brought me to Bath. For you alone I think and plan. I can hardly write. Every instant I hear something which overwhelms me... You do believe in true love and devotion in men! Believe it to be most fervent, most unchanging in F. W.*
>
> *I must go, uncertain of my fate, but I shall return. A word, a look will be enough to decide whether I enter your father's house this evening, or never.*

Anne was overwhelmed, and had not recovered when Mary, Charles and Henrietta came in ten minutes later. She had to excuse herself, saying she felt ill. They were all very concerned.

"We can call a carriage to take you home," said Mrs. Musgrove.

But Anne could not bear to miss the chance of meeting Captain Wentworth on the way home, and protested that she would walk. Charles insisted on accompanying her.

She could do no more, and left with Charles. A quick, familiar step behind them soon brought Captain Wentworth. He looked at her; Anne's cheeks glowed; he walked by her side.

Then an idea occurred to Charles, "Captain Wentworth, perhaps you could walk Anne home? She is not feeling well, and I was supposed to meet a fellow in town."

Persuasion

Of course, there was no objection, just polite smiles and dancing spirits, followed by bliss. Soon after Charles left, enough had been said for them to be certain of exquisite happiness. They exchanged the same feelings and promises as years before, this time more tender, more tested, more certain.

And there, slowly pacing up the hill, they talked of everything that had led to that point. She was right – he had been horribly jealous of Mr. Elliot. Gradually he had felt rising hope, and then, when he heard her words to Captain Harville, he had been certain.

He had thought himself indifferent when he had been angry. He had been unjust about her character because he had suffered by it. Now he thought she was perfect: both strong and gentle.

He had, he admitted, *tried* to become fond of Louisa Musgrove, but no one compared to Anne. In Lyme, he had learned the difference between determination and obstinacy. But then, he said, "Harville told me he thought I was engaged! So I went away, to visit my brother, to weaken that supposition if possible."

He continued, "Then I saw you at the concert, with Mr. Elliot, and thought they would all persuade you to take him, not me!"

"If I gave in to persuasion once, at least it was on the side of caution, not risk," Anne said. "Nothing could have persuaded me to marry a man I do not love."

Anne found herself home again. And she was happier than anyone in that house could have imagined.

The evening came, the drawing rooms were lit up, everybody was there. It was only a card party, but to Anne, glowing and lovely with happiness, the evening danced by. She spoke to everyone, occasionally meeting with Captain Wentworth. It was in one of those short meetings, each apparently admiring the greenhouse plants, that she said, "I have been thinking about whether I was wrong to be guided by my friend. To me, she was in the place of a parent. I am not saying that she did not err in her advice – but I think I was right to allow myself to be persuaded."

"I have been wondering whether there may have been a worse enemy than that lady…" he admitted, "…*me*. Tell me, if I had written to you, when I had a few thousand pounds and a posting on a ship, would you have renewed our engagement?"

"Would I?" was all she answered, but her tone said it all.

"You would!" he cried. "It is not that I did not think of it. I was too proud to ask again. I could have spared us six years of suffering… I used to think I deserved everything I had earned. Now I must get used to the idea of being happier than I deserve."

Who can doubt what followed? Anne Elliot and Captain Wentworth could have faced down a lot more opposition than they received to their marriage. Sir Walter made no objection. After all, Captain Wentworth was no longer a nobody. He was quite worthy enough to propose to the daughter of a foolish, spendthrift baronet. And, when the time came, Sir Walter happily wrote the marriage details into his most treasured book.

Mr. Elliot left Bath, followed by Mrs. Clay. They were soon heard of living in London together. He was so determined to avoid being cut off by her, he had lured her away from Sir Walter himself.

As for Lady Russell, all she had to do was admit that she had been wrong. And this she readily did, for her biggest concern was, and had only ever been, the happiness of Anne Elliot.

Captain Wentworth came to value Lady Russell as a friend, and became a good friend to Mrs. Smith too. He took it upon himself to recover her husband's property from the West Indies, so restoring her wealth and place in society.

Anne was full of happiness in Captain Wentworth's affection. And nothing but the distant threat of war could dim her sunshine.

Lady Susan

In a series of letters, a story emerges about Lady Susan, a terrible flirt. Newly widowed, she goes around taking advantage of both married and unmarried men, and creating utter mayhem in the houses of polite, upper-class England.

Lady Susan Vernon

The most famous flirt in England. A recently widowed 35-year old woman, whose sole ambition is to get what she can from rich men.

Frederica

Lady Susan's teenage daughter. Her mother sends her to boarding school and then tries to marry her off, all to benefit herself.

Charles & Catherine Vernon

Lady Susan's brother-in-law via her late husband, and his wife, who dislikes Lady Susan.

Mr. Reginald de Courcy

Catherine Vernon's younger brother, who falls for Lady Susan's wily charms.

Mr. Johnson

Alicia's husband, who has banned Lady Susan from his house.

Mrs. Alicia Johnson

Lady Susan's confidante, who helps in her schemes.

Mrs. Mansvaring

After catching Lady Susan flirting with her husband, she orders her to leave their house.

Mr. Mansvaring

A married man. Unfortunately for his wife, his head is totally turned by Lady Susan. He will do anything she asks.

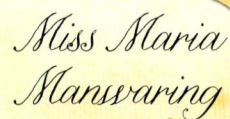

Sir James Martin

A rich young man. Lady Susan lures him away from Miss Maria Manwaring, intending to marry him to her daughter.

Miss Maria Mansvaring

Looking for a rich husband, she is sure of Sir James Martin, until Lady Susan lures him away with her charms.

Sir Reginald & Lady C. de Courcy

Catherine Vernon and Reginald's parents, who worry about their son's interest in Lady Susan.

369

Lady Susan

Lady Susan to her brother-in-law, Mr. Charles Vernon

I can no longer resist your kind invitation to stay with you at Churchill, your delightful country house, and therefore if convenient to you, I shall arrive in a few days. My friends here urge me to remain longer but their merry hospitality is too much for me. I need the quietness of your home. I have always wanted to get to know your wife Catherine – now my sister – and your dear little children, in whose hearts I hope to dwell. I shall need all my strength as I am on the point of being separated from my own daughter, Frederica. Her father's long illness and death prevented me from giving her the attention she deserved, and so I am sending her to one of the best private schools in London. I will leave her there on my way to you. I am determined, you see, that you will grant my wish to come to you. It would hurt me deeply if you refused me.
    Your most obliged and affectionate sister,
    S. Vernon

Lady Susan to her friend, Mrs. Johnson

    You were wrong to suppose me happily settled here at Langford for the winter. True, the last three months have been charming, but now nothing is going smoothly. The women of the family hate me. Mr. Manwaring, of course, is exceedingly pleasant. I was discreet; being only four months a widow, I allowed myself to flirt with nobody but him, except perhaps a little with Sir

Lady Susan

James Martin, but that was only to detach Sir James from Miss Manwaring. It was for Frederica that I led him on. I want him to marry her. But Frederica, the greatest simpleton on earth and born to be the torment of my life, has set herself against the match, so I have laid my scheme aside for the moment. I am sorry I did not marry Sir James myself, and if he had been one degree less ridiculously weak, I certainly should.

The result of all this is very annoying. Sir James has gone, Miss Manwaring is furious, and Mrs. Manwaring is jealous of me – and angry – and Manwaring hardly dares to speak to me.

It is time for me to leave. The whole family is at war.

Yes, I really am going to Churchill. It is my last resort, until I have something better to do. I dislike my brother-in-law, Charles Vernon, and I am afraid of his wife. I shall leave Frederica at school until she becomes more reasonable. The price is immense, and much beyond what I can ever attempt to pay.

Adieu, I will send you a line as soon as I arrive in town.

Yours ever,

S. Vernon

Catherine Vernon to her mother, Lady de Courcy

I am sorry to say we will not be spending Christmas with you as promised. Lady Susan has declared her intention of visiting us immediately, and it is impossible to know for how long. Why does she want to come, I wonder? Langford's elegant and expensive style of living appeared to suit her very well. Charles, I think, has been a great deal too kind to her. Her behaviour to him over our marriage

Lady Susan

was unforgivable, but he is so amiable that he overlooks it all, and I suppose it was proper of him to give her some money, since she is a widow in impoverished circumstances. Still, I feel asking her to Churchill was unnecessary. Her display of grief softened his heart, but I am unconvinced. She says she wants to get to know my children, but any woman who could be so unkind to her own child can hardly be looking to dote on any of mine. Frederica is to be sent to school in London, which I am glad of. It will be good for her to be separated from her mother, and a girl of sixteen without any education would not be a very desirable companion here.

My brother Reginald has long wished to meet this captivating Lady Susan, so we shall doubtless see him soon.

Yours ever,
Catherine Vernon

Mr. Reginald de Courcy to his sister, Catherine Vernon

I congratulate you and Mr. Vernon on receiving into your home the most famous flirt in England. I have heard of her behaviour at Langford. She does not confine herself to that sort of honest flirtation which satisfies most people, but aspires to the more delicious pleasure of making a whole family miserable. By her behaviour to Mr. Manwaring, she made his wife jealous and unhappy, and by her attentions to a younger man previously attached to Mr. Manwaring's sister, she deprived a harmless girl of a growing romance. What a woman she must be! I long to see her, and shall certainly be at Churchill very soon.

Your affectionate brother,
R. de Courcy

Lady Susan

Lady Susan to Mrs. Johnson

I have arrived safely at Churchill, dear Alicia. Charles received me kindly, but I am not satisfied with Catherine. I can tell she does not like me. I am being as amiable as possible; I want her to like me, but all in vain. To be sure, I did try quite hard to stop Charles from marrying her, but it shows in her an unforgiving spirit for what took place six years ago. Charles wanted to buy Vernon Castle when we had to sell it to raise money. I would not have minded if we could have kept him single, then we could have lived there with him, but he was on the point of marrying. I was right to stop him from buying it. What would I have gained by him having Vernon Castle? My actions may perhaps have given his wife a bad impression.

This house is elegant, and everything in it shows wealth and fashion. Charles is very rich; when a man has once got his name in a banking house, he rolls in money. But they do not know what to do with their fortune. They never entertain – so dull!

I mean to win my sister-in-law's heart through her children. I know all of their names already, and am going to attach myself to one in particular.

I miss Manwaring. I received a dismal letter from him on arrival here, which I passed off as being from his wife. When I write to him, it must be under cover to you.

Ever yours,
S. Vernon

Lady Susan

Catherine Vernon to her brother Reginald de Courcy

Well, my dear Reginald, Lady Susan is here. I have never seen a woman as lovely. She really is excessively pretty. Fair, with grey eyes and dark eyelashes; she looks no more than twenty-five, though she must be ten years older. Her manner is sweet, uniting brilliance and grace; her voice winningly mild. She is clever and interesting, and talks well, with a knowledge of the world which makes conversation easy. Her attitude to me is so open and affectionate, that if I had not known that she has always disliked me for marrying Charles, and if I had not met her before, I could have imagined her a real friend.

What else is this but deceit?

She has almost persuaded me that she loves her daughter, but I remember how many times she was in town, leaving her child to the care of servants or an indifferent governess.

I cannot believe the story about Mr. Manwaring. She corresponds with his wife regularly.

Yours,
Catherine Vernon

Lady Susan to Mrs. Johnson

My dear Alicia,

You are very good in taking notice of Frederica, but do not overdo it. She is a stupid girl, and has nothing to recommend her. I intend her to marry Sir James within the year. I will succeed. It must be humiliating for a girl of Frederica's age to be still at school,

Lady Susan

and on that account, I beg you not to invite her any more, as I wish her to find her situation as unpleasant as possible. I do not want her to learn much. To be mistress of French, Italian, German, music, singing, drawing etc. will gain a woman some applause but will not add one lover to her list. Ask Sir James to your house and talk of Frederica so that he does not forget her.

Enough of this tiresome girl.

My first week here was insufferably dull. Now it begins to improve. Mrs. Vernon's brother Reginald has joined us, a handsome young man who promises to be some amusement. He may be an agreeable flirt.

I have unsettled him already by my gentleness. I will shame these self-important de Courcys; show Catherine her sisterly warnings are unnecessary and persuade Reginald she has scandalously misrepresented me.

Yours ever,
S. Vernon

Mrs. Vernon to her mother, Lady de Courcy

My dear mother,

Do not expect Reginald home for some time. He is fascinated by Lady Susan. I am not enjoying his visit as much as I hoped. This unprincipled woman upsets all that is pleasant.

What greater proof of her dangerousness than this… Reginald came here convinced she was entitled neither to sympathy nor respect but now he is delighted with her. Yesterday he actually said that he could not be surprised at any effect on a man's heart by such loveliness.

Lady Susan's attentions are of course those of absolute

Lady Susan

flirtation, or a desire for universal admiration. It saddens me to see Reginald, who is usually so steady, so deceived by her.
   Catherine Vernon

Mrs. Johnson to Lady Susan

My dear friend,
   I congratulate you on Mr. de Courcy's arrival, and advise you to marry him. His father is very rich. He is also ill, so not likely to stand in your way for long. I have seen Sir James several times. He is so far from forgetting either you or your daughter that I am sure he would marry either of you. He is as silly as ever.
   Yours faithfully,
   Alicia

Lady Susan to Mrs. Johnson

   Thank you for your advice regarding Mr. de Courcy. But I cannot think of anything as serious as marriage, especially as I do not need money at present. I would not benefit much from the match till the old gentleman's death.
   I am enjoying making Reginald like me. I have never behaved less like a flirt in my life. I have subdued him by my dignity and serious conversation. He is inferior to Manwaring, less polished, but agreeable enough to give me some amusement.
   Your account of Sir James is pleasing. I shall give Frederica a hint about him soon.
   Yours,
   S. Vernon

Lady Susan

Mrs. Vernon to her mother, Lady de Courcy

I wish you could get Reginald to go home again. Lady Susan's power over him seems boundless. He is completely taken in. He says the rumour of her flirtation at Langford with Mr. Manwaring and the young man Miss Manwaring was engaged to must be nothing but a scandalous invention.

How sincerely sorry I am that she ever entered this house!
Yours,
Catherine Vernon

Sir Reginald de Courcy to his son, Reginald de Courcy

I hope you will allow a father's anxiety. I fear you may be drawn in by a lady whom your whole family mistrusts. Be aware, you are an only son and the representative of an ancient family.

Lady Susan's age is one objection, but that is outdone by her misconduct. Her neglect of her husband, her encouragement of other men, and her extravagance cannot be forgotten. Also, please remember that she did, from selfish motives, attempt to stop Charles from marrying Catherine.

It would destroy every comfort of my life to know that you were married to Lady Susan Vernon. It would be the death of my pride in you.

Sir Reginald de Courcy

Lady Susan

Mr. de Courcy to his father, Sir Reginald

My dear sir,

I am to thank my sister Catherine, I suppose, for giving you all this alarm. I assure you I have no plans of marriage.

My sister is prejudiced beyond hope against Lady Susan. She believes it was selfishness that made Lady Susan try to prevent her marriage to Charles. But Lady Susan has been grossly misunderstood. She had heard something to the disadvantage of Catherine that persuaded her that Charles, to whom she is very attached, would not be happy with her.

I blame myself for having so easily believed the tales against Lady Susan. None of them are true. She is a most excellent mother; her prudence and economy are exemplary. I admire her. Your fears have been most idly created.

R. de Courcy

Mrs. Vernon to her mother, Lady de Courcy

My dear mother,

I am happy that my father is reassured by Reginald's letter. But I believe only that he has no intention of marrying Lady Susan at present, not that he will never do so.

I cannot help but pity her. She has received a letter from Frederica's school demanding Frederica's instant removal. The girl had tried to run away. Mr. Vernon is going to London to persuade them to keep her, or to bring her here if he fails. Lady Susan is comforting herself by strolling in the shrubbery with Reginald.

Lady Susan

However, she talks about it to me too lightly, I fear, to feel very deeply.
 Yours ever,
 Catherine Vernon

Lady Susan to Mrs. Johnson

Never have I been so angry. That horrid girl of mine has tried to run away. I had no idea she was such a little devil; she seemed to have all the Vernon mildness, but on receiving my letter, in which I told her my intention about Sir James, she attempted to flee.

She shall be punished; she shall have him. I have sent Charles to town to mend matters, for I do not want her here.

I like Reginald, but he is ridiculously careful. He wants a full explanation of what he has heard to my disadvantage. This sort of love does not satisfy me. I prefer Manwaring, who is dying to see me again, and speaks of taking a cottage near here so that we can meet secretly. I forbid anything of the kind. I cannot forget I owe the world a good opinion of me.
 Yours ever,
 S. Vernon

Mrs. Vernon to her mother, Lady de Courcy

My dear mother,
Frederica is here, and I have never in my life seen a creature look so frightened. Lady Susan shows her no tenderness, though the child seems so unhappy. My heart aches for her. Lady Susan

Lady Susan

is surely too severe; Frederica does not have the sort of nature to make severity necessary.

She is very pretty, though not as beautiful as her mother. She is a true Vernon, with gentle, dark eyes and a mild, sweet expression. Her mother says she has a horrid temper, but I never saw a face less likely to express it. I believe her mother has no real love for her.

She is meant to practise the piano for hours in Lady Susan's dressing room, but I seldom hear any noise. What she does there, I do not know. Lady Susan makes sure she spends very little time alone with me. But in the brief times when I do see her, we have become great friends. Her little cousins are all very fond of her. She has a most loving heart.

Reginald still thinks Lady Susan the best of mothers – still condemns Frederica as a worthless girl. But she admires him. I often see her eyes fixed on him, and she listens to all he says.

I remain,
Catherine Vernon

Lady Susan to Mrs. Johnson

I was perfectly right. Frederica ran away because of my letter about Sir James. It frightened her so much that the little fool fled, without realizing she could not escape my authority. She only got two streets away when she was missed, pursued and returned to Wigmore Street.

Such was the first distinguished exploit of Miss Frederica Vernon and if we consider it was achieved at the age of sixteen, we can expect much of her. She now spends her time falling in love with Mr. Reginald de Courcy. To disobey her mother by refusing an offer is not enough. She also gives her affections without her

Lady Susan

mother's permission.

Her aunt likes her – because she is so unlike myself, of course. Do not imagine for a moment that I have given up plans for her marriage. I have not decided how I shall bring it about. Miss Frederica must therefore wait a little.

Yours ever,
S. Vernon

Mrs. Vernon to her mother, Lady de Courcy

My dear mother,

An unexpected guest arrived yesterday. I was sitting with my children when Frederica, pale as ashes, rushed in, crying, "Oh! He is come! Sir James! What am I to do?"

We went down to find Sir James Martin in the breakfast room, the man Lady Susan had detached from Miss Manwaring. It seems she means him to marry her daughter, but the poor girl dislikes him. Mr. Vernon and I think him a very weak young man.

That evening, Lady Susan spoke to me privately. Sir James, she said, was a good match for Frederica, and she demanded my congratulations. I gave them awkwardly, for the suddenness of the request took away my power of speaking clearly. She thanked me, saying, "God bless you for your kindness to me and my girl," and "I had no idea that I could love you as I do now."

What can one say of such a woman?

I think Reginald is confused at her allowing the attention of such a man to her daughter.

Something must be done for this poor girl.

I remain,
Catherine Vernon

Lady Susan

Frederica Vernon to Mr. Reginald de Courcy

Sir,

I hope you will excuse this letter. I am forced by the greatest distress to write it, or I would be ashamed to trouble you. I am very miserable about Sir James, and have no other way in the world to save myself, other than by writing to you. I am forbidden to speak to my uncle and aunt about it, but if you do not take my part and persuade my mother to break it off, I shall be so unhappy, for I cannot bear him. I would rather work for my bread than marry him. I have always disliked him, so it is not a sudden feeling. Please help me. I am aware how dreadfully angry Mama will be with me for writing, but I must run the risk. No human being but you has any power over her.

I am, sir, your most humble servant,
F.S.V.

Lady Susan to Mrs. Johnson

This is insufferable! My dearest friend, I was never so enraged before. Who should come on Tuesday but Sir James Martin? Guess my astonishment and vexation – I never intended him to be seen at Churchill. He actually invited himself to stay here for a few days. I could have poisoned him. I told Frederica she must behave politely and that she must marry him. She said something of her misery but that was all. I am even more resolved on the match, because I see the rapid increase of her feelings for Reginald, and fear it will awaken a response in his affection. Reginald has praised Frederica twice lately.

Lady Susan

I have persuaded Reginald that the match is desirable, and I forbade Frederica from complaining to her uncle and aunt. They see that Sir James is weak, but they had no reason to interfere, though I could see Catherine was waiting for a chance to do so.

Everything was going smoothly and I was satisfied. But then my schemes were disrupted. Reginald came into my dressing room this morning, informing me of my unkindness in allowing Sir James to address my daughter. He told me that Frederica had actually written to him to request his help, and that he had spoken to her, in order to understand her real wishes.

I am perfectly certain, by his manner, that she took this opportunity to make him fall in love with her. Much good may such love do him! I shall always despise him now. He can have no real feelings for me or he would not have listened to her. I am amazed at her: her rebellious little heart has made her throw herself at a man she scarcely knows. And Reginald! How dare he believe what she told him! Where was his belief in me!

He has gone now to shut himself up in his room. How unpleasant his thoughts must be. But some people's feelings are incomprehensible.

I am too angry to see Frederica. She shall not soon forget the occurrences of today. She shall find she has exposed herself to the contempt of the whole world, and the severest resentment of her own mother.

Your affectionate,
S. Vernon

Lady Susan

Mrs. Vernon to her mother, Lady de Courcy

I am so delighted, dearest Mother, that I can hardly hold my pen. Reginald is coming home to you. His passion for Lady Susan is finished.

I was sitting in the breakfast room when he came in. You know how eager his manner is when his mind is set afire. Instantly I saw something was the matter.

"Catherine," he said. "I am going home today. But before I leave you," – speaking with even greater energy – "do not let Frederica be made unhappy by that Sir James Martin. She is a sweet girl, and deserves a better fate than being tied to him. He is a fool."

Soon after, he left. I guessed Lady Susan and Reginald had quarrelled about Frederica. I sense Reginald's affection for her. We must wait – indeed, dear Mother, you could not have a sweeter daughter-in-law than Frederica.

When next I write, I hope to tell you that Sir James is gone, Lady Susan defeated, and Frederica at peace.

Yours ever,
Catherine Vernon

From the same to the same

Little did I think, dear Mother, that the news I wrote but two hours earlier should be reversed!

I found Frederica crying in her bedroom, and I made her tell me everything. She was afraid she had caused a quarrel between her mother and Reginald. "She will never forgive me," she wept. I assured her she was safe, and that her mother had no right to make her unhappy.

Lady Susan

I left her calm, but imagine my surprise to see Reginald coming out of Lady Susan's dressing room.

"Are you leaving us now?" I asked.

"I am not. I find I have entirely misunderstood Lady Susan. Frederica does not know her mother; Lady Susan means nothing but her good, but Frederica will not be friendly to her. Lady Susan therefore does not always know what will make her happy. She wishes to speak to you."

"Certainly," I sighed.

Lady Susan tried to exonerate herself. Pretending to cry, she said that Frederica was afraid of her. She was completely unaware of her child's unhappiness. Reginald thinking badly of her distressed her, because of the affection she felt for our entire family.

She finished, "I trust you think no worse of me."

I could have said, "Not much," but I left her in silence. It was the greatest stretch of tolerance I could manage.

Sir James's carriage was at the door. Merry as usual, he took his leave. How easily does her ladyship encourage or dismiss a lover!

Prepare for the worst. Reginald is in deeper danger of marriage to Lady Susan. He is more securely hers than ever. When it takes place, Frederica must be wholly ours.

Yours ever,
Catherine Vernon

Lady Susan to Mrs. Johnson

Congratulate me! I am myself again – triumphant.

I managed easily to soften Reginald, and now his tenderness is restored. I have much to do: punish Frederica, punish Reginald for listening to her. I must torment Catherine for her insolent

Lady Susan

expression since Sir James left. In reconciling Reginald to me, I was not able to save that young man, and I must take revenge for the humiliations I have endured these last few days.

I owe it to my character to marry Frederica immediately to Sir James, after having so long intended it. I will take her to London to achieve my goal, and reward myself with your company after ten weeks' penance at Churchill.

Your most attached,
S. Vernon

Mrs. Johnson to Lady Susan

You must come to town and leave Frederica. You should think of yourself before your daughter. She will not shine in society like you. Let her punish herself at Churchill.

I have another reason for urging this. Manwaring is in town, miserable about you, and jealous of de Courcy. If you take my advice and marry de Courcy, you can send Manwaring back to his jealous wife. Silly woman, to expect such a charming man to be faithful to her. She was silly to marry him at all, she, an heiress, and he, with nothing.

You cannot stay here, dear friend. Mr. Johnson forbids your company. I thought he would be in Bath, but he has a fit of gout, and remains with me.

Adieu. Yours ever,
Alicia

Lady Susan

Lady Susan to Mrs. Johnson

What a mistake you made in marrying a man of Mr. Johnson's age, old enough to have gout but too young to die.

I am in town, at the lodgings you found me. I arrived last night. I had scarcely eaten my dinner when Manwaring called. I prefer him to Reginald, who has agreed to be in town soon. I am not sure about marrying Reginald. If the old man were to die, I might not hesitate, but a state of dependence on his life would not suit my free spirit. Manwaring thinks I have only the lightest of flirtations with Reginald. They must not meet. I will write to Reginald to delay his coming. I will say I am ill.

Yours ever,
S. Vernon

Mrs. Johnson to Lady Susan

I am in agonies and know not what to do. Mrs. Manwaring arrived here, just at the same time as Mr. de Courcy. She had wormed the knowledge out of Manwaring's servant that he visits you every day. For your comfort, she is thinner and uglier than ever. However, de Courcy now knows everything.

Yours faithfully,
Alicia

Lady Susan to Mrs. Johnson

Silly woman! What does she expect by such manoeuvres?

Lady Susan

No matter. I can make up some story to tell Reginald. I am sure he will be a little enraged at first, but all will be well.
Adieu!
S.V.

Mr. de Courcy to Lady Susan

I write to bid you farewell. The spell is removed. I now see you as you really are.

I have received from an indisputable authority – Mrs. Manwaring herself – the truth about your conduct.
R. de Courcy

Lady Susan to Mr. de Courcy

I am astonished and bewildered. I cannot suppose you believe that old story of Mrs. Manwaring's jealousy. Come to me immediately and explain. To be sunk in your opinion is a humiliation I cannot bear.
S.V.

Mr. de Courcy to Lady Susan

Your misconduct has been proved beyond a doubt. You have written to Manwaring ever since leaving Langford, and all this time I was your encouraged, accepted lover. You have robbed his family

Lady Susan

of its peace. Can you, dare you deny it? How is Mrs. Manwaring to be consoled?

You know how I have loved you. You can judge my present feelings, but I am not so weak as to describe them to a woman who will glory in having excited their anguish.

R. de Courcy

Lady Susan to Mr. de Courcy

I am satisfied and will trouble you no more. The engagement which you were eager to form a fortnight ago will not take place. I rejoice to find that you will obey the prudent advice of your family. I flatter myself I will survive this disappointment.

S.V.

Mrs. Johnson to Lady Susan

I am not surprised at your rupture with Mr. de Courcy.

You have heard of course that the Manwarings are to part. I fear she will come to us. She frets so much about her broken marriage that perhaps she may not live long. Miss Manwaring is coming to town to pursue Sir James.

If I were you, I would certainly get him myself.

Yours sincerely attached,
Alicia

Lady Susan

Lady Susan to Mrs. Johnson

Manwaring is more devoted to me than ever, and were he free, I could not resist marrying him. If his wife lives with you, the violence of her feelings must wear her out, and you can easily irritate them. I rely on your friendship for this.

I shall bring Frederica here and make her marry Sir James. She may whimper and the Vernons may storm. I do not care. I am tired of submitting my will to others.

Unalterably yours,
S. Vernon

Lady de Courcy to Mrs. Vernon

I have charming news. Reginald has returned! He and Lady Susan are parted for ever. This is the most joyful day since the hour of his birth! My only wish now is to have you here. Come as soon as you can, and bring all the grandchildren – and Frederica, who occupies my thoughts. It has been a sad season, worrying about Reginald and seeing nothing of you, but our happy meeting will make me young again.

Your affectionate mother,
C. de Courcy

Mrs. Vernon to Lady de Courcy

We, with our little ones, will be with you next Thursday. I wish we could bring Frederica, but her mother arrived at Churchill and

Lady Susan

has taken her to London. The poor child's heart was broken.
Yours ever,
Catherine Vernon

Conclusion

Anxious to retrieve Frederica from her mother, Mrs. Vernon went to see them in London. Lady Susan was in excellent spirits; Frederica as pale and sad as before. Mrs. Vernon suggested that Frederica was sickening, possibly with influenza. That was enough for Lady Susan. Of all things, she feared illness. Frederica was returned to Churchill with Mrs. Vernon, and within three weeks, Lady Susan married Sir James Martin.

Lady Susan wrote twice to her daughter, and then, in the space of two months, ceased to write to her at all.

Frederica was therefore fixed in the family of her uncle and aunt. Within a year, Reginald de Courcy recovered from his attachment to her mother, and his mistrust of the entire female sex, and settled into great affection for her.

Whether Lady Susan was happy in her marriage can never be ascertained. She had nothing against her but her husband and her conscience. Sir James suffered a harder fate than his foolishness warranted, and deserved all the pity that anyone could give him.

Perhaps Miss Manwaring earned the most pity. She came to London in pursuit of Sir James, putting herself to great expense in buying clothes which impoverished her for two years, and was cheated of her expectations by a woman who was ten years older than herself.

Jane Austen:
Life and Times

Early village life

Jane Austen is one of the greatest novelists in the English language. Much of what we have discovered about her comes from the letters she wrote to friends and family, particularly her beloved sister, Cassandra. Her writing and an early biography by her nephew, James Edward Austen-Leigh, also reveal details about her views and lifestyle. But much about her emotional life remains a mystery. She left no diaries, and after her death, many of her letters were burned by her sister, perhaps to guard her private life.

Jane Austen was born on December 16th 1775, the seventh of eight children – six of them brothers – in the village of Steventon in Hampshire. Her father was a vicar who, in addition to his church duties, farmed, and tutored boys in the family home.

Austen grew up in a large house with few luxuries, but her father kept a library, and reading and writing were always encouraged. The children also enjoyed singing and putting on plays – in the barn in summer and in the dining room in winter. At the age of seven, Austen was sent away with her sister to be educated by a relative, and later at a boarding school for girls. But at 10, she came back with her sister to continue her education at home.

Soon after her return from school, Austen began to write plays, stories and comic versions of popular novels. At 15, she wrote a comic history of England, which mocked the history books of the time. These early writings were not intended for publication, but they were passed around and enjoyed by friends and family.

Jane Austen: Life and Times

In her late teens, Austen spent more time writing novels, and by 21, she had completed early drafts of three books, *Susan* (later entitled *Northanger Abbey*), *Elinor and Marianne* (*Sense and Sensibility*), and *First Impressions* (*Pride and Prejudice*). Her father was so entertained by *First Impressions* that he wrote to a publisher in London, but the book was rejected by return of post.

Around this time, Austen grew close to a law student and family friend named Tom Lefroy. They met and danced together on several occasions, but a month later he returned to his studies and their friendship ended, possibly because neither had enough money for the families to consider a marriage between them.

Bath to Chawton

WHEN AUSTEN'S FATHER RETIRED AS VICAR OF STEVENTON in 1801, the family moved to a house in Bath, much to Austen's dismay at leaving the countryside. Here she was thrown into a social whirl of tea and supper parties, concerts and balls, the type of events which are described to great comic effect in her novels. In 1802, aged 26, she accepted a marriage proposal from a wealthy landowner. But the next morning, she swiftly broke off the engagement. Although her heroines were all to secure marriage in the closing pages of her books, Austen remained single all her life.

She was delighted when her first novel, *Susan* (*Northanger Abbey*), was accepted by a publisher. But the publisher decided not to print the book after all, and it remained unpublished throughout Austen's lifetime.

The sudden death of her father in 1805 left Austen and her mother and sister virtually penniless. They spent the next few years moving between homes and staying with family. After a short time in Southampton, they finally settled in Chawton, a pretty village in Hampshire. The house belonged to her brother Edward, who had inherited a nearby estate from a wealthy, childless couple, who had adopted him when he was a teenager. Austen may have drawn on this experience when writing about Fanny Price, the main character in *Mansfield Park*, who is taken in by her rich uncle and aunt.

Once settled in Chawton, Austen had the peace and quiet at last to concentrate on her writing, although she had to fit it in between her busy domestic duties.

The Georgian Era

JANE AUSTEN LIVED THROUGH A TIME OF GREAT CHANGE. After the French Revolution in 1789, Britain and France were almost constantly at war. In 1811, the Prince Regent, later George IV, began to rule in place of his father, George III, who was unwell. The years 1811-1820 are known as the Regency period, after the Prince Regent. As political unrest grew over unjust laws, rising food prices and new factories, it became too dangerous for writers to question the government openly. This may be one reason why Austen only hints at these turbulent times in her novels.

But many great works of literature were produced at this time. There was a new focus on feeling and imagination in the works of poets such as Burns, Byron, Wordsworth and Coleridge, and a surge of interest in books of horror, mystery and romance, known as Gothic novels. Austen gently mocks these books, including *The Mysteries of Udolpho* by Ann Radcliffe, Catherine Morland's enthralling novel in *Northanger Abbey*. Austen may also have been influenced by Mary Wollstonecraft's *A Vindication of the Rights of Women* in 1792, an early feminist work that argued for women to be better educated, in a more rational manner. Austen touches on these ideas in novels such as *Northanger Abbey* and *Persuasion*.

Jane Austen: Life and Times

Women, class and society

Jane Austen belonged to a society in which the wealthiest landowners earned enough money to build magnificent houses and parks, employ hundreds of servants, keep horses and carriages and hold splendid balls. Many of them spent several months of the year in fashionable town houses in London or Bath, and had inherited titles, such as Lord, Lady or Count, that gave them a higher rank at social events.

Beneath them was the educated upper-middle class, known as the gentry, to which Jane Austen's family and most of her heroines belonged. The gentry included vicars, military officers, doctors and lawyers, and although they were considered to be socially less important, they mixed with the wealthy landowners. Beneath the gentry were farmers, servants and tradesmen – who had to work for a living.

Women in the gentry had little control over money and most could only hope to gain a comfortable living through marriage. Unmarried women, like Austen, were often considered a burden, and depended on family members for their support. Upon a father's death, everything passed to the eldest son, and the wife and daughters were often left poor. It was even harder for a daughter to marry if she had no wealth to offer her husband. Women could not go to university or gain a career, so a good marriage was the most important ambition for a woman in the gentry.

Although reading was a popular pastime in Georgian England, earning a living as an author was generally frowned upon, especially for women. This is probably why Jane Austen's name did not appear on any of her books during her lifetime. On the title page of *Sense and Sensibility*, for instance, it merely stated 'By a Lady', while beneath the title of *Pride and Prejudice* was written 'By the author of *Sense and Sensibility*'.

Jane Austen: Life and Times

The novels

Austen had no private study in the house at Chawton, but worked on a small desk in the dining room. It was here that she revised her first three books and wrote three more. After her brother Henry contacted a publisher on her behalf, *Sense and Sensibility* was published in 1811, when Austen was 35. The reviews were good, the book became popular among the fashionable upper classes, and in two years the first edition had sold out.

Pride and Prejudice was published in 1813 to even greater success, and a second edition was printed later that year. Perhaps Austen's best known novel, it contains one of the most famous opening lines in English literature: "It is a truth universally acknowledged, that a single man in possession of a good fortune, must be in want of a wife." The brilliant wit of this sentence only becomes clear after the reader discovers that this "truth" is not in fact "universally acknowledged," but reflects the views of eager individuals such as Mrs. Bennet, who has five daughters to find husbands for.

When *Mansfield Park* appeared in 1814, the first edition of 1,500 copies sold out in six months. *Emma* followed in 1815. It is thought by some to be Austen's greatest masterpiece for its choice of an intelligent but problematic heroine and its gentle mocking of English country life.

That same year, Austen began writing *Persuasion*, which is set in Dorset which Austen visited as a child. She may have touched on her own experience when writing about Anne Elliot, who falls in love early in life, but is dissuaded from marrying a man with no fortune. By this time Austen was suffering from an illness, thought to be Addison's disease. She finished the novel, but by 1817 was so unwell, she moved to Winchester to seek medical help. Austen died on July 18th 1817 in her sister's arms, at the age of 41.

Jane Austen: Life and Times

She was buried in Winchester Cathedral, where three memorials to her remain to this day. *Persuasion* and *Northanger Abbey* were published as a joint edition at the end of 1817. She also left two unfinished books, *The Watsons* and *Sanditon,* and a short novel of letters called *Lady Susan,* printed long after her death in 1871.

A mocking eye

AUSTEN'S HEROINES WERE REMARKABLE AT THE TIME FOR THEIR mistakes and flaws, their strong will, and desire to be treated as men's equals. Her characters were also realistic people from her own time, in contrast to those in most novels of the day. Austen experimented with a way of writing that let her reveal the secret feelings and inner lives of characters from the view of the narrator. This technique, known as 'free indirect style', helped Austen show her heroines change as they learn to know themselves.

In her last six years, Austen gained many admirers, including the Prince Regent, to whom she dedicated *Emma*. As her reputation grew, more and more readers became captivated by her work. Lord Alfred Tennyson wrote: "Miss Austen understood the smallness of life to perfection. She was a great artist, equal in her small sphere to Shakespeare…" Tennyson even visited Lyme Regis in Dorset just to see the steps where Louisa fell in *Persuasion*. Austen's stories still inspire millions today, which is evident from the books, movies and television series based on her work that continue to be made.

Not only is she known for her wit, elegant style and sparky dialogue, but also for her heart-warming scenes and clever observations about English society and married life. From foolish mothers and controlling fathers, to interfering, wealthy ladies and handsome scoundrels, no one is safe from her mocking eye.

Find out more at Usborne Quicklinks

For links to websites where you can find out more about the life and times of Jane Austen, and the books she wrote, go to the Usborne Quicklinks website at www.usborne.com/quicklinks and type in the keywords 'Complete Jane Austen'. Please follow the online safety guidelines at the Usborne Quicklinks website.

Here are some things you can do at the recommended websites:

• See places where Jane Austen lived and worked

• Watch video clips of performances from movies and plays based on some of Jane Austen's books

• Find out about everyday life in Georgian times, including Regency fashion, balls and dancing

Jane Austen consultant: Freya Johnston,
Associate Professor, St. Anne's College, Oxford

'Jane Austen: Life and Times' by Minna Lacey
Additional design by Catherine Mackinnon
Digital manipulation by John Russell
Editors: Anna Milbourne and Jane Chisholm
Managing designer: Stephen Moncrieff

First published in 2018 by Usborne Publishing Ltd., Usborne House, 83–85 Saffron Hill, London, EC1N 8RT, United Kingdom. www.usborne.com Copyright © 2018 Usborne Publishing Ltd. UE. The name Usborne and the devices ⊕ ⊛ are Trade Marks of Usborne Publishing Ltd. All rights reserved. No part of this publication may be reproduced, stored in any retrieval system, or transmitted in any form or by any means, electronic, mechanical, photocopying, recording or otherwise, without the prior permission of the publisher. Printed in UAE.

The websites recommended at Usborne Quicklinks are regularly reviewed but Usborne Publishing is not responsible and does not accept liability for the availability or content of any website other than its own, or for any exposure to harmful, offensive or inaccurate material which may appear on the Web. Usborne Publishing will have no liability for any damage or loss caused by viruses that may be downloaded as a result of browsing the sites it recommends.